Comments from readers of

"Whether you are a newcomer to Excel or already a user of an earlier version, this is THE book to get you up to speed on Excel 2007. Not only did it teach me how to use the many new features of 2007, such as the ribbon, but it is also stuffed full of general Excel hints and tips, all presented in a way which makes them easy to practice and assimilate."
– *A reader from Four Marks, England*

"Finally I've found a book that teaches the way that I teach; Covers everything fast if the student knows the area and slower where the skill is new. And using interesting example spreadsheets (Fastest cars in the world, Best-selling music albums of all time and so on). The layout is really easy to read with each step title summarized in bold font so you can see where to skip the stuff you (or your students) know and where to concentrate. Overall, I've seen many books on Excel but this one is the best I've found so far."
– *A reader from Canberra, Australia*

"This Excel 2007 Essential Skills manual by Mike Smart is fantastic. I have little experience using Excel and after training with the manual, I now consider myself at the intermediate level. I can highly recommend it as a starting point for all those who need to learn Excel."
– *A reader from New York, USA*

"Before I bought this book I went to a couple of bookstores and checked-out what was available. I found two broad categories: super-intensive and utterly superficial. The Smart Method gave me just what I wanted: a broad overview and straight-forward how-to examples. Now the jargon makes sense and I have enough insight into the numerous features to know where to look to learn more. This book is a great resource for someone who wants to learn Excel and needs a place to start." – *A reader from Oregon USA.*

 "The Smart Method is all I will be using to train our company's Administrative, Customer Service, and Management employees. After extensively searching the web for the right training materials, I have found "Essential Skills" to be the easiest training for self study or classroom presentation. The Smart Method is great for those with no Excel experience or for those that are upgrading from a previous Excel version."
– *A reader from Atlanta, Georgia, USA*

"Early on in the book the author makes the bold claim that 'even the most advanced Excel user will find some nugget of extremely useful information in every session'. This is a bold statement that I put to the test by reading the book through from cover to cover. It is true! Although thought of by my peers as an advanced Excel user, the book taught me some very useful tips that either I had missed altogether in 2003 or were new to 2007. I can thoroughly recommend the clear teaching style and love the A4 layout. It is well worth getting if you are new to Excel or you are in the progress of upgrading."
– *A reader from Portsmouth, UK*

"If you want to learn to use Excel 2007 effectively from a starting point of zero, all the way to using charts and graphics, this is a great book. The book is well laid out, the Smart Method engenders easy learning, with short snappy lessons on, in this book, seven different areas including one which a lot of teaching methods forget - how to make your results look good. If you need a start in Excel 2007, buy this book, you won't regret it."
– *A reader from the UK*

"I have used a number of books and courseware to learn excel but have always been left confused. Most books showed too many ways of doing the same thing and I never perfected a single way. Also, other books tended to focus on simple and complex topics together. To sum up, the book is 'Simply Awesome'."
– *A reader from Ohio, USA*

"I am an intermediate Excel user and this book is just what I needed. It has tips and tricks for doing routine tasks more efficiently, and adding details that give my workbooks that 'Wow' factor. This book took me from being an Excel user to the 'go to' person for Excel help in my office. I couldn't be more pleased with this purchase." – *A reader from Maryville, Tennessee, USA.*

Who Is This Book For?

If you need good Excel skills for your work, or want to add Excel skills to your CV, you've found the right book.

If you've never used Excel 2007 before, this book will give you all of the skills you need to be thoroughly competent. By the end of the book your Excel skills will be better than most office workers with many years of experience.

This book is for Excel 2007 users who:

- Need to acquire essential Excel skills quickly.

- Have never used Excel before, or who have only basic Excel skills.

- Want to learn Excel skills from first principles.

- Are moving to Excel 2007 from an earlier version.

Use of this book as courseware

This book is also the official courseware for The Smart Method's Excel 2007 Essential Skills course.

Smart Method courses have been taken by a varied cross-section of the world's leading companies. We've had fantastic feedback from the vast number of professionals we've empowered with Excel skills.

This book is also suitable for use by other training organizations, teachers, schools and colleges to provide structured, objective-led, and highly effective classroom courses.

Learn Excel 2007 Essential Skills with The Smart Method

Mike Smart

Published by:

The Smart Method Ltd
Burleigh Manor
Peel Road
Douglas, IOM
Great Britain
IM1 5EP

Tel: +44 (0)845 458 3282 Fax: +44 (0)845 458 3281

E-mail: info@LearnMicrosoftExcel.com
Web: www.LearnMicrosoftExcel.com (this book's dedicated web site)

Printed and bound in the EEC

FIRST EDITION

International Standard Book Number (ISBN10): 0-9554599-1-5
International Standard Book Number (ISBN13): 978-0-9554599-1-7

The Smart Method is a trade mark of The Smart Method Ltd.

European Edition – This book may not be sold in the United States of America or Canada.

4 6 8 10 9 7 5 3

Contents

Introduction

Welcome to *Learn Excel 2007 Essential Skills With The Smart Method*. This book has been designed to enable students to master Excel 2007 by self-study. The book is equally useful as courseware in order to deliver courses using The *Smart Method* teaching system.

Smart Method publications are continually evolving as we discover better ways of explaining or teaching the concepts presented.

Feedback

At The Smart Method we love feedback – both positive and negative. If you have any suggestions for improvements to future versions of this book, or if you find content or typographical errors, the author would always love to hear from you via e-mail to:

feedback@LearnMicrosoftExcel.com

Future editions will always incorporate your feedback so that there are never any known errors at time of publication.

If you have any difficulty understanding or completing a lesson, or if you feel that anything could have been more clearly explained, we'd also love to hear from you. We've made hundreds of detail improvements to our books based upon reader's feedback and continue to chase the impossible goal of 100% perfection!

Downloading the sample files

In order to use this book it is sometimes necessary to download sample files from the Internet. The sample files are available from:

http://www.LearnMicrosoftExcel.com

Type the above URL into your web browser and you'll see the link to the sample files at the top of the home page.

Problem resolution

If you encounter any problem downloading or using the sample files please send an e-mail to:

feedback@LearnMicrosoftExcel.com

We'll do everything possible to quickly resolve the problem.

Typographical Conventions Used In This Book

This guide consistently uses typographical conventions to differentiate parts of the text.

When you see this	Here's what it means
This edition was written using *Microsoft Excel 2007 Service Pack 1* running under the *Microsoft Vista Service Pack 1* operating system	Italics may sometimes be used for emphasis or distinction.
Click the *Windows Start Button* ⊕ at the bottom left of your screen.	Italics are sometimes also used when you need to click on a control.
Click: Home→Font→Underline.	Click on the Ribbon's *Home* tab and then look for the *Font* group. Click the *Underline* button within this group (that's the left-hand side of the button, not the drop-down arrow next to it). Don't worry if this doesn't make sense yet. We cover the Ribbon in depth in session one.
Click: Home→Font→Underline Drop Down→Double Underline.	Click on the Ribbon's *Home* tab and then look for the *Font* group. Click the drop-down arrow next to the Underline button (that's the right-hand side of the button) within this group and then choose *Double Underline* from the drop-down list.
Click Office→Excel Options→ Popular→Edit Custom Lists→Import **Office Button**	This is a more involved example. The *Office Button* is at the top left hand corner of the Excel screen. 1. Click the *Office Button*, and then click the *Excel Options* button. A new dialog pops up. 2. Choose the *Popular* list item and then click the *Edit Custom Lists* button. Yet another new dialog pops up. 3. Click the *Import* button.
Type **European Sales** into the cell.	Whenever you are supposed to actually type something on the keyboard it is shown in bold faced text.
Press <Ctrl> + <Z>.	You should hold down the **Ctrl** key and then press the **Z** key.

Σ AutoSum ▾

When a lesson tells you to click a button, an image of the relevant button will often be shown either in the page margin or within the text itself.

note

In Excel 2007 there are a possible 16,585 columns and 1,048,476 rows. This is a great improvement on previous versions.

If you want to read through the book as quickly as possible, you don't have to read notes.

Notes usually expand a little on the information given in the lesson text.

important

Do not click the Delete button at this point as to do so would erase the entire table.

Whenever something can easily go wrong, or when the subject text is particularly important, you will see the *important* sidebar.

You should always read important sidebars.

tip

Moving between tabs using the keyboard

You can also use the <Ctrl>+<PgUp> and <Ctrl>+<PgDn> keyboard shortcuts to cycle through all of the tabs in your workbook.

Tips add to the lesson text by showing you shortcuts or time-saving techniques relevant to the lesson.

The bold text at the top of the tip box enables you to establish whether the tip is appropriate to your needs without reading all of the text.

In this example you may not be interested in keyboard shortcuts so do not need to read further.

anecdote

I ran an Excel course for a small company in London a couple of years ago...

Sometimes I add an anecdote gathered over the years from my Excel classes or from other areas of life.

If you simply want to learn Excel as quickly as possible you can ignore my anecdotes.

trivia

The feature that Excel uses to help you out with function calls first made an appearance in Visual Basic 5 back in 1996 and had the wonderful name: *IntelliSense*. The Excel...

Sometimes I indulge myself by adding a little piece of trivia in the context of the skill being taught.

Just like my anecdotes you can ignore these if you want to. They won't help you to learn Excel any better!

The World's Fastest Cars

When there is a sample file (or files) to accompany a lesson, the file name will be shown in a folder icon.

You can download the lesson or file from: *www.LearnMicrosoftExcel.com.*

Putting the Smart Method to Work

Excel version and service pack

This edition was written using *Microsoft Excel 2007 Service Pack 1* running under the *Microsoft Vista Service Pack 1* operating system. You'll discover how to confirm that your computer is running these versions during session 1.

If you are using an earlier or later operating system (for example Windows XP or Windows 7) this book will be equally relevant, but you may notice small differences in the appearance of some of the screen grabs in the book. This will only occur when describing an operating system (rather than an Excel) feature.

This book is written purely for Excel 2007 and, due to huge changes in this version, will not be useful for earlier versions (97, 2000, 2002 and 2003).

Sessions and lessons

The book is arranged into Sessions and Lessons. In a *Smart Method* course a Session would generally last for between sixty and ninety minutes. Each session would represent a continuous period of interactive instruction followed by a coffee break of ten or fifteen minutes.

When you use this book for self-instruction I'd recommend that you do the same. You'll learn better if you lock yourself away, switch off your telephone and complete the whole session without interruption. The memory process is associative, and we've ensured that each lesson within each session is very closely coupled (contextually) with the others. By learning the whole session in one sitting, you'll store all of that information in the same part of your memory and should find it easier to recall later.

The experience of being able to remember all of the words of a song as soon as somebody has got you "started" with the first line is an example of the memory's associative system of data storage.

We'd also highly recommend that you do take a break between sessions and spend it relaxing rather than catching up on your e-mails. This gives your brain a little idle time to do some data sorting and storage!

Read the book from beginning to end

Many books consist of disassociated self-contained chapters, often all written by different authors. This approach works well for pure reference books (such as encyclopedias). The problem with this approach is that there's no concept of building knowledge upon assumed prior knowledge, so the text is either confusing or unduly verbose as instructions for the same skill are repeated in many parts of the book.

This book is more effective as a learning tool because it takes a holistic approach. You will learn Excel in the same way you would be taught during one of our *Smart Method* courses.

In our classroom courses it's often the case that a delegate turns up late. One golden rule is that we can't begin until everybody is present, as each hands-on lesson builds upon skills taught in the previous lesson.

I strongly recommend that you read the book from beginning to end in the order that it is written. Because of the unique presentational style, you'll hardly waste any time reading about things that you already know and even the most advanced Excel user will find some nugget of extremely useful information in every session.

How this book avoids wasting your time

> Nobody has things just as he would like them. The thing to do is to make a success with what material I have.
>
> *Dr. Frank Crane (1861–1928), American clergyman and journalist*

The only material available to me in teaching you Excel is the written word and sample files. I'd rather have you sitting next to me in a classroom, but Frank Crane would have told me to stop complaining and use the tools I have in the most effective way.

Over the years I have read many hundreds of computer text books and most of my time was wasted. The big problem with most books is that I have to wade through thousands of words just to learn one important technique. If I don't read everything I might miss that one essential insight.

This book utilizes some of the tried and tested techniques developed after teaching vast numbers of people to learn Excel during many years of delivering *Smart Method* classroom courses.

As you'll see in this section, many presentational methods are used to help you to avoid reading about things you already know how to do, or things that are of little interest to you.

Why our classroom courses work so well

In *Smart Method* classroom courses we have a 100% success rate training delegates to *Essential Skills* level in one day (the subject matter of this book) and to *Expert* level in a further single day (the subject matter of our follow-on *Expert Skills* book).

One of the reasons we can teach so much in a single day is that we don't waste time teaching skills that the delegates already know. Class sizes are small (six maximum) and the instructor stands behind the delegates monitoring their screens. The instructor will say "Open the sample file *Sales* that you'll find in the *Samples* folder on the C drive". If everybody does this no time is wasted explaining how. If anybody has difficulty, more information is given until all delegates demonstrate success.

Another key to learning effectively is to only teach the best way to accomplish a task. For example, you can save a workbook by clicking the Save button on the Quick Access Toolbar or you can press the <Ctrl>+<S> keys on the keyboard. Because clicking the Save button is the easiest, fastest and most intuitive method we only teach this in the classroom. In the book we do mention the alternatives, but only in a sidebar.

How this book mimics our classroom technique

Here's a lesson step:

Note

You can also use the <Ctrl>+<S> keyboard shortcut to save your work.

1 Save the workbook.

When you are editing a workbook the changes you make are only held in the computer's memory. If there is a power cut or your computer crashes, you will lose any work that has been done since the last save. For this reason you should get into the habit of regularly saving your work.

Click the *Save button* on the *Quick Access Toolbar* at the top left of the screen.

If you already know how to save a workbook read only the line: *Save the workbook* and just do it. Don't waste your time reading anything else.

Read the smaller print only when you don't already know how to do something.

If you're in a hurry to learn only the essentials, as fast as possible, don't bother with the sidebars either unless they are labeled **important**.

Read the sidebars only when you want to know everything and have the time and interest.

Avoiding repetition

2	Create a new worksheet and name it *January*.
	This was covered in: *Lesson 1-5: Save a workbook.*

A goal of this book (and our classroom courses) is not to waste your time by explaining any skill twice.

In a classroom course, a delegate will sometimes forget something that has already been covered earlier in the day. The instructor must then try to get the student to remember and drop little hints reminding them about how they completed the task earlier.

This isn't possible in a book, so I've made extensive use of cross references in the text pointing you back to the lesson in which the relevant skill was learned. The cross references also help when you use this book as a reference work but have forgotten the more basic skills needed to complete each step.

Use of American English

American English (rather than British English) spelling has been used throughout. This is because the Excel help system and screen elements all use American English spelling, making the use of British English confusing.

Examples of differences are the British English spelling: *Colour* and *Dialogue* as opposed to the American English spelling: *Color* and *Dialog*.

Because this book is used all over the world much care has been taken to avoid any country-specific terminology. In most of the English speaking world, apart from North America, the symbol # is referred to as the **hash sign**. I use the term *hash* throughout this book.

First page of a session

1/ The first page begins with a quotation, often from an era before the age of the computer, that is particularly pertinent to the session material. As well as being fun, this helps us to remember that all of the real-world problems we solve with technology have been around for a long time.

3/ The session objectives *formally* state the precise skills that you will learn in the session.

At the end of the session you should re-visit the objectives and not progress to the next session until you can honestly agree that you have achieved them.

In a *Smart Method* course we never progress to the next session until all delegates are completely confident that they have achieved the previous session's objectives.

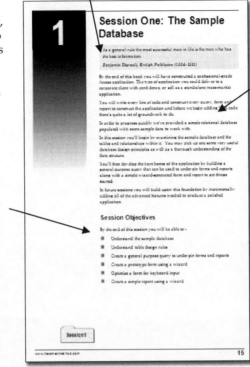

2/ In the next few paragraphs we *informally* summarise why the session is important and the benefits that you will get from completing it.

This is important because without motivation adults do not learn. For adults, learning is a means to an end and not an end in itself.

The aim of the introduction is to motivate your retention of the skills that will be taught in the following session by allowing you to preview the relevance of the material that will be presented. This may subconsciously put your brain into "must remember this" mode—assuming, of course, that the introduction convinces you that the skills will be useful to you!

Every lesson is presented on two facing pages

Pray this day, on one side of one sheet of paper, explain how the Royal Navy is prepared to meet the coming conflict.
Winston Churchill, Letter to the Admiralty, Sep 1, 1939

Winston Churchill was well aware of the power of brevity. The discipline of condensing thoughts into one side of a single sheet of A4 paper resulted in the efficient transfer of information.

A tenet of our teaching system is that every lesson is presented on *two* facing sheets of A4. We've had to double Churchill's rule as they didn't have to contend with screen grabs in 1939!

If we can't teach an essential concept in two pages of A4 we know that the subject matter needs to be broken into two smaller lessons.

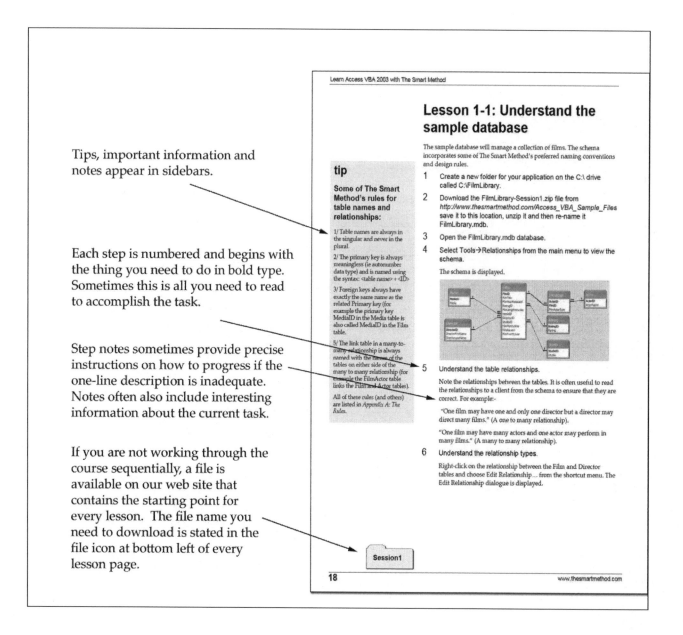

Tips, important information and notes appear in sidebars.

Each step is numbered and begins with the thing you need to do in bold type. Sometimes this is all you need to read to accomplish the task.

Step notes sometimes provide precise instructions on how to progress if the one-line description is inadequate. Notes often also include interesting information about the current task.

If you are not working through the course sequentially, a file is available on our web site that contains the starting point for every lesson. The file name you need to download is stated in the file icon at bottom left of every lesson page.

Learning by participation

Tell me, and I will forget. Show me, and I may remember. Involve me, and I will understand.

Confucius (551-479 BC)

Confucius would probably have agreed that the best way to teach IT skills is hands-on (actively) and not hands-off (passively). This is another of the principal tenets of the *Smart Method* teaching system. Research has backed up the assertion that you will learn more material, learn more quickly, and understand more of what you learn, if you learn using active, rather than passive methods.

For this reason pure theory pages are kept to an absolute minimum with most theory woven into the hands-on sessions either within the text or in sidebars. This echoes the teaching method in Smart Method courses, where snippets of pertinent theory are woven into the lessons themselves so that interest and attention is maintained by hands-on involvement, but all necessary theory is still covered.

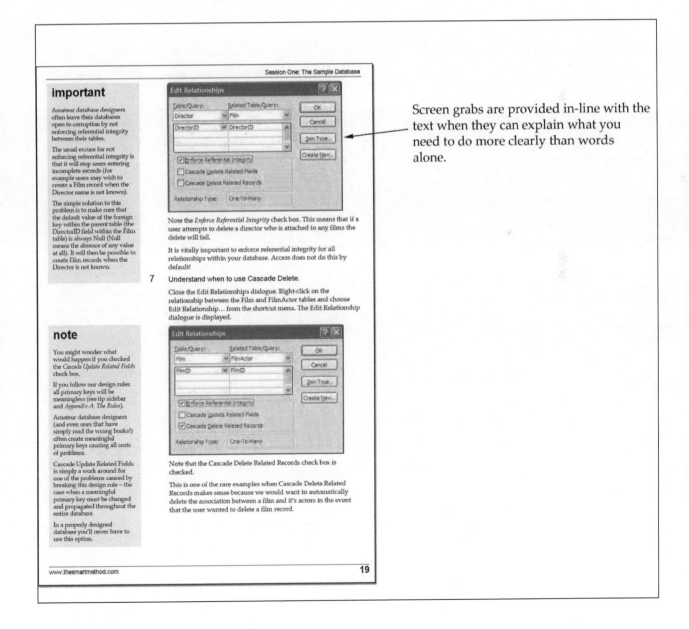

Session One: The Sample Database

important

Amateur database designers often leave their databases open to corruption by not enforcing referential integrity between their tables.

The usual excuse for not enforcing referential integrity is that it will stop users entering incomplete records (for example users may wish to create a Film record when the Director name is not known).

The simple solution to this problem is to make sure that the default value of the foreign key within the parent table (the DirectorID field within the Film table) is always Null (Null means the absence of any value at all). It will then be possible to create Film records when the Director is not known.

note

You might wonder what would happen if you checked the *Cascade Update Related Fields* check box.

If you follow our design rules all primary keys will be meaningless (see tip sidebar and *Appendix A: The Rules*).

Amateur database designers (and even ones that have simply read the wrong books!) often create meaningful primary keys causing all sorts of problems.

Cascade Update Related Fields is simply a work around for one of the problems caused by breaking this design rule – the case when a meaningful primary key must be changed and propagated throughout the entire database.

In a properly designed database you'll never have to use this option.

Note the *Enforce Referential Integrity* check box. This means that if a user attempts to delete a director who is attached to any films the delete will fail.

It is vitally important to enforce referential integrity for all relationships within your database. Access does not do this by default!

7 Understand when to use Cascade Delete.

Close the Edit Relationships dialogue. Right-click on the relationship between the Film and FilmActor tables and choose Edit Relationship... from the shortcut menu. The Edit Relationship dialogue is displayed.

Note that the Cascade Delete Related Records check box is checked.

This is one of the rare examples when Cascade Delete Related Records makes sense because we would want to automatically delete the association between a film and it's actors in the event that the user wanted to delete a film record.

Screen grabs are provided in-line with the text when they can explain what you need to do more clearly than words alone.

Session One: Basic Skills

> A bad beginning makes a bad ending.
>
> *Euripides, Aegeus (484 BC - 406 BC).*

Even if you are a seasoned Excel user, I urge you to take Euripides' advice and complete this session. You'll fly through it if you already know most of the skills covered.

In my classes I often teach professionals who have used Excel for over ten years and they *always* get some nugget of fantastically useful information from this session.

In this session I teach you the absolute basics you need before you can start to do useful work with Excel 2007.

I don't assume that you have any previous exposure to Excel (in any version) so I have to include some very basic skills.

If you're moving to Excel 2007 from an earlier version this session will de-mystify Microsoft's new fluent user interface (Ribbon).

Session Objectives

By the end of this session you will be able to:

- Start Excel and check your program version
- Maximize, minimize, re-size, move and close the Excel window
- Understand the Application and Workbook windows
- Open and navigate a workbook
- Save a workbook
- Pin a document and understand file organization
- View, add, rename, delete and navigate worksheet tabs
- Use the Ribbon
- Understand Ribbon components
- Customize the Quick Access Toolbar and preview the printout
- Use the Mini Toolbar, Key Tips and keyboard shortcuts
- Understand Views
- Use full screen view
- Use the help system

Video

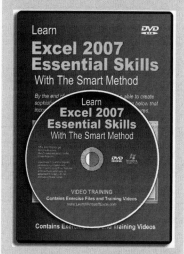

I've recorded a video walk-through for all of the lessons in this book.

The videos show you a full-size recorded Excel screen with my voice-over as I walk you through each lesson.

You can watch a free video for each of the lessons in this session at:

www.LearnMicrosoftExcel.com

Lesson 1-1: Start Excel and check your program version

If you are using Windows XP or Windows 7 the procedure is almost the same as described here. You should be able to figure out the differences!

1 Click the *Windows Start Button* at the bottom left of your screen.

2 Click the *All Programs* item at the bottom of the pop-up menu.

3 Scroll down the list and click on the Microsoft Office item.

4 Pin *Microsoft Office Excel 2007* to the start menu.

You'll be using Excel a lot so it makes sense to pin it to the start menu. This will make it appear at the top of the list in future so you'll be able to start Excel with just two clicks.

To pin to the start menu, point to *Microsoft Office Excel 2007* in the list, right-click your mouse and then choose *Pin to Start Menu* from the shortcut menu.

5 Left-click Microsoft Office Excel 2007 to start the application.

Excel starts and is displayed on the screen:

6 Check the program version.

Click the *Microsoft Office button* at the top left of the screen and then click the *Excel Options* button at the bottom right of the dialog.

Click *Resources* from the left hand sidebar and you'll see the version number at the bottom of the dialog:

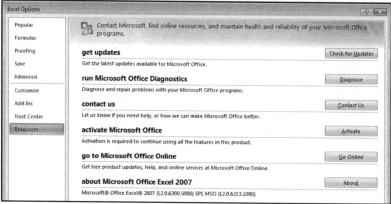

In this example the Excel version is:

about Microsoft Office Excel 2007
Microsoft® Office Excel® 2007 (12.0.6300.5000) SP1 MSO (12.0.6213.1000)

The important part is the *SP1* denoting that you have *service pack one* installed. If this says SP2, SP3 or an even larger number this is also fine. It simply means that Microsoft have fixed even more bugs in their product since this book was published.

If you do not see any reference to SPn, you have an early, un-patched version of Excel 2007 and you should update it (the update is free) via the Internet.

7 Check the Operating System version.

Click the *About Button* next to *about Microsoft Excel 2007*. A dialog is displayed with information about your copy of Excel.

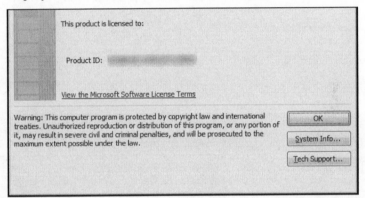

Click the *System Info...* button. The Operating System (OS) Name and Version will then be visible at the top right of the dialog:

Vista

Item	Value
OS Name	Microsoft® Windows Vista™ Ultimate
Version	6.0.6001 Service Pack 1 Build 6001

Windows XP

Item	Value
OS Name	Microsoft Windows XP Professional
Version	5.1.2600 Service Pack 2 Build 2600

Once again, it doesn't matter if you have Vista running a later service pack than SP1 (or Windows XP running a later service pack than SP2).

If you're running Vista or Windows XP, any edition will suffice (it doesn't have to be the Ultimate or Professional edition).

8 Click the close button ☒ on the top right corner of each dialog to return to the Excel screen.

Lesson 1-2: Maximize, minimize, re-size, move and close the Excel window

The great successful men of the world have used their imaginations, they think ahead and create their mental picture, and then go to work materializing that picture in all its details, filling in here, adding a little there, altering this a bit and that bit, but steadily building, steadily building.

Robert Collier, American motivational author, (1885-1950)

Now that Excel is open you are confronted with a dazzling array of buttons, switches and other artifacts.

For now let's explore the big picture by looking at how the Excel window can be sized and moved. The details will come later.

1   Understand the Maximize, Minimize and Restore Down buttons

At the top right corner of the Excel window you'll see three buttons.

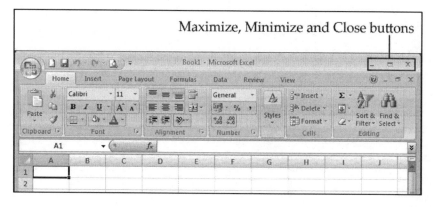

The buttons that you see will depend upon how the Excel window was left last time the application closed down. Normally the Excel screen is Maximized to fill the screeen and you'll see:

But if you had reduced the size of the Excel window so that it didn't fill the screen you'll see this instead:

Try clicking the *Maximize, Minimize* and *Restore Down* buttons but be careful to click the group of three buttons at the very top of the

window and not the similar group beneath (we'll be visiting those in the next lesson).

- *Maximize* makes the Excel window completely fill the screen.
- *Minimize* reduces Excel to a button on the bottom task bar.

Click this button again to restore the window to its previous size.

- *Restore Down* makes the Excel window smaller allowing you to re-size the window.

2   Re-size the window

After clicking the *Restore Down* button you are able to re-size the window. Hover over either the side of the window, or a corner of the window, with your mouse cursor. The cursor shape will change to a double-headed arrow.

When you see either cursor shape, hold down the left mouse button and move the mouse (this is called *click and drag*) to re-size the window.

Clicking and dragging a corner allows you to change both the height and width of the window.

Clicking an edge allows you to change only one dimension.

3   Move the window.

Click and drag the Title Bar (the bar at the very top of the window) to move the Excel Application window around the screen.

4   Close Excel

There are two common ways to close down Excel and three lesser used methods (see sidebar). Most people will use one of the following methods:

Click on the *Close button* ☒ at the top right of the Excel application window.

OR

Click on the *Office button* 🔘 at the top left of the screen and then click on the *Exit Excel* button at the bottom right of the dialog.

---

note

Other ways to close down Excel

There are three expert ways of closing Excel that will save a second or two of your time.

1. Double click the Office button at the top left of your screen.

2. Press the **<Ctrl>+<W>** keys on your keyboard. We'll be learning more about keyboard shortcuts later in this session.

3. Press the **<Alt>+<F4>** keys on your keyboard.

Lesson 1-3: Understand the Application and Workbook windows

Excel can be thought of as a frame (the *Application window*) containing one or more *Workbook windows*. Most of the time you will work with one *Application window* containing one *Workbook window*.

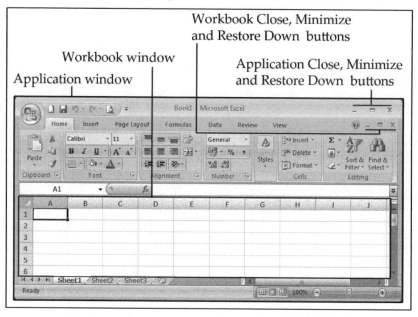

The screen grab above shows the normal way of working. The Workbook window is maximized within the Application window.

If the Workbook (that's the lower group of three buttons) *Restore Down* button is clicked the workbook window floats within the frame provided by the Application window.

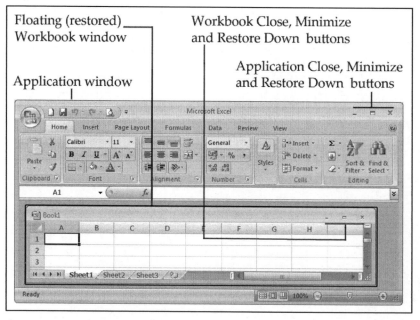

1   Close Excel down and re-start it again.

note

What's the point of having a floating workbook window?

At this stage in your journey of discovery, none at all.

You need to know how to maximize, minimize and restore down the workbook window because you might do it by accident and need to fix things up again.

In *Lesson 2-2: Create a new workbook and view two workbooks at the same time,* you'll see how Excel is able to display more than one Workbook window within the Application window. This allows you to view two workbooks at the same time.

2   Click the Workbook's Restore Down button (that's the one in the lower group of three buttons).

The workbook floats within the Application window:

Notice that the workbook's *Maximize, Minimize* and *Restore Down* buttons have now moved to the top right corner of the floating window.

3   Click the Workbook's Maximize button.

The workbook completely fills the Application window:

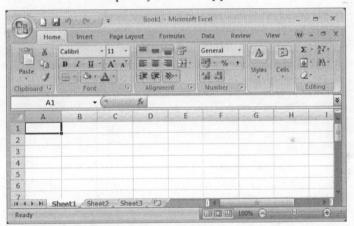

4   Understand the two close buttons.

You've probably noticed that there are two close buttons on screen. One for the Application window, and one for the Workbook window. How these buttons work is quite quirky.

Application close button

- Closes both the application and workbook windows when only one workbook is open, or no workbooks are open.
- Closes only the active workbook (that's the one that is currently on display), when more than one workbook is open.

Workbook close button

- Closes the workbook but always leave the application window open.

important

Organizing your sample files folder!

When you complete a lesson that involves a sample file that is changed, you will be instructed to save the file with a suffix.

By the time you've completed the course you'll have sample files such as:

Sales
Sales-1
Sales-2
Sales-3 ... etc

The first file is a sample file that you downloaded, and the others (with the number postfix) are interim versions as you complete each lesson.

The sample file set includes the sample file *and all interim versions.*

The interim versions are provided for three reasons:

1. If your work-in-progress becomes unusable (for example after a system crash) you can continue without starting at the beginning again.

2. If a lesson doesn't seem to give the results described, you can view the example to get some clues about what has gone wrong.

3. When you have completed the course you will use this book as a reference. The interim versions allow you to work through any of the lessons in isolation if you need to remind yourself how to use a specific Excel feature.

It is a good idea to place the sample files in a different folder to your saved work. If you don't do this you'll be over-writing the sample interim files (such as Sales-1, Sales-2 etc) with your own finished work.

The Wealth of Nations

Lesson 1-4: Open and navigate a workbook

Excel uses the analogy of a book that has many pages. In Excel terminology we use the term: *Workbook* for the book and *Worksheet* for each of the pages. We'll be learning more about worksheets later in this session in *Lesson 1-7: View, add, rename, delete and navigate worksheet tabs.*

1   Download the sample files (if you haven't already done so).

    1.   Open your web browser and type in the URL:

        www.learnmicrosoftexcel.com

    2.   Click the download link on the top left of the home page.

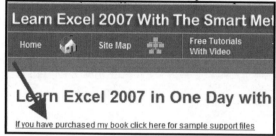

    3.   Download the sample files.

2   Open the sample workbook: *The Wealth of Nations*.

    1.   Open Excel and then click on the Office button at the top left of the screen.

    2.   Select *Open* from the drop down menu. Navigate to the folder containing the sample files and double click *The Wealth of Nations* to open the sample workbook.

        If you prefer to use the keyboard, another way to open a workbook is to hold down the **<Ctrl>** key and then press the **<O>** key.

3   Go to Cell ZZ3 using the Name box.

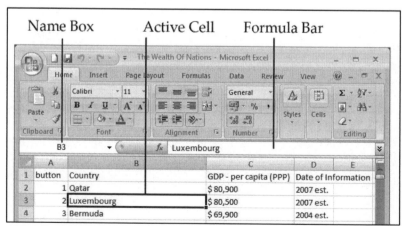

Excel uses the letter of the column and the number of the row to identify cells. This is called the *cell address*. In the above example the cell address of the active cell is B3.

note

Excel 2007 is big!

"Space is big - really big - you just won't believe how vastly, hugely mind-bogglingly big it is. You may think it's a long way down the road to the chemist, but that's just peanuts to space".

Douglas Adams, The Hitchhikers' Guide to the Galaxy

A compelling reason to upgrade from Excel 2003 to the new 2007 version is the sheer size of worksheets that can now be manipulated.

Excel versions 97-2003 were limited to 65,536 rows and 256 columns.

Many of my clients have needed to overcome the "65,000 row problem" in earlier Excel versions. Until now that meant moving to Access (Microsoft's database management application).

Excel 2007 worksheets can have up to 1,048,576 rows and 16,585 columns.

Put into more understandable terms.

- You could create a single worksheet with the name of every human being on the planet and you wouldn't run out of cells (in fact, you wouldn't have even used half of your worksheet).

- If you filled every cell and printed out the worksheet it would be 3.25 miles (5.24 kilometres) long and 320 yards (293 Metres) wide – that's a lot of paper.

Believe it or not, some of my clients aren't even happy with this and are now running into the "million row problem"!

In Excel 2007 there are a little over a million rows and a little over sixteen thousand columns. You may wonder how it is possible to name all of these columns with only 26 letters in the alphabet.

When Excel runs out of letters it starts using two: X,Y,Z and then AA, AB, AC etc. But even two letters is not enough. When Excel reaches column ZZ it starts using three letters: ZX, ZY, ZZ and then AAA, AAB, AAC etc.

The currently selected cell is called the *Active Cell* and has a black line around it. The Active Cell's address is always displayed in the *Name Box* and its contents are displayed in the *Formula Bar*.

We can also use the Name Box to move to a specific cell.

To see this in action, type **ZZ3** into the *Name Box* and then press the **<Enter>** key. You are teleported to cell ZZ3:

ZZ3				f_x			
	ZS	ZT	ZU	ZV	ZW	ZX	ZY	ZZ
1								
2								
3								
4								

4   Return to Cell A1 by pressing <Ctrl>+<Home>.

5   Go to the end of the worksheet by pressing <Ctrl>+<End>.

6   Use the Scroll Bars.

There are two scroll bars for Excel's workbook window.

The vertical scroll bar runs from top to bottom of the worksheet window and allows you to quickly move up and down the worksheet.

The horizontal scroll bar is at the bottom right hand side of the workbook window and allows you to move to the left and right in wide worksheets.

Here's how the scroll bars work:

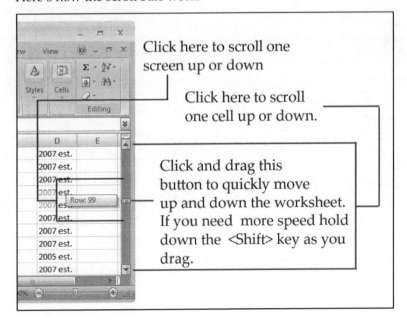

Click here to scroll one screen up or down

Click here to scroll one cell up or down.

Click and drag this button to quickly move up and down the worksheet. If you need more speed hold down the <Shift> key as you drag.

Lesson 1-5: Save a workbook

1 Save the workbook

When you are editing a workbook, the changes you make are only held in the computer's memory. If there is a power cut or your computer crashes you will lose any work that has been done since the last save.

For this reason you should get into the habit of regularly saving your work.

Even though we haven't changed this worksheet, let's save it now by clicking the Save button on the Quick Access Toolbar at the top left of the screen.

2 Save the workbook with a different name.

Click the *Office button* and then hover the mouse cursor over the *Save As* item in the drop-down dialog.

You can see that it is possible to save your file in many different formats.

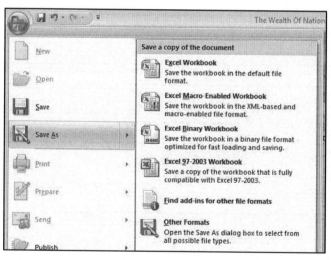

3 Understand file formats.

Excel Workbook (the Open XML format)

Until very recently every program stored its information on the hard disk in a completely different way. These incompatible formats are called *binary formats*. This made it very difficult to write applications that could be used together.

All of this has changed with the new file format: *Office Open XML*.

The Wealth of Nations

note

How users of earlier office versions can read your OpenXML files

Microsoft has a free download: The Microsoft Office Compatibility Pack.

If users of Excel XP (2002) or 2003 install this they will be able to read and save Word, Excel and PowerPoint 2007 files in the new OpenXML format.

If the user has Office 97 or Office 2000 they are out of luck. You'll have to save your files in the old 97-2003 format if you need to share them.

The Smart Method still runs many Excel 2000 courses (especially for clients in the banking and finance sector). These users have no solution to read an Open XML workbook other than to upgrade.

Of course, as the years pass this will become less of an issue.

Microsoft have published exactly how this format works and given it away free to the world's developer community. This allows other programs to easily work with Excel workbook files. For example, Apple's iPhone already supports Office Open XML Email attachments.

Unfortunately the future has to co-exist with the past and there are a lot of people in the world using the older versions of Office (97, 2000, 2002 and 2003). If you save your files in the new Open XML format only people running Office 2007 will be able to read them (but see the sidebar for a potential solution to this problem).

Excel Macro Enabled Workbook

The Excel Macro Enabled Workbook is simply a workbook that has program code (called Macro code) embedded within it. Macros are beyond the scope of this book but are covered in our *Excel Expert Skills* book

Macro programming (also called VBA programming) is a vast subject of its own and is not useful to the vast majority of Excel users. The Smart Method run comprehensive Excel VBA courses but they are usually only taken by scientists and engineers who need to add very advanced functionality to Excel.

Earlier versions of Excel could potentially allow a workbook to infect your machine with a macro virus because all Excel files were capable of carrying macros. By separating the formats it is easier to avoid opening potentially infected files.

Excel 97-2003 Workbook

This is the old binary format that allows users with earlier versions of Excel to read your workbooks. Some features won't work in earlier versions and if you've used those in your workbook Excel will display a warning and tell you which features will be lost.

Excel Binary Workbook

An oddity in Excel 2007 is a new binary format: Excel Binary Workbook. This is a binary alternative to Open XML but it can't be read by earlier versions of Excel. The advantage of this format is that it loads and saves more quickly than Open XML.

4   Save the workbook with a different name.

1. Click on the *Excel Workbook* icon.

2. Type: **The Wealth of Nations Copy** into the *File name* text box.

3. Click the *Save* button.

   Notice that the name of the workbook in the title bar (at the top of the window) has now changed indicating that you are now viewing the new workbook that you have just saved.

File name: The Wealth of Nations Copy
Save as type: Excel Workbook

Lesson 1-6: Pin a document and understand file organization

tip

Increasing the number of items in the recent documents list.

Excel remembers the seventeen most recently opened documents.

As you open more documents the seventeenth oldest is removed from the Recent Documents list unless you pin it.

If you'd like to increase Excel's memory up to a maximum of fifty items here's how it's done:

1. Click the Office button at the top left of the screen.

2. Click the *Excel Options* button at the bottom right of the dialog.

3. Choose *Advanced* from the left hand pane.

4. Scroll down the right-hand list until you find the *Display* category. You'll see *Show this number of Recent Documents: 17*.

5. Change the number to the number of recent documents you'd prefer Excel to remember (up to a maximum of fifty).

1 Close down and restart Excel.

2 Pin a workbook to the Recent Documents list.

1. Click the Office Button at the top left of the screen.

On the right hand side of the dialog is a list of all recently opened documents beginning with the most recent (probably the *Wealth of Nations* worksheet opened during the last lesson).

Note that there is a pin icon ⊞ next to each workbook name.

When you hover the mouse cursor over the pin a tooltip is displayed saying: *Pin this document to the Recent Documents list.*

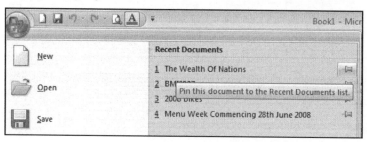

This can be a great time saver as it enables any workbook that you use a lot to always be in the *Recent Documents* list. You won't have to waste time looking for it on the hard drive.

2. Click the pin icon. The icon changes from unpinned ⊞ to pinned.

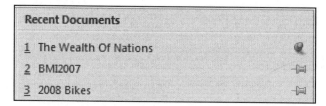

3. Click on *The Wealth of Nations* to open the workbook.

3 Understand file organization.

By default Excel saves all workbooks into your documents folder along with other Office documents (such as Word and PowerPoint files). This clearly is going to cause problems when you have a few hundred files.

Better to organize yourself from the start by setting up an orderly filing system.

I create a folder called *Excel* beneath the *Documents* folder (Windows Vista) or the *MyDocuments* folder (Windows XP). In this folder I create subfolders to store my work. You can see a screen

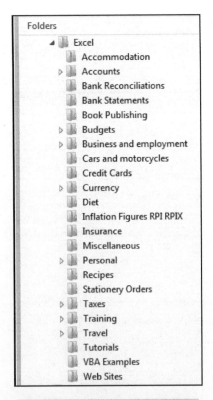

tip

Learning more about file organization.

Microsoft have some good ideas about good file organization. You can read their recommendations at:

www.microsoft.com/atwork/manageinfo/files.mspx

grab of my Excel folder in the sidebar (of course, your needs will be different to mine).

4 Set the default file location.

If you take my advice and create an Excel folder you will waste a mouse click every time you open a file because Excel will take you to the *documents* folder by default.

Here's how to reset the default file location to your new Excel folder:

1. Click the Office button 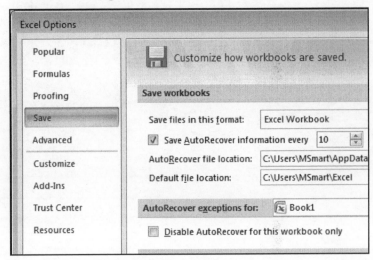 at the top left of the screen.

2. Click the Excel Options button at the bottom right of the dialog.

3. Choose the Save category from the left hand side of the dialog.

4. Change the default file location.

   You have to actually type in the default file location. Microsoft seems to have forgotten to add a browse button!

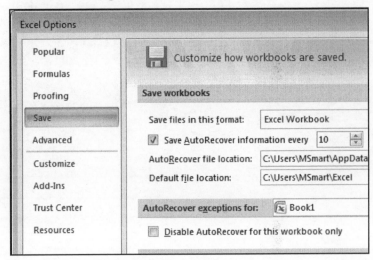

When you click Office→Open in future you'll automatically be taken to your Excel folder ready to choose a category.

During the remainder of the book I'll explain the above sequence of choices like this:

Click: Office→Excel Option→Save, and then change the default file location.

This will save a lot of time and forests!

Lesson 1-7: View, add, rename, delete and navigate worksheet tabs

When you save an Excel file onto your hard disk, you are saving a single workbook containing one or more worksheets.

You can add as many Worksheets as you like to a Workbook.

There are two types of worksheet. Regular worksheets contain cells (just like the one you're looking at now). Chart sheets, as you would expect, each contain a single chart (we'll be exploring charts in depth in: *Session Five: Charts and Graphics*).

1   Open *The Wealth of Nations* from your sample files folder (if it isn't already open).

2   Move between worksheets.

Look at the tabs on the bottom left corner of your screen. Notice that this sample workbook contains three worksheets: GDP, Life Expectancy and Mobile Phones. Click on each tab in turn to view the different worksheets.

3   Add a new worksheet.

1.   Click the Insert Worksheet tab (the tiny tab next to Mobile Phones). A new tab appears named *Sheet1*.

2.   Double-click the *Sheet1* tab.

3.   Type the word **Population** followed by the **<Enter>** key.

4   Move a worksheet's tab.

1.   Click on the Population tab (you may have to do this twice).

2.   Drag to the left. As you drag you'll notice an icon of a page and a black arrow telling you where the tab will be placed.

3.   Release the mouse button to move the tab to the location of your choice.

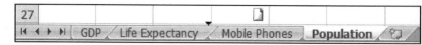

5   Understand the tab scroll buttons

Because this workbook only has four tabs, there's no need to use the tab scroll buttons (in fact, they won't work at all when all tabs are visible).

The Wealth of Nations

When there are more tabs than will fit on the screen the *tab scroll buttons* are used to move between tabs.

6   **Move between worksheets using the keyboard.**

You can move between worksheets using only the keyboard by pressing the **<Ctrl>+<PgUp>** and **<Ctrl>+<PgDn>** keyboard shortcuts to cycle through all of the tabs in your workbook.

7   **Change tab colors.**

The colored tab feature was only added in Excel 2003 and most users have yet to discover that they can color code their tabs. Others will be very impressed if you color code yours!

1.   Right-click on any of the tabs and choose *Tab Color* from the shortcut menu.

2.   Choose any color.

3.   Repeat for the other tabs on the worksheet.

8   **Delete a worksheet.**

Right click on the Population tab and select *Delete* from the shortcut menu.

9   **Delete several worksheets at the same time.**

1.   Hold down the **<Ctrl>** key.

2.   Click each tab you want to delete in turn. Don't select them all as it isn't possible to delete every worksheet in a workbook.

3.   Right click any of the selected tabs and select Delete from the shortcut menu.

Don't worry about the missing tabs. We're going to close the workbook without saving it so you won't overwrite the original workbook.

10   **Close the workbook without saving it.**

1.   Click Office→Close.

A dialog is displayed:

2.   Click *No* so that you don't over-write the workbook.

Because you haven't saved the workbook it will remain in its original state when you next open it.

note

Older versions of Excel hid all of their best features underneath an arcane system of menu navigation. Many users didn't know that half of the features were there at all.

Because only the standard and formatting toolbars were visible on screen, users didn't explore the menu options and, instead, used only a tiny subset of Excel's features.

The Ribbon makes Excel seem overwhelming because all of those features are right in your face.

Hardly anybody in the workplace today understands every one of Excel's features. You'll be doing productive work with Excel by session two of this book while using a tiny subset of the full feature set. By the end of the book you'll be thoroughly competent working with Excel.

note

The Ribbon shows more if you have a wide screen

When I work with Excel I use a 22 inch widescreen monitor running at 1,680*1,050 pixels.

Excel uses the extra screen space to display extended descriptions of each feature on the Ribbon.

For example, the Styles pane on the Home Ribbon expands to show buttons for nine common cell styles allowing them to be applied with a single click rather than two clicks.

Lesson 1-8: Use the Ribbon

Look what they've done to my song, Ma
Look what they've done to my song
Well it's the only thing I could do half right
And it's turning out all wrong, Ma
Look what they've done to my song

Song lyric by Melanie (M. Safka)

The Ribbon causes huge frustration for seasoned Excel 97 to 2003 users as everything seems to be in the "wrong place". "Look what they've done to Excel" they cry. But it's a better, and an entirely new, way of working.

The sheer breadth of Excel features can seem overwhelming. This book will gently introduce all of the most important features, one at a time. By the end of the book you'll be really comfortable and productive with the Ribbon.

1 Start Excel and open a new workbook.

1. Click Office→New.

The New Workbook dialog appears.

2. Double-click the *Blank Workbook* icon to create a new blank workbook.

2 Use Ribbon tabs.

Each Ribbon tab has its own toolkit available to you. By far the most important tab is the *Home* tab which has buttons for all of the most common and useful features.

Click each tab in turn and view the buttons. The screen grab below has the *Insert Tab* selected. Don't worry if the buttons seem cryptic at the moment. Most of them will make complete sense by the end of this book.

If you later go on to complete the Expert course too, Excel will have no mysteries left at all!

note

contextual tabs

If you are doing something special, such as previewing a worksheet, Excel doesn't want to bother you with a lot of commands that are irrelevant.

For this reason you'll often see a cut-down version of the Ribbon, listing only the commands that are available at that time. For example, when you change to print preview view (we cover that later in *Lesson 1-10: Customize the Quick Access Toolbar and preview the printout*), you'll see a cut-down Ribbon with only one tab containing all of the things you are able to do when previewing a printout.

Sometimes Excel will show you even more tabs. For example, when you select a picture, a *Picture Tools* tab group will magically appear containing a *Format* tab. This enables you to enhance the picture.

note

Other ways to show and hide the Ribbon

1. Press <Ctrl>+<F1>.

2. Right-click anywhere on the Ribbon and choose *minimize the Ribbon* from the shortcut menu.

You can do any of the above a second time to bring the Ribbon back.

If you close Excel with the Ribbon hidden it will still be hidden when you re-open it.

Customize Quick Access Toolbar Button

3   Type the word **Test** into any blank cell and then press the <Enter> key on the keyboard once.

Notice how the Active Cell moves to the cell beneath.

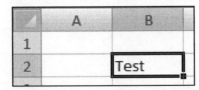

4   Make the cell with the word *Test* into the active cell.

Click once on the word *Test* or use the arrow keys on the keyboard to navigate back to the cell. Be very careful not to double-click otherwise Excel will think that you want to edit the cell.

5   Click the *Home* tab on the Ribbon and focus upon the Font panel (it's the second panel from the left). Try clicking each of the buttons and you will see the word *Test* change to reflect your choices.

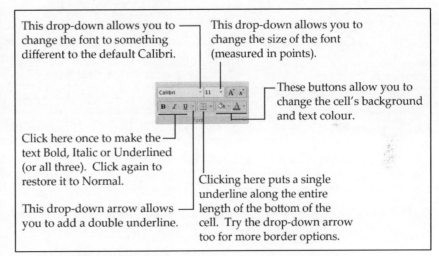

This drop-down allows you to change the font to something different to the default Calibri.

This drop-down allows you to change the size of the font (measured in points).

These buttons allow you to change the cell's background and text colour.

Click here once to make the text Bold, Italic or Underlined (or all three). Click again to restore it to Normal.

This drop-down arrow allows you to add a double underline.

Clicking here puts a single underline along the entire length of the bottom of the cell. Try the drop-down arrow too for more border options.

6   Minimize the Ribbon.

To minimize the Ribbon in order to save screen space, click the *Customize the Quick Access Toolbar* button (see sidebar) and choose *Minimize the Ribbon* from the drop-down menu. Notice how the Ribbon now takes up far less screen space.

An even quicker way of doing the same thing is to double-click any of the tabs.

Double-click once more to bring the Ribbon back to full size.

7   Save your work with the name *Ribbon Test* and close Excel.

Click Office→Save As→Excel Workbook, type in the file name (Ribbon) and then click the Save button.

Lesson 1-9: Understand Ribbon components

The whole is more than the sum of its parts.
Aristotle, Greek critic, philosopher, physicist & zoologist (384 BC – 322 BC)

The Ribbon is made up of several different artifacts.

Normal button

Simply executes a command when clicked. The Bold button on the Home tab is a good example.

Menu button

This type of button has a little down-arrow on it. It will display a Menu or Gallery when clicked.

Split button

This is the hardest button to understand because these buttons look almost the same as the *menu or gallery* button. When you hover the mouse cursor over a split button, the icon and drop-down arrow highlight seperately as different "buttons within a button".

A good example is the *underline* button on the Home toolbar.

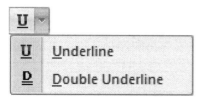

Clicking the icon part of a split button (the <u>U</u>) will perform the default action of the button (in this case a single underline). Clicking the arrow part of the button will display a menu of further choices (in this case the choice between a single and double underline).

Check box

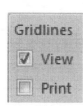

A little square box that you can click to switch an option on or off.

In this example (from the *Page Layout* Ribbon) you are able to switch the gridlines on and off for the screen display and/or the printout.

Command group

Similar actions are grouped into a cluster. For example, every component relating to numbers is clustered into the Number group.

Dialog launcher

Dialog launchers appear on the bottom right-hand corner of some command groups. Dialogs offer more choice than it is possible for the Ribbon to express graphically. Many of the dialog launchers will present a dialog that is identical to the old dialogs from Excel 2003.

Drop down list

I often shorten this to simply "Drop Down" in this book. A drop down is a simple menu listing several choices.

If you see an ellipsis (…) after a drop down list item this means that a dialog will be displayed after you click, offering further choices.

Drop down gallery

This is a little like a drop down list but has graphics to visually demonstrate the effect of each choice.

Rich menu

The rich menu is Microsoft's way of trying to coerce you into being brave enough to use a feature that you might not have understood in previous Excel versions. A sort of an "in your face" help system.

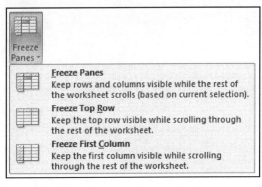

This rich menu can be found at:

View→Window→Freeze Panes

You'll find out what it is used for later in the book in: *Lesson 3-16: Freeze columns and rows.*

note

If you are used to an earlier version of Excel you might wonder where all of the toolbars have gone?

In earlier versions of Excel it was possible to create as many of your own custom toolbars as you wanted.

The new Ribbon based user interface (Microsoft calls this the *Fluent Interface*) means that you don't need to create toolbars to the same extent in Excel 2007, because every panel on the Ribbon is, essentially, a toolbar.

Lesson 1-10: Customize the Quick Access Toolbar and preview the printout

In Excel 2007 you may have just one custom toolbar: the *Quick Access Toolbar*. In this lesson we'll add some useful buttons to the Quick Access Toolbar to save a few clicks.

The Quick Access Toolbar is one of the keys to being really productive with Excel 2007. This lesson will introduce you to the main features.

1   Open *The Wealth of Nations* from your sample folder, (if it isn't already open).

2   Preview how the *Life Expectancy* worksheet will look when printed.

   1.   Click the *Life Expectancy tab* at the bottom of the worksheet.

   2.   Click Office→Print→Print Preview:

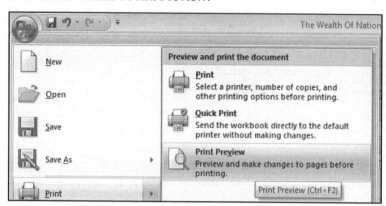

A preview of how the page will print is displayed.

Notice that the Ribbon now displays a contextual menu because there are only a few options open to you when previewing.

   3.   Click the *Next Page* and *Previous Page* buttons to move through the print preview.

   4.   Use the *Zoom* button to magnify the page for a clearer view.

   5.   Click the *Close Print Preview* button to return to the workbook.

3   Add a Print Preview button to the Quick Access Toolbar.

Print Preview is a very useful feature and you'll probably use it a lot. Every time you use it, however, it is going to take three clicks of the mouse. Wouldn't it be better if you could show a print preview with just one click?

   1.   Click the *Customize Quick Access Toolbar button* (see sidebar).

   2.   Click the *Print Preview* item in the drop-down list.

The Wealth of Nations

note

Some amazing Excel features cannot be used at all without customizing the Quick Access Toolbar!

One of my favourite features in Excel 2007 is its ability to read the workbook to me via its *Text to Voice* facility.

When I need to input lots of numbers from a sheet of paper and want to check them I get Excel to read them to me as I tick each off my list. This is much faster and nicer than continuously looking first at the screen, then at the paper, for each entry.

This feature is covered in depth in the Expert Skills book in this series.

You can't use this feature at all unless you add some custom buttons to the Quick Access Toolbar!

tip

The Quick Access Toolbar is one of the keys to being really productive with Excel 2007.

Always try to minimize the number of mouse clicks needed to do common tasks.

If you find yourself forever changing tabs to use a button, change two clicks into one by adding the button to the Quick Access Toolbar.

All of those extra clicks add up to a lot of time over the weeks and years.

A new button now appears on the Quick Access Toolbar. You are now able to Print Preview your work with a single click of the mouse.

4   Add a Font Color button to the Quick Access Toolbar.

The *More Commands...* option is available when you click the *Customize Quick Access Toolbar* button. This enables you to add any command in Excel to the toolbar. But there's an easier way!

1.   Click the *Home tab* on the Ribbon (if it isn't already selected)

2.   Right-click on the *Font Color* button in the *Font Group*.

3.   Click *Add to Quick Access Toolbar*.

A *Font Color* button is added to the Quick Access Toolbar.

5   Remove a button from the Quick Access Toolbar.

1.   Right-click on the *Font Color* button you've just added to the Quick Access Toolbar.

2.   Click *Remove from Quick Access Toolbar* on the shortcut menu.

6   Add separators to make heavily customized Quick Access toolbars more readable.

1.   When you add many items to the Quick Access toolbar it is a good idea to use separators to split icons into logical groups.

2.   Click the Customize Quick Access Toolbar button.

3.   Click More Commands... on the shortcut menu.

4.   Click the   <Separator>   item at the top of the Commands list.

5.   Click the Add>> button.   Add >>

6.   Use the up and down buttons to move the separator to the required location.

Here's a screen grab of my own Quick Access Toolbar:

note

Keyboard shortcuts are one of the secrets of maximizing productivity with Excel

Many years ago I took my mouse and stuck it to the back of my monitor with sticky tape.

For a whole day I struggled to work without it.

The first few hours weren't much fun but after that my work became faster and faster. It became a challenge to figure out how to do things without the mouse.

You will be far more productive if you can get into the same habit.

These days, there are some things that you simply need the mouse for, and some things that are genuinely faster (or easier) with the mouse. For most common tasks, however, there are keyboard shortcuts and Excel 2007 has just made things a lot easier with the new Key Tips feature.

Lesson 1-11: Use the Mini Toolbar, Key Tips and keyboard shortcuts

1 Open the *Wealth of Nations* sample worksheet (if it isn't already open).

2 Select cell B2 (Qatar) on the GDP worksheet.

1. Click on the *GDP* tab.

2. Click on cell B2 (Qatar).

Make sure that you only click once otherwise Excel will think that you are trying to edit the cell.

	A	B	C
1	button	Country	GDP - per capita (PPP)
2	1	Qatar	$ 80,900

3 Make cell B2 (Qatar) bold, italicized and underlined.

1. Click Home→Font→Bold

2. Click Home→Font→Italic

3. Click Home→Font→Underline

	A	B	C
1	button	Country	GDP - per capita (PPP)
2	1	*Qatar*	$ 80,900

4 Display Key Tips.

Hold down the **<Alt>** key on the keyboard.

Notice how Key Tips are now displayed on the Ribbon and the Quick Access Toolbar:

5 Use the Key Tips to show a print preview using only the keyboard.

The key tips reveal the key you need to press to simulate clicking any of the Ribbon and Quick Access Toolbar icons.

Hold down the **<Alt>** key and press the relevant number to show a print preview.

NB: Your toolbar, and the number you need to press, may look different to the screen grab above. For example, the print preview

The Wealth of Nations

button will not be on the Quick Access Toolbar unless you added it during: *Lesson 1-10: Customize the Quick Access Toolbar and preview the printout.*

6   Click the Close Print Preview button to return to normal

7   Use the mouse to select the text *Qatar* in cell B2.

   1.   Double-click the cell containing the text.

       You'll see the cursor flashing in the cell.

   2.   Position the cursor just after the word *Qatar* and hold down the left mouse button.

   3.   Drag the mouse across the complete word until it is highlighted like this:

       Qatar

8   Observe the *Mini Toolbar*.

Hover the mouse cursor over the selected text and you should see a "ghost" image of the Mini Toolbar just above the cell:

When you move the mouse cursor up and over the Mini Toolbar it will light up.

9   Use the Mini Toolbar to restore the text to non-bold and non-italic.

Click on the Bold [B] and Italic [I] buttons to remove the bold and italic attributes from the text.

       Qatar

10   Show a bigger Mini Toolbar with a right-click.

Right-click on *Bermuda* (Cell B4). Notice that, as well as the shortcut menu (see sidebar) you now get an even better Mini Toolbar with a few extra buttons.

11   Remove the underline from Qatar.

   1.   Click on Qatar again (cell B2).

   2.   Press the **<Ctrl>+<U>** keys on the keyboard to remove the underline.

But how can you remember cryptic keyboard shortcuts like <Ctrl>+<U>? Fortunately you don't have to. Hover the mouse over the underline button [U] and you'll see the keyboard shortcut listed in the tooltip.

Lesson 1-12: Understand views

Views are different ways to look at your worksheet.

Excel 2007 has three views. They are:-

View	Icon	What it is used for
Normal		This is the view you've been using until now. It's the view most users use all of the time when they are working with Excel.
Page layout		This is a fantastic new view for Excel 2007. It allows you to see (almost) exactly what the printout will look like. Unlike running a Print Preview you are able to edit cells just as you can in Normal view.
Page break preview		A page break is when the printer advances onto a new sheet of paper. We'll use this view in : *Lesson 7-5: Insert, delete and preview page breaks* to make sure that the page breaks in the right place.

1   Open the *Wealth of Nations* sample worksheet (if it isn't already open).

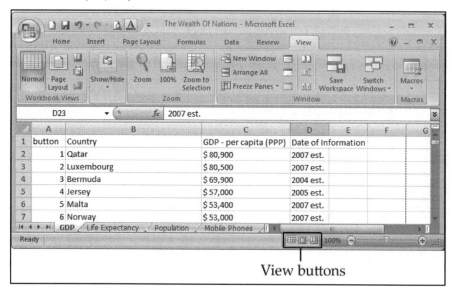

View buttons

2   Click on the GDP tab and then click on the *page layout view* button at the bottom of the screen.

The worksheet is displayed in *page layout view*. It is a little like *Print Preview view* as you are able to see (almost) exactly what will be printed. Headers, footers and margins are all shown.

Unlike *Print Preview* view you are able to edit the worksheet.

The Wealth of Nations

You may wonder why we don't use page layout view as the default when editing worksheets. While some users may prefer to do this, most will want to see the maximum amount of data possible on screen and so will prefer the Normal view.

3 Click the *page break preview button*.

The worksheet is displayed in page break preview view (you may also see a help dialog first).

This view shows each page with a watermark to indicate which sheet of paper it will be printed on:

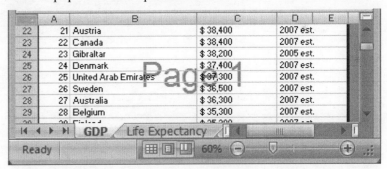

It also shows the break between each page as a dotted line:

It is possible to click and drag the dotted line to change the place where the page breaks. This will be covered in depth in: *Lesson 7-6: Adjust page breaks using Page Break Preview.*

Lesson 1-13: Use full screen view

1   Open the *Wealth of Nations* from your sample files folder (if it isn't already open) and click the *Life Expectancy* tab.

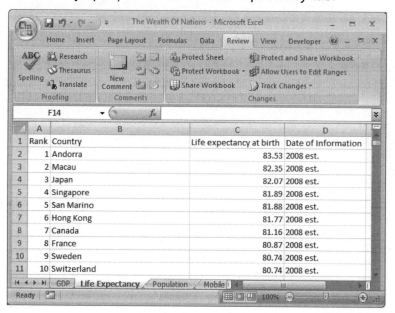

Notice that the Ribbon, formula bar and status bar are all taking up space that could be used to display information. In the example above only the first eleven rows are visible.

1   Double-click on any of the Ribbon tabs to hide the Ribbon.

With the Ribbon hidden things are a little better. Sixteen rows are now visible. Perhaps you may need to view even more. This is what *Full Screen View* is for.

2   Click View→Workbook Views→Full Screen.

The Wealth of Nations

Note that the Quick Access Toolbar, the Ribbon, the formula bar and the status bar have all vanished. On the above example shown at 1,024*768 screen resolution 34 rows are visible.

On my own 22 inch monitor running at 1,680*1,050 pixels in portrait mode I can view 81 rows of information on one screen.

3   Switch back to normal view.

To return to normal view either:

Press the **<Esc>** key on the keyboard.

OR

Right click in any cell and then click *Close Full Screen*.

Lesson 1-14: Use the help system

1 Click the Help button at the top right of your screen.

The help dialog is displayed:

If your screen doesn't look like this, click the *show/hide table of contents* button.

Tip

The *Keep On Top* button

When this button is pinned in like this: the help window will stay on top of all open Office windows.

When the button is unpinned like this the window will be hidden if you move other Office windows on top of the help window.

Note that this is only the case with Microsoft Office windows and not with windows from other applications.

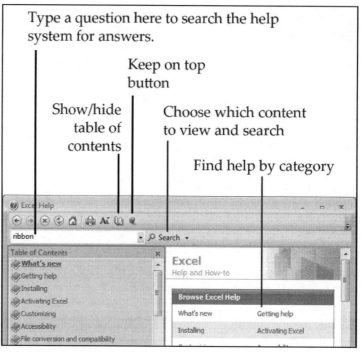

2 Type **how do I save a file** into the search box followed by the **<Enter>** key.

The help system provides many potential answers to the question:

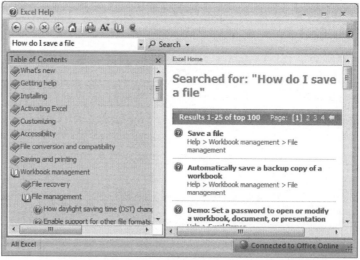

3 Click on the most likely answer to read the help topic.

Step by step instructions are displayed showing how to save a file.

4 Find help by category.

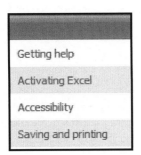

Let's do the same thing now using the category pane. The category pane is a little like a web page. You find the answer to your question by navigating a series of hyperlinks.

Close down the help system and re-start it. Look at all of the categories and decide which is most relevant. See if you can find a help topic for saving a file by navigating the hyperlinks. On my system I got there by clicking Workbook Management→Saving and Printing→Save a File but your links may differ.

The same help topic found earlier is displayed.

5 Choosing which content to search.

Excel is a huge application and just one help reference wouldn't be enough. As well as the help files stored on your hard disk you can also search a perpetually updating help resource on-line at Microsoft via the Internet.

Click the drop-down arrow next to the *Search* button at the top of the Help dialog.

The Search drop-down menu appears:

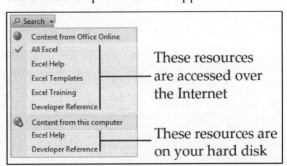

The Developer Reference contains topics only of interest to programmers who understand VBA macro code. This is a very advanced subject and is covered in the *Excel Expert Skills* book in this series.

6 Get help directly from the Ribbon.

1. Click the *Home tab* on the Ribbon and hover the mouse cursor over the drop down arrow to the right of the word *General* in the *Number group*.

   If you keep the mouse still, after a short delay a screen tip pops up providing a short description of what the drop-down list is for and also advising that you can obtain more help by pressing the <F1> key on your keyboard.

2. Press the <F1> button (at the top left of your keyboard) to obtain help about topics relevant to this control.

7 Obtain help directly from a dialog.

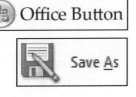

Click Office→Save As.

At the top right corner of the *Save As* dialog there is a help button

(if you are using Windows Vista).

Click it for detailed help about the Save As dialog.

Session 1: Exercise

In this exercise you'll try to remember the name of each of the Excel screen elements. The answers are on the next page so you might want to recap by turning the page for a little revision before you start.

Keep trying until you are able to name each of the screen elements from memory. We'll be using this terminology during the remainder of the book so it's important that you can correctly identify each element.

If you need help slide the page to the left

Session 1: Exercise answers

Ribbon

Office button

Name Box

Quick Access
Toolbar

Active Cell

Formula Bar

Title bar

Column Header

Minimize, Maximize
and Close buttons:
For Excel application
For this worksheet

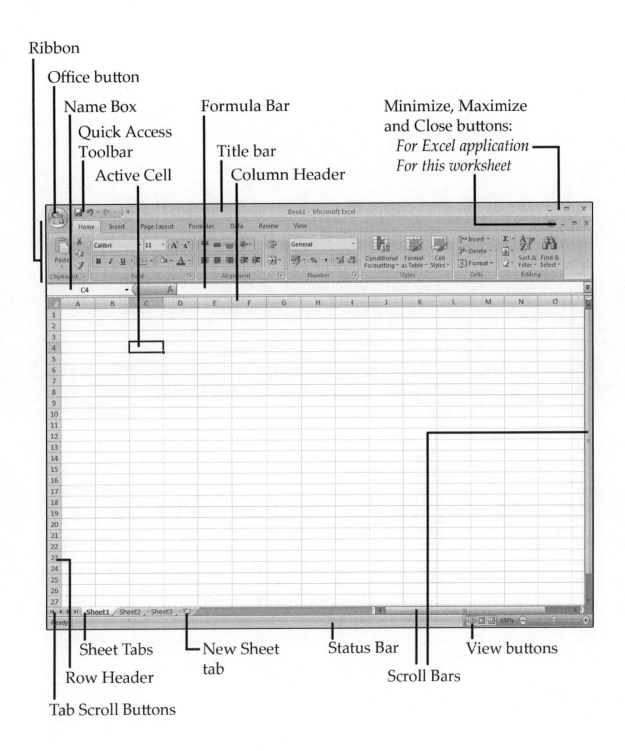

Sheet Tabs

Row Header

New Sheet
tab

Status Bar

View buttons

Scroll Bars

Tab Scroll Buttons

2

Session Two: Doing Useful Work with Excel

Only those who have the patience to do simple things perfectly ever acquire the skill to do difficult things easily.

Unknown author

Now that you've mastered the basics you are ready to do really useful work with this amazing tool. In this session you will learn to use all of Excel's basic features properly. This will put you way ahead of anybody that hasn't been formally trained in Excel best practice. You'll be doing simple things, but you'll be doing them perfectly!

Even after years of daily use many users are unable to properly use Excel's fundamental features. They often reach their goal, but get there in a very inefficient way simply because they were never taught how to do things correctly. By the end of this session you'll be astonished with how well you are working with Excel. What originally seemed like a baffling array of little colored buttons will suddenly all begin to make sense.

Session Objectives

By the end of this session you will be able to:

- Enter text and numbers into a worksheet
- Create a new workbook and view two workbooks at the same time
- Use AutoSum to quickly calculate totals
- Select a range of cells and understand Smart Tags
- Enter data into a range and copy data across a range
- Select adjacent and non-adjacent rows and columns
- Select non-contiguous cell ranges and view summary information
- Re-size rows and columns
- Use AutoSum to sum a non-contiguous range
- Use AutoSum to quickly calculate averages
- Create your own formulas
- Resize a column and create functions using Formula AutoComplete
- Use AutoFill for text and numeric series
- Use AutoFill to adjust formulas
- Use AutoFill Options
- Speed up your AutoFills and create a custom fill series
- Use the zoom control
- Print out a worksheet

Lesson 2-1: Enter text and numbers into a worksheet

Excel beginners tend to reach for the mouse far too often. One of the keys to productivity with Excel is to avoid using the mouse when entering data. In this lesson we'll quickly populate a worksheet without using the mouse at all.

1   Open the Sample file: *First Quarter Sales and Profit*.

	A	B	C	D
1	Sales and Profit Report - First Quarter 2008			
2				
3		Jan	Feb	Mar
4	New York	22,000	29,000	19,000
5	Los Angeles			
6	London			
7	Paris			
8	Munich			

2   Notice the difference between values and text.

Cells can contain values or text. Values can be numbers, dates or formulas (more on formulas later).

Excel usually does a great job of recognizing when there are values in a cell and when there is text. The giveaway is that text is always (by default) left aligned in the cell and values are right aligned.

Look at the numbers on this worksheet. Notice how they are all right aligned. This lets you know that Excel has correctly recognized them as values and will happily perform mathematical operations using them.

3   Save a value into a cell.

1.   Type the value 42000 into cell B5. Notice that the mouse cursor is still flashing in the cell.

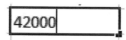

At this stage the value has not been saved into the cell.

If you change your mind, you can still undo the value by pressing the <ESC> key at the top left of your keyboard or by clicking the *Cancel button* on the left hand side of the Formula Bar.

2.   Decide that you want to keep this value in the cell by either pressing the <Enter>, <Tab> or an <Arrow> key on the keyboard, or by clicking the *Confirm button* on the Formula Bar.

4   Enter a column of data without using the mouse.

When you enter data into a column there's no need to use the mouse. Press the <Enter> key after each entry and the active cell moves to the cell beneath. Try this now with the following January sales data:

important

The many ways of entering numbers

Negative numbers

-123.56
(123.56)

Currency prefixes

Excel is quite happy for you to prefix a number with a currency symbol. The currency symbol it will accept depends upon how you defined the regional options in your operating system.

$123.56 (works in USA)
£123.56 (works in UK)

See *Lesson 4-3: Format numbers using built-in number formats* for an easy method of setting $, £ and € currency prefixes whatever your locale.

Commas

12,234,567.78

Fractions

You must leave a space between a number and a fraction for this to work.

6 1/4
(six, space, one, /, four)

The above will appear on the worksheet as 6.25 after you enter it in this way.

0 1/4
(zero, space, one,/,four)

The above will appear on the worksheet as 0.25. The leading zero is needed to prevent Excel from thinking that you are entering a date.

1. Type **18,000** into cell B6.

2. Press the **<Enter>** key to move to cell B7.

3. Do the same to enter the relevant values into the next two cells.

3		Jan	Feb	Mar
4	New York	22,000	29,000	19,000
5	Los Angeles	42,000		
6	London	18,000		
7	Paris	35,000		
8	Munich	12,000		

5 Enter a row of data without using the mouse.

When you enter a row of data you also don't have to use the mouse.

1. Click in Cell C5.

2. Type **39,000** and then press the **<Tab>** key on your keyboard.

    The <Tab> key is on the left hand side of the keyboard above the <Caps Lock> key. Notice how pressing the <Tab> key saves the value into the cell and then moves one cell to the right.

3. Type **43,000** in cell D5 and press the **<Enter>** key.

4. You magically move to cell C6 as Excel assumes you want to begin entering the next row.

6 Complete the table without using the mouse.

By using the <Tab> or <Enter> key in the right place you should be able to complete the table now without using the mouse:

	A	B	C	D
3		Jan	Feb	Mar
4	New York	22,000	29,000	19,000
5	Los Angeles	42,000	39,000	43,000
6	London	18,000	20,000	22,000
7	Paris	35,000	26,000	31,000
8	Munich	12,000	15,000	13,000

7 Change the text in cell B3 to January.

1. Double-click cell B3. Notice that there is now a flashing cursor in the cell.

    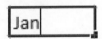

2. Type **uary** on the keyboard to change Jan to January.

3. Press the **<Enter>** key.

8 Change the text in cell B3 back to **Jan** using the formula bar.

Click once in cell B3 and then change the text in the formula bar (see sidebar).

9 Save your work as First Quarter Sales and Profit-2.

Lesson 2-2: Create a new workbook and view two workbooks at the same time

tip

Other ways of creating a new workbook

- Use the keyboard shortcut <Ctrl>+<N>.

- Add a button to the Quick Access Toolbar.

See more details of how this is done in: *Lesson 1-10: Customize the Quick Access Toolbar and preview the printout.*

note

What are templates?

The vast majority of users know nothing about templates and simply base every worksheet upon the *Blank Workbook* default template supplied by Microsoft.

The *Blank Workbook* template has no information in the worksheet itself, but contains all of the Excel Option settings such as the default font size and type.

Templates can also contain anything that a worksheet can contain and are used to store worksheet frameworks to give you a flying start when you find that you often create very similar worksheet layouts.

If you explore the *New Workbook* dialog a little more you'll see that there are hundreds of pre-built templates provided by Microsoft.

Later in this book, in: *Lesson 3-14: Create a template* you'll learn how to create your own template library to personalize the appearance of your workbooks.

1 Create a new workbook by opening Excel

The easiest way to create a new workbook is to simply open Excel. Excel helpfully creates a workbook, unimaginatively named Book1. If you already have a workbook open called Book1, the new workbook will be called Book2... and so on.

Open Excel now and see this in action. Notice that *Book1 – Microsoft Excel* is displayed on the Title Bar.

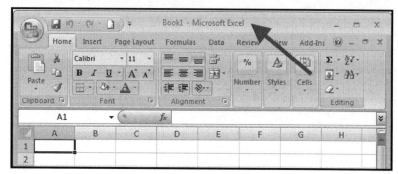

2 Create another new workbook.

You wouldn't want to have to open and close Excel every time you needed a new workbook.

1. Click the Office button at the top left of the screen and click the *New* button on the dialog:

2. The New Workbook dialog is displayed:

3. Double-Click the Blank Workbook template. A new blank workbook called Book2 is displayed in the workbook window.

note

Finding a workbook when many are open

An alternative way to quickly find a workbook when many are open is to click View→Window→Switch Windows.

This presents you with a list of all open workbooks.

You can also use the <Ctrl>+<Tab> keyboard shortcut to cycle through all open workbooks.

Arrange All

Tile all open program windows side-by-side on the screen.

You could be forgiven for thinking that nothing has happened but you can see that the Title Bar now says: *Book2 – Microsoft Excel,* showing that you are now looking at a different workbook.

See the *What are templates* sidebar for more information about templates.

3 **Use the buttons on the taskbar to move between workbooks.**

You'll see two buttons on the taskbar at the bottom of the screen:

Click on the buttons to show each workbook in the worksheet window. The only difference you will see is the Title Bar changing from Book1 to Book2 because both workbooks are empty.

See the sidebar for other methods of switching windows.

4 **Show both Book1 and Book2 in the worksheet window at the same time.**

This skill often draws a gasp of amazement from my students. Believe it or not, most Excel users don't know how to do this.

1. Click View→Window→Arrange All. The *Arrange Windows* dialog is displayed.

2. Choose the Horizontal arrangement and click the OK button.

Both workbooks are now shown within the workbook window:

Notice that as you click each workbook window the title bar lights up and the *Close/Minimize/Restore Down* buttons appear, to show that this is the active workbook.

5 **Close Book2 and Maximize Book1 to restore the display to a single workbook.**

If you've forgotten how to do this, refer back to: *Lesson 1-3: Understand the Application and Workbook windows.*

Lesson 2-3: Use AutoSum to quickly calculate totals

Excel's AutoSum feature is a really useful and fast way to add the values in a range of cells together.

1   Open *First Quarter Sales and Profit-2* from your sample files folder (if it isn't already open).

2   In cell A9 Type the word **Total** followed by the **<Tab>** key.

The cursor moves to the right and is now in cell B9:

	A	B	C	D
7	Paris	35,000	26,000	31,000
8	Munich	12,000	15,000	13,000
9	Total			

3   Click Home→Editing→ Σ (this is the Autosum button).

Something interesting has happened to the worksheet:

	A	B	C	D
3		Jan	Feb	Mar
4	New York	22,000	29,000	19,000
5	Los Angeles	42,000	39,000	43,000
6	London	18,000	20,000	22,000
7	Paris	35,000	26,000	31,000
8	Munich	12,000	15,000	13,000
9	Total	=SUM(B4:B8)		
10		SUM(**number1**, [number2], ...)		

Excel has placed a marquee around the number range that AutoSum has guessed we want to work with. The pattern of dots that marks the boundary of the marquee is called the *marching ants* (that really is the technical term for them)!

The marching ants surround all of the numbers in the column above, up to the first blank cell or text cell (in this case, up to the word Jan).

=Sum(B4:B8) is your first glimpse of an Excel Formula. Formulas always begin with an equals sign. This formula is using the SUM function to compute the Sum (or total) of the values in cells B4 to B8.

First Quarter Sales and Profit-2

tip

Entering an AutoSum using only the keyboard

You can also execute an AutoSum using the keyboard shortcut:

<Alt>+<=>

4   Press the **<Enter>** key or click the AutoSum button 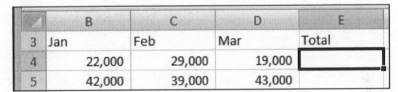 once more to display the total January sales:

	A	B	C	D
3		Jan	Feb	Mar
4	New York	22,000	29,000	19,000
5	Los Angeles	42,000	39,000	43,000
6	London	18,000	20,000	22,000
7	Paris	35,000	26,000	31,000
8	Munich	12,000	15,000	13,000
9	Total	129,000		

5   Type the word **Total** in cell E3 and press the **<Enter>** key once.

The cursor moves down one row and is now in cell E4.

	B	C	D	E
3	Jan	Feb	Mar	Total
4	22,000	29,000	19,000	
5	42,000	39,000	43,000	

6   Use AutoSum to calculate sales for New York.

1.   Click Home→Editing→AutoSum.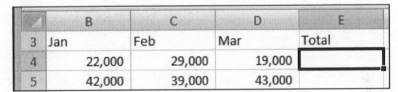

This time AutoSum correctly guesses that you want to sum the values to the left of cell E4:

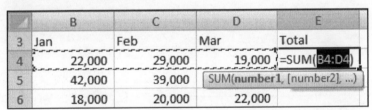

	B	C	D	E
3	Jan	Feb	Mar	Total
4	22,000	29,000	19,000	=SUM(B4:D4)
5	42,000	39,000	43,000	SUM(**number1**, [number2], ...)
6	18,000	20,000	22,000	

2.   Press the **<Enter>** key, or click the AutoSum button once more.

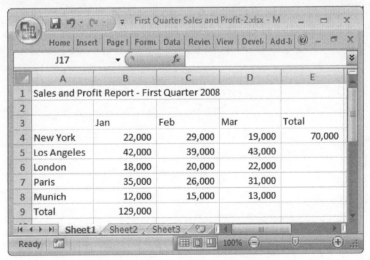

7   Save your work as First Quarter Sales and Profit-3.

Lesson 2-4: Select a range of cells and understand Smart Tags

Sometimes you don't want to add all of the values in a column. You only want to add a selection of cells that you define yourself.

This lesson shows you how to do this with a different AutoSum technique.

1   Open *First Quarter Sales and Profit-3* from your sample files folder (if it isn't already open).

2   Observe the formula behind the value in cell B9.

Click on cell B9 or move to it with the arrow keys on your keyboard.

Look at the *formula bar* at the top of the screen. Notice that the cell displays the *value* of a calculation and the formula bar shows the *formula* used to calculate the value:

B9		▼		fx	=SUM(B4:B8)
	A	B		C	D
8	Munich	12,000		15,000	13,000
9	Total	129,000			
10		Value		Formula	
11					

3   Delete the contents of cell B9.

The easiest way to delete the contents of a cell is to press the **<Delete>** key on your keyboard but you can also right-click the cell and then click *Clear Contents* from the shortcut menu.

4   Change the word *Total* in cell A9 to *USA Sales* and press the **<Tab>** key once.

8	Munich	12,000
9	USA Sales	
10		

You don't have to delete the word *Total* before typing *USA Sales*. When you click in a cell and immediately begin to type, the existing cell contents are replaced.

The cursor moves to cell B9.

5   Select cells B4:B5 with your mouse.

When the mouse cursor hovers over a cell there are three possible cursor shapes:

First Quarter Sales and Profit-3

note

Selecting cells with the keyboard

To select cells with the keyboard hold down the **<Shift>** key and then use the **<Arrow>** keys to select the range needed.

note

Selecting a large range of cells with the <Shift>-click technique

If you need to select a very large range of cells it is sometimes useful to use this technique:

1. Click the cell in the top left corner of the required range.

2. If necessary, use the scroll bars to make the bottom right corner of the required range visible.

3. Hold down the **<Shift>** key.

4. Click in the bottom right corner of the required range.

Cursor	What it does
⊕1.6	The white cross (Select) cursor appears when you hover over the centre of the cell. You can then click and drag to select a range of cells.
1.6 ┿	The black cross (AutoFill) cursor appears when you hover over the bottom right-hand corner of a cell. We'll be covering AutoFill later in this session.
1.6 ✥	The four headed arrow (Move) cursor appears when you hover over one of the black edges of the cell (but not the bottom right corner).

Beginners often have difficulty selecting cells and end up moving them or AutoFilling them by mistake.

Position the mouse at the centre of cell B4 so that you see the White Cross (select) cursor. When you see the white cross, hold down the left mouse button and drag down to cell B5.

You have now selected cells B4 and B5 (in Excel speak we say that you have selected the *range* B4:B5).

	A	B
3		Jan
4	New York	22,000
5	Los Angeles	⊕2,000

6   Click the Autosum button. **Σ**

USA sales are shown in cell B9. Notice the small green triangle at the top left of B9. This is Excel's way of saying: "I think you may have made a mistake".

9	USA Sales	64,000

Select cell B9 and you will see an Exclamation Mark icon. This is called a *Smart Tag*.

7   Hover the mouse cursor over the Smart Tag.

A tip box pops up telling you what Excel thinks you may have done wrong (see below). Of course, in this case, everything is fine. The Smart Tag thinks that perhaps we didn't want just the USA sales – but the Smart Tag is mistaken!

The formula in this cell refers to a range that has additional numbers adjacent to it.

8   Examine the remedial actions suggested by the Smart Tag.

Click the drop-down arrow next to the exclamation mark icon. A list of possible remedial actions is displayed. In this case you can choose *Ignore Error* to remove the green triangle from the corner of the cell.

9   Save your work as First Quarter Sales and Profit-4.

Lesson 2-5: Enter data into a range and copy data across a range

Now that you have mastered the technique of selecting cells, you can use it to speed up data entry.

When you select a range of cells prior to entering data, Excel knows that all data entered belongs in that range. Several key combinations are then available to greatly speed up data entry.

1   Open a new workbook and save it as *Data Range Test*.

2   Select cells B2:D4.

3   Type **London.**

The text appears in Cell B2, the top left cell in the range selected.

4   Press the **<Enter>** Key.

The cursor moves to cell B3 as it normally would.

5   Type **Paris** followed by the **<Enter>** key.

The cursor moves to cell B4 as it normally would.

6   Type **New York** followed by the **<Enter>** key.

This time something new happens. The cursor doesn't move to cell B5 as you might expect but jumps to cell C2.

7   Type **150,000** followed by the **<Enter>** key.

The value appears in C2 and Excel moves down the column again to cell C3.

8   Press the **<Enter>** key without entering a value to leave C3 blank.

Excel moves down the column to cell C4.

9   Type **225,000** followed by the **<Enter>** key.

The cursor jumps to cell D2.

10   Press **<Shift>+<Enter>** twice to change your mind about leaving Paris blank.

1. Press **<Shift>+<Enter>** to move backwards to New York sales.

2. Press **<Shift>+<Enter>** a second time and you are back to the Paris cell.

	A	B	C	D	E
1					
2		London	150,000		
3		Paris			
4		New York	225,000		
5					

11   Type **180,000** followed by the **<Tab>** key.

<Tab> moves you across the range, to cell D3.

	A	B	C	D	E
1					
2		London	150,000		
3		Paris	180,000		
4		New York	225,000		
5					

You can now appreciate how to use this technique of <Enter>, <Tab>, <Shift>+<Tab> and <Shift>+<Enter> to save a lot of time when entering a whole table of data.

12   Select cells D2:D4.

13   Type **50%** but don't press the <Enter> or <Tab> keys.

The challenge this time is to place the same value into cells D3 and D4 without having to type the value two more times.

14   Press **<Ctrl>+<Enter>**.

The value is replicated into all of the other cells in the range.

	A	B	C	D	E
1					
2		London	150,000	50%	
3		Paris	180,000	50%	
4		New York	225,000	50%	
5					

Lesson 2-6: Select adjacent and non-adjacent rows and columns

1   Open *First Quarter Sales and Profit-4* from your sample files folder (if it isn't already open).

2   Select all of column A.

Hover the mouse cursor over the letter **A** at the top of the column. The button lights up and the mouse cursor changes to a black down arrow:

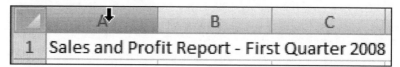

	A	B	C
1	Sales and Profit Report - First Quarter 2008		

Click to select the entire column. The column becomes slightly shaded and a black line surrounds all of the cells.

	A	B
1	Sales and Profit Report - Firs	
2		
3		Jan
4	New York	22,000

3   Click Home→Font→Bold to bold face the column.

Because the whole column was selected, all of the values become bold faced.

4   Click Home→Font→Bold once more to change the type back to normal.

5   Select all of row 4.

To select a row, hover the mouse cursor over the number on the left hand side of the row. The button lights up and the mouse cursor changes to a black arrow pointing across the row:

3		Jan
→	New York	22,000
5	Los Angeles	42,000

Click to select the row.

6   Select columns B and C.

Hover over the letter at the top of column B until you see the black down arrow. When you see the arrow, click and drag to the right to select both columns.

First Quarter Sales and Profit-4

◢	A	B	C	D
1	Sales and Profit Report - First Quarter 2008			
2				
3		Jan	Feb	Mar
4	New York	22,000	29,000	19,000

7   Select rows 6 and 7.

Hover over the number at the left of row 6 until you see the black arrow pointing across the row. When you see the arrow, click and drag down to row 7 to select both rows.

5	Los Angeles	42,000	39,000
6	London	18,000	20,000
→ 7	Paris	35,000	26,000
2R	Munich	12,000	15,000

8   Select columns A, B, C, D and E.

Sometimes you will need to select a large number of adjacent columns or rows. You could drag across them but it is often easier to use the following technique:

1. Select Column A.

2. Hold down the **<Shift>** key.

3. Select Column E.

Columns A to E are selected.

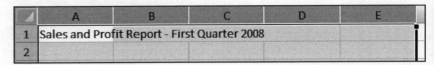

◢	A	B	C	D	E
1	Sales and Profit Report - First Quarter 2008				
2					

9   Select rows 4 and 6.

Perhaps you need to perform an operation on two non-adjacent rows. To select rows 4 and 6 you need to:

1. Select row 4.

2. Hold down the **<Ctrl>** key on the keyboard.

3. Select Row 6.

3		Jan	Feb	Mar
4	New York	22,000	29,000	19,000
5	Los Angeles	42,000	39,000	43,000
6	London	18,000	20,000	22,000
7	Paris	35,000	26,000	31,000

Lesson 2-7: Select non-contiguous cell ranges and view summary information

Non-contiguous is a very impressive word! It simply means a range of cells that is split across two blocks of cells in different parts of the worksheet.

Non-contiguous ranges can be selected using both the mouse and keyboard. The keyboard method may seem a little involved at first but you'll find it much faster once you have the hang of it.

1   Open *First Quarter Sales and Profit-4* from your sample files folder (if it isn't already open).

2   Select the contiguous range B4:D8 with the keyboard.

When you need to select a contiguous range with the keyboard here's how it's done:

1.   Use the arrow keys on the keyboard to navigate to cell B4

2.   Hold down the **<Shift>** key on the keyboard

3.   Still holding the **<Shift>** key down, use the arrow keys on the keyboard to navigate to cell D8

The contiguous range B4:D8 is selected.

	A	B	C	D	E
1	Sales and Profit Report - First Quarter 2008				
2					
3		Jan	Feb	Mar	Total
4	New York	22,000	29,000	19,000	70,000
5	Los Angeles	42,000	39,000	43,000	
6	London	18,000	20,000	22,000	
7	Paris	35,000	26,000	31,000	
8	Munich	12,000	15,000	13,000	
9	USA Sales	64,000			

3   Select the non-contiguous range B4:B8,D4:D8 using the mouse.

1.   Select the range B4:B8.

2.   Hold down the **<Ctrl>** key and select the range D4:D8.

The non-contiguous range **B4:B8,D4:D8** is selected:

	A	B	C	D	E
1	Sales and Profit Report - First Quarter 2008				
2					
3		Jan	Feb	Mar	Total
4	New York	22,000	29,000	19,000	70,000
5	Los Angeles	42,000	39,000	43,000	
6	London	18,000	20,000	22,000	
7	Paris	35,000	26,000	31,000	
8	Munich	12,000	15,000	13,000	
9	USA Sales	64,000			

First Quarter Sales and Profit-4

4   Select the same non-contiguous range with the keyboard.

This is a little more involved than using the simple **<Shift>+<Arrow keys>** method used earlier.

Here's how it's done:

1. Use the arrow keys on the keyboard to navigate to cell B4

2. Press the **<F8>** key (it is on the very top row of your keyboard)

3. Use the arrow keys to navigate to cell B8

4. Press **<Shift>+<F8>**

5. Use the arrow keys to navigate to cell D4

6. Press **<F8>**

7. Use the arrow keys to navigate to cell D8

8. Press **<Shift>+<F8>** one last time

The non-contiguous range B4:B8,D4:D8 is selected:

	A	B	C	D	E
1	Sales and Profit Report - First Quarter 2008				
2					
3		Jan	Feb	Mar	Total
4	New York	22,000	29,000	19,000	70,000
5	Los Angeles	42,000	39,000	43,000	
6	London	18,000	20,000	22,000	
7	Paris	35,000	26,000	31,000	
8	Munich	12,000	15,000	13,000	
9	USA Sales	64,000			

5   Obtain a total sales figures for January and March using the status bar.

The status bar contains summary information for the currently selected range.

Look at the bottom right of your screen. You can see the average sales and total sales (sum of sales) for January and March:

Average: 25,700	Count: 10	Sum: 257,000

6   View the Maximum and Minimum sales for January and March using the status bar.

Right-click the status bar and click *Maximum* and *Minimum* on the pop-up menu (see sidebar).

The status bar now also displays Maximum and Minimum values.

Average: 25,700	Count: 10	Min: 12,000	Max: 43,000	Sum: 257,000

7   Close the workbook without saving.

✓	Average	25,700
✓	Count	10
	Numerical Count	
✓	Minimum	12,000
✓	Maximum	43,000
✓	Sum	257,000
✓	View Shortcuts	
✓	Zoom	100%
✓	Zoom Slider	

Lesson 2-8: AutoSelect a range of cells

When data is arranged in a block (as it is in the Sales and Profit Report) it is referred to as a *range* (in previous versions of Excel it used to be called a database or list).

You will often want to select a row or column of cells within a range, or even the entire range.

You can select ranges by using any of the techniques covered so far but this could be very time consuming if the range encompassed thousands of rows and columns.

In this lesson you'll learn how to select range rows, range columns and entire ranges with a few clicks of the mouse.

1   Open *Sales Report* from your sample files folder.

This report contains a range of cells. The range is the block of cells from A3 to E19.

	A	B	C	D	E
1	Weekly Sales Report				
2					
3	Invoice No	Date	Customer	Country	Total
4	10918	10 March 2008	Bottom-Dollar Markets	Canada	1,700.81
5	10917	10 March 2008	Romero y tomillo	Spain	429.92
6	10926	10 March 2008	Ana Trujillo Emparedados y helados	Mexico	604.42
7	10929	11 March 2008	Frankenversand	Germany	1,380.33
8	10934	11 March 2008	Lehmanns Marktstand	Germany	587.50
9	10939	11 March 2008	Magazzini Alimentari Riuniti	Italy	749.05
10	10939	11 March 2008	Magazzini Alimentari Riuniti	Italy	- 749.05
11	10925	12 March 2008	Hanari Carnes	Brazil	558.29
12	10944	12 March 2008	Bottom-Dollar Markets	Canada	1,204.75
13	10923	12 March 2008	La maison d'Asie	France	879.83
14	10937	13 March 2008	Cactus Comidas para llevar	Argentina	757.64
15	10947	13 March 2008	B's Beverages	UK	258.50
16	10933	13 March 2008	Island Trading	UK	1,081.71
17	10938	14 March 2008	QUICK-Stop	Germany	3,209.95
18	10949	14 March 2008	Bottom-Dollar Markets	Canada	5,195.85
19	10945	14 March 2008	Morgenstern Gesundkost	Germany	287.88
20					
21	Thsi report excludes sales to Asia and South Africa.				**Range**

H ◀ ▶ H   Sheet1   Sheet2   Sheet3

2   Select all cells within the range to the right of cell A7.

1. Click in cell A7 to make it the active cell.

2. Hover over the right hand border of cell A7 until you see the four headed arrow cursor shape.

7	10929 11
8	10934 11

3. When you see this cursor shape hold down the **<Shift>** key and double-click.

All cells to the right of A7, but within the range, are selected.

7	10929	11 March 2008	Frankenversand	Germany	1,380.33

Sales Report

note

Other ways to AutoSelect a range

Using the keyboard.

Here's how you would select the entire range in the Weekly Sales Report (excluding the header row) using the keyboard method.

Make cell A4 the active cell by navigating to it with the **<Arrow>** keys.

1. Press: **<Ctrl>+<Shift>+ <DownArrow>**

    Cells A4:A19 are selected.

2. Press: **<Ctrl>+<Shift>+ <RightArrow>**

    The entire range (excluding the header row) is selected.

Using shortcut keys.

The shortcut keys method is the fastest way to select the entire range *including* the header row.

1. Click anywhere inside the range.

2. Press: **<Ctrl>+<A>**

    The entire range (including the header row) is selected.

From the Ribbon.

The Ribbon method isn't as powerful as the other methods but does provide a way to select the current range (described as the *region* in the dialog).

Make sure that the active cell is within the range.

1. Click:

    Home→Editing→ Find & Select→ GoTo Special...

    The *GoTo Special* dialog is displayed.

2. Click the *Current Region* option button and then click the OK button.

The entire range (including the header row) is selected.

3   Select all cells within the range except the header row.

1. Click in cell A4 to make it the active cell.

2. Hover over the right hand border of cell A4 until you see the four headed arrow cursor shape.

    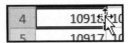

3. When you see this cursor shape hold down the **<Shift>** key and double-click.

    All cells to the right of cell A4, but within the range, are selected.

4. Hover over the bottom border of the selected range until you see the four headed arrow cursor shape.

	Customer
March 2008	Bottom-Dollar Markets
March 2008	Romero y tomillo

5. When you see this cursor shape hold down the **<Shift>** key and double-click.

The entire range (except the header row) is selected.

	A	B	C	D	E
1	Weekly Sales Report				
2					
3	Invoice No	Date	Customer	Country	Total
4	10918	10 March 2008	Bottom-Dollar Markets	Canada	1,700.81
5	10917	10 March 2008	Romero y tomillo	Spain	429.92
6	10926	10 March 2008	Ana Trujillo Emparedados y helados	Mexico	604.42
7	10929	11 March 2008	Frankenversand	Germany	1,380.33
8	10934	11 March 2008	Lehmanns Marktstand	Germany	587.50
9	10939	11 March 2008	Magazzini Alimentari Riuniti	Italy	749.05
10	10939	11 March 2008	Magazzini Alimentari Riuniti	Italy	- 749.05
11	10925	12 March 2008	Hanari Carnes	Brazil	558.29
12	10944	12 March 2008	Bottom-Dollar Markets	Canada	1,204.75
13	10923	12 March 2008	La maison d'Asie	France	879.83
14	10937	13 March 2008	Cactus Comidas para llevar	Argentina	757.64
15	10947	13 March 2008	B's Beverages	UK	258.50
16	10933	13 March 2008	Island Trading	UK	1,081.71
17	10938	14 March 2008	QUICK-Stop	Germany	3,209.95
18	10949	14 March 2008	Bottom-Dollar Markets	Canada	5,195.85
19	10945	14 March 2008	Morgenstern Gesundkost	Germany	287.88
20					
21	Thsi report excludes sales to Asia and South Africa.				

Sheet1   Sheet2   Sheet3

You can also use this technique to select cells to the left of the active cell or above the active cell.

4   Close the workbook without saving.

Lesson 2-9: Re-size rows and columns

1 Open *First Quarter Sales and Profit-4* from your sample files folder (if it isn't already open).

Notice that columns B, C, D and E are far too wide for their contents. It would be useful to make them narrower to keep the worksheet compact.

2 Re-size column B so that it is just wide enough to contain the January sales figures.

Hover over the line separating the letters B and C until you see the re-size cursor shape:

When you see this shape, keep the mouse still and click and drag to the left. Column B will re-size as you drag. Make it narrower so that the values just fit in the column. Notice that the column width in points and pixels are displayed as you drag (one point = 1/72 inch).

A1		▼	Width: 8.86 (67 pixels)	Profit R
	A	B ✛	C	D
1	Sales and Profit Report -	First Quarter 2008		
2				
3		Jan	Feb	Mar
4	New York	22,000	29,000	19,000

3 Re-size column B so that it is too narrow to contain the January sales figures.

Notice that when the column isn't wide enough to contain the contents, hash signs are shown instead of values (if you're used to hashes being called **pound signs** or **number signs** see the sidebar).

	A	B	C	D
1	Sales and Profit Report - First Quarter 2008			
2				
3		Jan	Feb	Mar
4	New York	#####	29,000	19,000

4 Automatically re-size column B so that it is a perfect fit for the widest cell in the column.

Hover over the line separating the letters B and C until you see the re-size cursor shape:

When you see this shape, double-click to automatically re-size column B.

First Quarter Sales and Profit-4

note

Other ways to re-size rows and columns

You can also re-size rows and columns using the Ribbon.

Click Home→Cells→Format.

A drop-down menu appears.

You can use the *Row Height* and *Column Width* settings to set the row or column to a specific number of points (a point is 1/72 of an inch).

You can also use the *AutoFit Row Height* and *AutoFit Column Width* options to automatically size the row or column (you achieved this more efficiently with a double-click in the lesson).

Default Width... often confuses as it doesn't appear to work. This is because it re-sets all columns to default width *except those that have already been re-sized*.

note

Making several columns or rows the same size.

Sometimes you will want to make several columns exactly the same width.

To do this, select the multiple columns and then click and drag the intersection of any of the selected columns. This will make each of the columns exactly the same width.

5   Automatically re-size every column in the worksheet in one operation.

1.   Select every cell in the workbook by clicking the *select all* button in the top left corner of the worksheet (you can also do this by clicking in any blank cell and then pressing **<Ctrl>+<A>**).

2.   Hover over the intersection of any two columns until you see

the re-size cursor shape and then double-click.

Every column is now perfectly sized.

Notice that Auto-resize has done its job rather too well. Column A is now wide enough to accommodate all of the text in cell A1.

	A	B	C
1	Sales and Profit Report - First Quarter 2008		

6   Automatically re-size column A so that it is only wide enough to contain the longest city name (Los Angeles).

	A	B	C	D	E
1	Sales and Profit Report - First Quarter 2008				
2					
3		Jan	Feb	Mar	Total
4	New York	22,000	29,000	19,000	70,000
5	Los Angeles	42,000	39,000	43,000	

1.   Select cells A4:A9.

2.   Click Home→Cells→Format→AutoFit Column Width.

This time the column is automatically sized so that it is wide enough to contain all of the text in the selected cells.

Notice that the text has spilled over from cell A1 into the adjoining columns B, C, D and E. This always happens when a cell contains text and the adjacent cells are empty.

7   Manually size row 3 so that it is about twice as tall as the other rows.

Do this in exactly the same way you re-sized the column but, this time, hover between the intersection of rows 3 and 4 until you see the re-size cursor shape, and then drag downwards.

1	Sales and Profit Report - First Quarter 2008			
	Height: 30.00 (40 pixels)	Jan	Feb	Mar
3	New York	22,000	29,000	19,000
4	Los Angeles	42,000	39,000	43,000

8   Auto-resize row 3 so that it is the same size as the other rows again.

Lesson 2-10: Use AutoSum to sum a non-contiguous range

In *Lesson 2-7: Select non-contiguous cell ranges and view summary information*, you learned how to view the sum of January and March sales using the status bar. But how can you put that value onto the worksheet?

Now that you have the hang of selecting non-contiguous ranges you can use this in conjunction with your AutoSum skills to create a formula that will calculate the total of a non-contiguous range.

1 Open *First Quarter Sales and Profit-4* from your sample files folder (if it isn't already open).

2 Enter the text **Jan/Mar Sales** in cell A10 and press the <Tab> key.

The active cell moves to cell B10.

3 Re-size column A so that it is wide enough to contain the text.

   1. Hover over the line separating the letters A and B until you see the re-size cursor shape:

   2. When you see this shape, keep the mouse still and click and drag to the right. Column A will re-size as you drag. Make it wider so that the words *Jan/Mar Sales* comfortably fit in the column:

3		Jan	Feb	Mar	T
4	New York	22,000	29,000	19,000	
5	Los Angeles	42,000	39,000	43,000	
6	London	18,000	20,000	22,000	
7	Paris	35,000	26,000	31,000	
8	Munich	12,000	15,000	13,000	
9	USA Sales	64,000			
10	Jan/Mar Sales				

4 Click Home→Editing→ 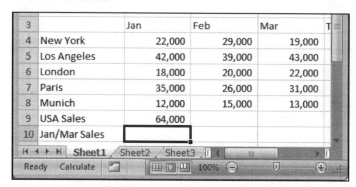 (the AutoSum button).

An AutoSum appears in cell B10 but it isn't anything like what we want yet. It guesses that we simply want to repeat the value in the USA Sales cell.

5 Select the range B4:B8 with the mouse.

6   Hold down the **<Ctrl>** key and select the range D4:D8 with the mouse.

Notice that the non-contiguous range **B4:B8,D4:D8** is shown in the AutoSum's formula:

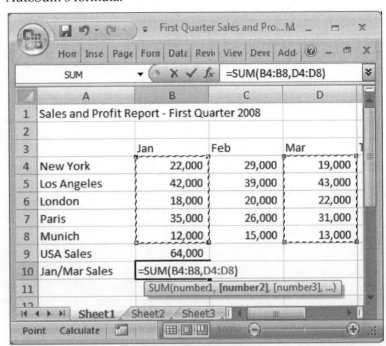

7   Press the **<Enter>** key or click the AutoSum button Σ again to view the sales for January and March in cell B10.

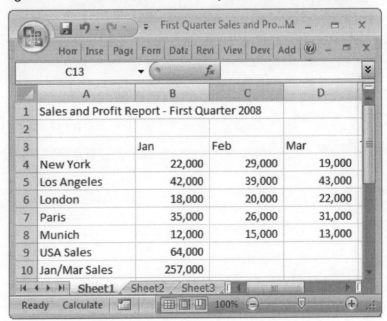

8   Save your work as *First Quarter Sales and Profit-5*.

Lesson 2-11: Use AutoSum to quickly calculate averages

Excel's *AutoSum* feature isn't only restricted to addition. It is also able to compute averages and maximum/minimum values.

In this lesson we'll use AutoSum to calculate the average sales for each month.

1   Open *First Quarter Sales and Profit 5* from your sample files folder (If it isn't already open).

2   Delete cells E3:E4.

Select cells E3 and E4 and press the **<Delete>** key on your keyboard.

3   Type the word *Average* in cell E3 and press the **<Enter>** key.

The cursor moves to cell E4:

4   Use AutoSum to create a formula that will show the Average New York sales.

1.   Click Home→Editing→AutoSum →Drop down arrow (see sidebar).

A drop down menu is displayed showing all of the different ways in which AutoSum can operate upon a range of cells:

2.   Click Average.

3.   Excel generates an Average function and inserts the cell range B4:D4. This is exactly what we want:

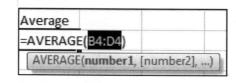

4.   Press the **<Enter>** key or click the AutoSum button Σ again to see the average sales for New York:

3		Jan	Feb	Mar	Average
4	New York	22,000	29,000	19,000	23,333

5   Type the word **Maximum** in Cell F3 and then press the **<Enter>** key.

6   Use AutoSum to create a formula in cell F4 that will show the Maximum New York Sales for this period.

Click Here

First Quarter Sales and Profit-5

1. Place an AutoSum in cell F4 but this time, choose Max from the drop-down menu.

   This time we have a small problem. AutoSum is including the average value (23,333) in the calculation.

Jan	Feb	Mar	Average	Maximum
22,000	29,000	19,000	23,333	=MAX(B4:E4)

2. Select cells B4:D4 with the mouse

   The marquee corrects and the average value in cell E4 is no longer included.

New York	22,000	29,000	19,000	23,333	=MAX(B4:D4)

   Notice that the Max function is now working with the range B4:D4.

3. Press the <Enter> key or click the AutoSum button Σ once more to see the maximum sales the New York office managed during the first quarter of the year:

3		Jan	Feb	Mar	Average	Maximum
4	New York	22,000	29,000	19,000	23,333	29,000

7 Change the words *USA Sales* in cell A9 back to *Sales* and press the **<Tab>** key.

8 Press the **<F2>** key on the keyboard (or double-click cell B9) to bring back the marquee (shown as a blue box).

9 Adjust the marquee using click and drag so that all offices are included in the Sales total.

tip

Another way to bring back the blue box showing a range is to click the range in the Formula bar.

Notice that there is a small blue spot on each corner of the range. These are called sizing handles.

1. Hover the mouse cursor over the bottom right (or bottom left) sizing handle until the cursor shape changes to a double headed arrow. It is really important that you see the double headed arrow and not the four headed arrow or white cross.

4	New York	22,000
5	Los Angeles	42,000
6	London	18,000

2. When you see the double headed arrow click and drag with the mouse down to cell B8.

3. Press the <Enter> key or click the AutoSum button again.

7	Paris	35,000
8	Munich	12,000
9	Sales	129,000

10 Save your work as First Quarter Sales and Profit-6.

Lesson 2-12: Create your own formulas

The AutoSum tool is very useful for quickly inserting Sum(), Average(), Count(), Max() and Min() formulas into cells. Many Excel users never get any further with their formulas than this.

In this session we'll create our own formulas without the use of AutoSum. You'll be amazed at how easy it is.

1   Open *First Quarter Sales and Profit*-6 from your sample files folder (if it isn't already open).

2   Select cells A10:B10 and press the **<Delete>** key once.

The previous contents of cells A10:B10 are removed.

3   Type the word **Costs** into cell A11 and **Profit** into cell A12.

4   Type the value 83,000 into cell B11 and press the **<Enter>** key to move down to cell B12.

11	Costs	83,000	
12	Profit		

5   Enter a formula into cell B12 to compute the profit made in January.

   1.   Type: = **B9-B11** into cell B12

   2.   Press the **<Enter>** key.

The profit for January is displayed:

9	Sales	129,000
10		
11	Costs	83,000
12	Profit	46,000

6   Enter the formula again using a better technique.

The method that you have just used to enter the formula works just fine but it isn't the best method. Sooner or later you will make a mistake. For example you could easily type **B8:B11** resulting in an incorrect answer.

To eliminate such errors you should always select cell references visually rather than simply type them in. You can visually select cells using either the mouse or the keyboard. First we'll use the mouse method.

   1.   Click in cell B12 and press the **<Delete>** key on the keyboard to clear the old formula.

   2.   Press the equals <=> key on the keyboard.

   3.   Click once on the value 129,000 in cell B9.

important

Formulas automatically recalculate whenever any of the cells in the formula change.

For example: If you were to change the Paris sales to 45,000 this would cause cell B9 to re-calculate to 139,000. Because B9 has changed this would, in turn, cause the profit to re-calculate to 56,000.

First Quarter Sales and Profit-6

4. Press the minus <-> key on the keyboard.

5. Click once on the value 83,000 in cell B11.

6. Press the <Enter> key on the keyboard.

If you followed the above steps carefully you will see that you have created the same formula but with a much lower possibility of making a mistake.

7   Enter the formula again using the visual keyboard technique.

The very best Excel experts hardly use the mouse at all. You waste valuable seconds every time you reach for the mouse.

Here's the expert technique of visual selection via keyboard:

1. Use the arrow keys to navigate to cell B12 and then press the <Delete> key on the keyboard to clear the old formula.

2. Press the <=> key on the keyboard.

3. Press the <Up Arrow> key three times to move to cell B9.

4. Press the <-> key on the keyboard.

5. Press the <Up Arrow> key once to move to cell B11.

6. Press the <Enter> key on the keyboard.

8   Enter a formula that uses the multiplication operator.

This employer is very generous and pays the staff ten percent of all profits as an incentive bonus.

In cell A13 type the words **10% Bonus** and then press the <Tab> key on the keyboard to move to cell B13.

<table>
<tr><td colspan="3">important</td></tr>
<tr><td colspan="3">The Excel Operators</td></tr>
<tr><td></td><td>Name</td><td>Example</td></tr>
<tr><td>+</td><td>Addition</td><td>1+2</td></tr>
<tr><td>-</td><td>Subtraction</td><td>7-5</td></tr>
<tr><td>*</td><td>Multiplication</td><td>6*3</td></tr>
<tr><td>/</td><td>Division</td><td>15/5</td></tr>
<tr><td>%</td><td>Percent</td><td>25%</td></tr>
<tr><td>^</td><td>Exponentiation</td><td>4^2</td></tr>
</table>

9   Enter a formula that uses the multiplication operator.

The multiplication operator is not an X as you might expect but an asterisk (*). The other Excel operators are shown in the sidebar.

You need to press <Shift>+<8> to enter an asterisk. If you are using a full size keyboard with a numeric keypad at the right-hand side you can also use the numeric keyboard's <X> key.

Whichever key you use you'll still see an asterisk in the formula.

Use either the *mouse click* technique or the *visual keyboard* technique to enter the formula shown below into cell B13 and then press the <Enter> key to see how much bonus was earned:

11	Costs	83,000
12	Profit	46,000
13	10% Bonus	=B12*.1

11	Costs	83,000
12	Profit	46,000
13	10% Bonus	4,600

10   Save your work as First Quarter Sales and Profit-7.

---

trivia

The feature that Excel uses to help you out with function calls first made an appearance in Visual Basic 5 back in 1996 and had the wonderful name: *IntelliSense*. The Excel implementation is called *Formula AutoComplete*.

In 1996 I was working in Switzerland developing a ski-school management application. I was extremely impressed by how easy *IntelliSense* made my job. I didn't have to remember hundreds of function names any more.

I was even slightly worried that just about anybody could now program (but, of course, I was wrong).

Recently I was in London being driven by a Hackney cab driver (Hackney cab drivers know every shortcut and back street in London). He was worried that Satellite Navigation would now mean that anybody could become a London cabbie.

Of course, he really had nothing to worry about either!

note

Enabling and disabling AutoComplete.

As with so many other features, Microsoft allows you to turn this very useful feature off.

You'd never want to do this but you may work on a machine that has had Formula AutoComplete switched off and you need to turn it on again.

Click Office→Excel Options→Formulas and make sure that the *Formula AutoComplete* box is checked.

First Quarter Sales and Profit-7

Lesson 2-13: Create functions using Formula AutoComplete

1   Open *First Quarter Sales and Profit*-7 from your sample files folder (if it isn't already open).

2   Type the words **USA Sales** into cell A15 and **European Sales** into cell A16.

Notice that the text *European Sales* spills over into column B because column A isn't wide enough to contain it.

3   Re-size column A so that it is wide enough for the words *European Sales* to fit within the column.

You learned how to do this in: *Lesson 2-9: Re-size rows and columns.*

	A	B
15	USA Sales	
16	European Sales	

4   Click into cell B15 and type **=S** into the cell.

Something amazing happens:

15	USA Sales	=S
16	European Sales	*fx* SEARCH
17		*fx* SECOND
18		*fx* SERIESSUM
19		*fx* SIGN

A list drops down showing every function in the Excel function library beginning with S. This is a great new feature for Excel 2007 that Microsoft call *Formula AutoComplete* (if AutoComplete didn't display as expected see the sidebar).

You've already encountered the Sum(), Average() and Max() functions courtesy of AutoSum.

You may be pleased (or dismayed) to know that there are over 300 functions in the Excel function library. The good news is that most untrained Excel users only ever get to understand Sum() and Average()!

When you typed =S Excel listed all functions beginning with S.

5   Continue typing: **=SU**.

Notice that the list now only shows functions beginning with SU and look... there's the *SUM()* function we need three down in the list.

You could simply click on it with the mouse but let's behave like an Excel pro and do it with the keyboard.

6   Press the **<Down Arrow>** key twice to move the cursor over the SUM function.

The Sum function now has a tip telling you what the function does:

15	USA Sales	=SU
16	European Sales	⨍ SUBSTITUTE
17		⨍ SUBTOTAL
18		⨍ SUM
19	Adds all the numbers in a range of cells

7   Display detailed information about the SUM() function.

The tip tells you a little about the SUM() function but to get the full story press the **<F1>** key while SUM is still highlighted in the dropdown list:

The Excel help system opens showing detailed help for the SUM() function.

Read the help text if you are interested and then close the help window.

Notice that Excel has now left you with only *=SU* in the cell. Complete the formula by typing **M(**

Notice that a little box has appeared beneath the function call. This is the *Syntax* (see sidebar for more information).

8   Select the cells that you need to sum (cells B4:B5) with the mouse or keyboard.

If you want to be a real pro you should select them with the keyboard. To do this:

1.   Press the **<Up Arrow>** key repeatedly until you reach cell B4.

2.   Hold down the **<Shift>** key and press the **<Down Arrow>** key once to select cells B4:B5.

9   Type a closing bracket to complete the formula and then press the <Enter> key.

The total USA sales are displayed in cell B15.

10   Use the same technique to create a SUM() function in cell B16 to show the total European sales (cells B6:B8).

1.   Click in cell B16.

2.   Type = **SU.**

3.   Press the **<Down Arrow>** key twice to move the cursor over the SUM function.

4.   Press the **<Tab>** key to automatically enter the SUM function into cell B16.

5.   Select the range B6:B8.

6.   Type the closing bracket followed by the **<Enter>** key. The formula should now be: **=SUM(B6:B8).**

11   Save your work as *First Quarter Sales and Profit 8.*

note

The syntax box

The Syntax box tells you what arguments (sometimes called parameters) the function needs. The first argument has no square brackets meaning that you can't leave it out. The argument in square brackets is optional.

For such a simple function as SUM() the syntax box is hardly needed but later we'll discover functions that require several arguments and then the syntax box will be invaluable.

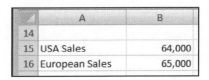

	A	B
14		
15	USA Sales	64,000
16	European Sales	65,000

Lesson 2-14: Use AutoFill for text and numeric series

1   Open *First Quarter Sales and Profit-8* from your sample files folder (if it isn't already open).

2   Delete the text **Feb** and **Mar** from cells C3:D3.

Select cells C3:D3 and then press the **<Delete>** key on your keyboard.

3   Make B3 the active cell.

Notice that there is a black border around the cell and a black spot on the bottom right-hand corner. This is the AutoFill handle. If you don't see it, refer to the sidebar.

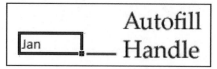

4   Hover over the AutoFill handle with your mouse until the cursor shape changes to a black cross.

Many of my students have great difficulty with this when they try it for the first time.

- You don't want the four-headed arrow: ✛ – that would move the cell.

- You don't want the white cross: ⊹ – that would select the cell.

- You want the black cross: ✚ – the AutoFill cursor.

5   When the black cross cursor is visible hold down the mouse button and drag your mouse to the right to AutoFill the other months: **Feb** and **Mar**.

Notice the tip that appears as you drag, previewing the month that will appear in each cell.

6   In cell A18 type **Monday** and AutoFill down to cell A24 to show the days of the week.

(If you are not using an English language version of Excel you will need to type **Monday** in your own language).

7   In cell B18 type the number **1** and in cell B19 type the number **2**.

8   Select cells B18 and B19.

9   AutoFill down to B24 to create sequential numbers:

18	Monday	1
19	Tuesday	2
20	Wednesday	3
21	Thursday	4

10   In cell C18 type **9** and in cell C19 type **18**.

11   Select cells C18 and C19.

12   AutoFill down to B24 to create the nine times table.

18	Monday	1	9
19	Tuesday	2	18
20	Wednesday	3	27

13   Use AutoFill to create sequential dates.

1.   Type 01-Jan-08 into cell D18.

2.   Type 02-Jan-08 into cell D19.

3.   Select Cells D18:D19.

4.   AutoFill down to D24 to create sequential dates.

14   Use AutoFill to quickly copy values.

Sometimes you will want to duplicate the value from one cell into many others to the right of, left of, beneath, or above the active cell.

When a cell containing text is the active cell and it isn't defined as a *fill series* (the built-in fill series are days of the week and months of the year), AutoFill will simply duplicate the contents of the cell:

Type the text **Adjusted** into cell E18 and then AutoFill it down as far as cell E24.

The same text is now shown in each of the cells:

18	Monday	1	9	01-Jan-08	Adjusted
19	Tuesday	2	18	02-Jan-08	Adjusted
20	Wednesday	3	27	03-Jan-08	Adjusted
21	Thursday	4	36	04-Jan-08	Adjusted
22	Friday	5	45	05-Jan-08	Adjusted
23	Saturday	6	54	06-Jan-08	Adjusted
24	Sunday	7	63	07-Jan-08	Adjusted

15   Save your work as First Quarter Sales and Profit-9.

Lesson 2-15: Use AutoFill to adjust formulas

AutoFill can save you a lot of time when extending or copying text and number ranges. But the story's not over yet.

AutoFill's ability to copy and adjust formulas is one of the most powerful tools in Excel's impressive armory.

1   Open *First Quarter Sales and Profit 9* from your sample files folder (If it isn't already open).

2   Consider the formula in cell B9.

Click onto cell B9 and view the formula displayed in the formula bar (the formula bar is at the top right of the screen grab below).

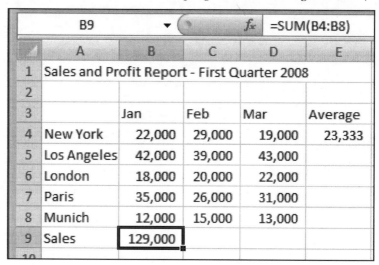

The formula is **=SUM(B4:B8)**. AutoSum created it for us in: *Lesson 2-3: Use AutoSum to quickly calculate totals*. The formula uses the SUM() function to add together the values in the range B4:B8.

Think about the formula that would work in cell C9 (the total sales for February). It would be: **=SUM(C4:C8)**. Similarly the formula that would work in cell D9 (the total sales for March) would be **=SUM(D4:D8)**.

As we move to the right all that is needed is to increment the letter for each cell reference in the formula and we'll get the right answer every time.

Now AutoFill is very clever and realizes this. When we AutoFill a cell containing a formula to the right, AutoFill increments the letters in each cell reference.

Most of the time that is exactly what we want.

Later, in *Lesson 3-12: Understand absolute and relative cell references,* we'll learn how to fine-tune the way in which AutoFill adjusts cell references. This will allow you to implement some more advanced AutoFill techniques.

First Quarter Sales and Profit-9

3   AutoFill cell B9 to the right as far as cell D9.

You may see a row of hashes in Cell C9. This is because the value is too wide to fit in the cell. If this is the case, AutoFit the column using the skill learned in: *Lesson 2-9: Re-size rows and columns.*

The correct answers for Feb and Mar sales are shown on the worksheet. Click on the Feb total cell (C9) and look at the formula in the formula bar.

C9		▼	f_x	=SUM(C4:C8)	
◢	A	B	C	D	E
3		Jan	Feb	Mar	Average
4	New York	22,000	29,000	19,000	23,333
5	Los Angeles	42,000	39,000	43,000	
6	London	18,000	20,000	22,000	
7	Paris	35,000	26,000	31,000	
8	Munich	12,000	15,000	13,000	
9	Sales	129,000	129,000	128,000	
10					

You can see that AutoFill has done its work perfectly, creating a sum of the values in cells C4:C8. Our five branches have sold exactly the same amount in both January and February, but a little less in March.

4   Consider the formula in cell E4.

Click onto cell E4 and view the formula displayed in the formula bar.

E4		▼	f_x	=AVERAGE(B4:D4)	
◢	A	B	C	D	E
3		Jan	Feb	Mar	Average
4	New York	22,000	29,000	19,000	23,333
5	Los Angeles	42,000	39,000	43,000	
6	London	18,000	20,000	22,000	

The formula is **=AVERAGE(B4:D4).** AutoSum created it for us in: *Lesson 2-11: Use AutoSum to quickly calculate averages.*

Think about the formula that would work in cell E5 (the average sales for Los Angeles). It would be: **=Average(B5:D5).** Similarly the formula that would work in cell E6 (the total sales for London) would be **=Average(B6:D6).**

As we move downward all that is needed is to increment the number for each cell reference in the formula. This is exactly what AutoFill will do.

E	F
Average	Maximum
23,333	29,000
41,333	43,000
20,000	22,000
30,667	35,000
13,333	15,000

5   AutoFill cell E4 down to E8 to see the Average sales for each branch.

6   AutoFill cell F4 down to F8 to view the maximum sales for each branch.

7   Save your work as First Quarter Sales and Profit-10.

Lesson 2-16: Use AutoFill options

Sometimes AutoFill begins to misbehave and actually gets in the way of efficient work by wrongly anticipating what you need.

1　Open *First Quarter Sales and Profit-10* from your sample files folder (If it isn't already open).

2　In cell F18 type the date **1-Jan-2009**.

3　AutoFill down as far as cell F24.

The cells are populated with sequential dates:

	A	B	C	D	E	F
18	Monday	1	9	01-Jan-08	Adjusted	01-Jan-09
19	Tuesday	2	18	02-Jan-08	Adjusted	02-Jan-09
20	Wednesday	3	27	03-Jan-08	Adjusted	03-Jan-09
21	Thursday	4	36	04-Jan-08	Adjusted	04-Jan-09
22	Friday	5	45	05-Jan-08	Adjusted	05-Jan-09
23	Saturday	6	54	06-Jan-08	Adjusted	06-Jan-09
24	Sunday	7	63	07-Jan-08	Adjusted	07-Jan-09

4　In cell G18 type the date **31-Mar-2009**.

5　AutoFill down as far as cell G24.

At some time you'll need to add transaction dates to a worksheet and will have four or five entries with the same date.

AutoFill is perfect for eliminating the need to re-type the date for each transaction, but its insistence upon incrementing the date every time could be very frustrating.

Fortunately we can change the default behavior.

6　Click the Auto Fill Options Smart Tag ⊞ at the bottom right corner of the filled cells.

First Quarter Sales and
Profit-10

7   Click *Copy Cells* to tell AutoFill not to increment the date.

The purpose of the *Fill Formatting* options will be clear later in the course when you have completed: *Session Four: Making Your Worksheets Look Professional.*

Here's what the other options will do:

Copy Cells	Fill Series	Fill Days	Fill Weekdays	Fill Months	Fill Years
This is what we just did. The first cell is copied to the other cells.	The default for dates that include the day. The date increments by one day at a time.	The date increments by one day at a time.	Because 3rd April 2009 is a Friday the weekend days are omitted and the series jumps from 3rd April to 6th April.	Normally this would show the same day number for each month. In this example, there are only 30 days in two of the months so 30th is shown instead of 31st.	The same calendar day is shown for each subsequent year.
31-Mar-09	31-Mar-09	31-Mar-09	31-Mar-09	31-Mar-09	31-Mar-09
31-Mar-09	01-Apr-09	01-Apr-09	01-Apr-09	30-Apr-09	31-Mar-10
31-Mar-09	02-Apr-09	02-Apr-09	02-Apr-09	31-May-09	31-Mar-11
31-Mar-09	03-Apr-09	03-Apr-09	03-Apr-09	30-Jun-09	31-Mar-12
31-Mar-09	04-Apr-09	04-Apr-09	06-Apr-09	31-Jul-09	31-Mar-13
31-Mar-09	05-Apr-09	05-Apr-09	07-Apr-09	31-Aug-09	31-Mar-14
31-Mar-09	06-Apr-09	06-Apr-09	08-Apr-09	30-Sep-09	31-Mar-15

8   Access fill options using right-click AutoFill.

1.   Click again on cell F18 to make it the active cell.

2.   AutoFill once more but, this time, hold down the right mouse button.

When you release the mouse button you are presented with the AutoFill options (see sidebar).

This method is preferred to the Smart Tag method because it is faster (one click instead of two)!

9   Change back to Fill Series or Fill Days.

In this example Fill Series and Fill Days produce exactly the same result.

10   Save your work as First Quarter Sales and Profit-11.

Lesson 2-17: Speed up your AutoFills and create a custom fill series

In this lesson we're going to learn some AutoFill techniques that will massively speed up your efficient use of the AutoFill feature.

1   Open *First Quarter Sales and Profit*-11 (if it isn't already open).

2   Delete the contents of cells G18:G24.

3   Type **31-Mar-09** into cell G18.

	A	B	C	D	E	F	G
17							
18	Monday	1	9	01-Jan-08	Adjusted	01-Jan-09	31-Mar-09
19	Tuesday	2	18	02-Jan-08	Adjusted	02-Jan-09	
20	Wednesday	3	27	03-Jan-08	Adjusted	03-Jan-09	
21	Thursday	4	36	04-Jan-08	Adjusted	04-Jan-09	
22	Friday	5	45	05-Jan-08	Adjusted	05-Jan-09	
23	Saturday	6	54	06-Jan-08	Adjusted	06-Jan-09	
24	Sunday	7	63	07-Jan-08	Adjusted	07-Jan-09	

4   Double click the AutoFill handle to automatically fill cells G19:G24.

This is a real master tip!

Hover over the AutoFill handle (the black spot at the bottom right hand corner). When you are sure that you have the correct black cross cursor shape, double click to automatically fill down.

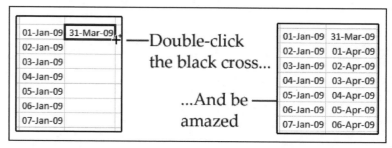

5   Delete all of the dates from cells G19:G24 leaving only the date 31-Mar-09 in cell G18.

6   Hold down the **<Ctrl>** key and AutoFill down as far as G24 by dragging the AutoFill handle down with the mouse.

Because you held the <Ctrl> key down AutoFill simply copies the cell instead of creating a series of values.

First Quarter Sales and Profit-11

B	C	D	E	F	G
1	9	01-Jan-08	Adjusted	01-Jan-09	31-Mar-09
2	18	02-Jan-08	Adjusted	02-Jan-09	31-Mar-09
3	27	03-Jan-08	Adjusted	03-Jan-09	31-Mar-09
4	36	04-Jan-08	Adjusted	04-Jan-09	31-Mar-09
5	45	05-Jan-08	Adjusted	05-Jan-09	31-Mar-09
6	54	06-Jan-08	Adjusted	06-Jan-09	31-Mar-09
7	63	07-Jan-08	Adjusted	07-Jan-09	31-Mar-09

This is even faster than using the right-click method when you want to prevent the date incrementing.

7   Click Office→Excel Options→Popular.

8   In the *Popular* category under *Top options for working with Excel* click the gray *Edit Custom Lists...* button.

   Edit Cus**t**om Lists...

   The Custom Lists dialog appears.

9   Click in the *List entries* window and add four custom list entries: North, South, East and West.

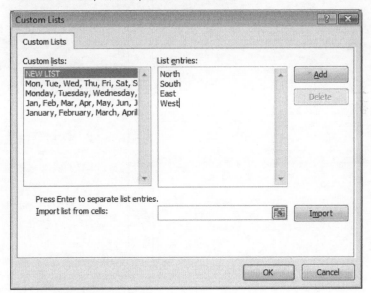

North
South
East
West
North
South
East
West

10   Click the OK button.

11   Type **North** in any cell and AutoFill down.

   As you AutoFill the custom list entries appear in the worksheet.

12   Delete the North, South, East, West… cells from the worksheet.

13   Save your work as First Quarter Sales and Profit-12.

Lesson 2-18: Use the zoom control

Zooming is used to magnify or reduce the worksheet. If you have a lot of rows in a worksheet and have good eyes you might want to zoom out sometimes to see more of the worksheet on one screen.

1   Open *First Quarter Sales and Profit-12* from your sample files folder (if it isn't already open).

2   Zoom in and out of a worksheet using the mouse wheel.

The fastest way to zoom a worksheet is by using the mouse.

Most mice these days have a wheel in the middle of the buttons. To zoom using this wheel hold down the **<Ctrl>** key on the keyboard and roll the wheel to zoom in and out.

3   Zoom in and out of a worksheet using the zoom control.

The zoom control is at the bottom right of your screen,

Click and drag on the zoom control slider to zoom in and out of your worksheet. You can also zoom by clicking the plus and minus buttons on either side of the Zoom control.

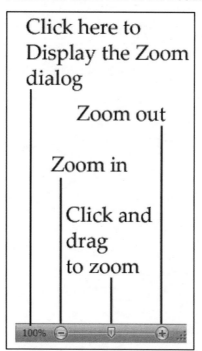

4   Select cells A3:D9.

We're going to use the zoom dialog to make this selection completely fill the screen.

5   Click the left hand side of the zoom bar.

The zoom dialog is displayed.

First Quarter Sales and Profit-12

6   Select the *Fit Selection* option button and click the OK button.

The worksheet is zoomed so that the selected cells completely fill the screen.

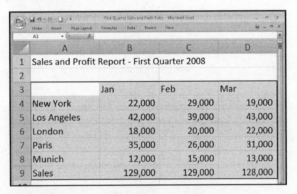

7   Zoom back to 100% using the Ribbon.

You'll probably find the zoom bar to be the quickest and most convenient way to zoom, but the View Ribbon also has a Zoom group containing three buttons:

Use the 100% button to restore the screen to normal.

Lesson 2-19: Print out a worksheet

We aren't going to explore every option for preparing and printing a worksheet in this lesson. Printing is such a huge subject that we devote a whole session to it in: *Session Seven: Printing Your Work.*

This lesson only aims to teach you the bare minimum skills you need to put your work onto paper.

1 Open First *Quarter Sales and Profit-12* from your sample files folder (if it isn't already open).

	A	B	C	D	E	F	G
1	Sales and Profit Report - First Quarter 2008						
2							
3		Jan	Feb	Mar	Average	Maximum	
4	New York	22,000	29,000	19,000	23,333	29,000	
5	Los Angeles	42,000	39,000	43,000	41,333	43,000	
6	London	18,000	20,000	22,000	20,000	22,000	
7	Paris	35,000	26,000	31,000	30,667	35,000	
8	Munich	12,000	15,000	13,000	13,333	15,000	
9	Sales	129,000	129,000	128,000			
10							
11	Costs	83,000					
12	Profit	46,000					
13	10% Bonus	4,600					
14							
15	USA Sales	-					
16	European Sales						
17							
18	Monday	1	9	01-Jan-08	Adjusted	01-Jan-09	31-Mar-09
19	Tuesday	2	18	02-Jan-08	Adjusted	02-Jan-09	31-Mar-09
20	Wednesday	3	27	03-Jan-08	Adjusted	03-Jan-09	31-Mar-09
21	Thursday	4	36	04-Jan-08	Adjusted	04-Jan-09	31-Mar-09
22	Friday	5	45	05-Jan-08	Adjusted	05-Jan-09	31-Mar-09
23	Saturday	6	54	06-Jan-08	Adjusted	06-Jan-09	31-Mar-09
24	Sunday	7	63	07-Jan-08	Adjusted	07-Jan-09	31-Mar-09

2 Click the Office button at the top left of the screen .

3 Hover the mouse cursor over the Print button at the left of the dialog.

4 Click Print Preview from the menu at the right hand side of the dialog.

5 A preview of the printout is shown on screen:

First Quarter Sales and Profit-12

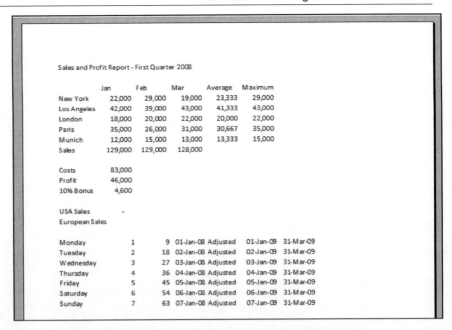

6 Click on the page to see the zoom feature working.

Each time you click on the page the page zooms in and out.

7 Click the Print button 🖶 at the top left of the Print Preview screen.

If you don't see this icon at the top of the Print Preview window it is because you have hidden the Ribbon. Unhide it by double-clicking the *Print Preview* Ribbon tab.

The print options dialog appears:

8 Click the **OK** button to print your work.

For this simple worksheet there's no need to change any of the options but you can probably figure out what most of them are for.

Session 2: Exercise

1   Open a new workbook.

2   Use AutoFill to put the three months Jan, Feb, and Mar into cells A4:A6.

3   Using only the keyboard add the following data:

	A	B	C	D	E
1	Profit Analysis				
2					
3		London	Paris	New York	Average
4	Jan	2,500	3,100	2,300	
5	Feb	2,200	2,700	2,600	
6	Mar	2,100	2,600	2,800	
7	Total				

4   Use AutoSum to compute London's total profit for Jan/Feb/Mar in cell B7.

5   Use AutoSum to compute the average January profit in cell E4.

6   Use AutoFill to extend the London total in cell B7, to the Paris and New York totals in cells C7 and D7.

7   Use AutoFill to extend the January average profit in cell E4, to the February and March average profits in cells E5 and E6.

8   Select all of Column A and all of Column E (at the same time) and bold face the values in them.

9   Select row 3 and row 7 (at the same time) and bold face the values in them.

	A	B	C	D	E
1	**Profit Analysis**				
2					
3		**London**	**Paris**	**New York**	**Average**
4	**Jan**	2,500	3,100	2,300	**2,633**
5	**Feb**	2,200	2,700	2,600	**2,500**
6	**Mar**	2,100	2,600	2,800	**2,500**
7	**Total**	**6,800**	**8,400**	**7,700**	

10 Select cells B4:B6 and cells D4:D6 at the same time and then read the total London and New York sales figure for Jan, Feb and March from the summary information displayed on the status bar.

11 Select cells B4:D6 and zoom the selection so that these cells fill the screen.

12 Save your work as Exercise2-End.

> If you need help slide the page to the left ➡

Session 2: Exercise answers

These are the four questions that students find the most difficult to remember:

Q 10	Q 8	Q 4 and 5	Q 2
1. Hover over the centre of cell B4 so that you see the white cross cursor shape. ⊹2,500 2. Click and drag down to cell B6. 3. Hold down the **<Ctrl>** key. 4. Hover over cell D4 until you see the white cross cursor shape. 5. Click and drag down to cell D6. This was covered in: *Lesson 2-7: Select non-contiguous cell ranges and view summary information.*	1. Click on the column A header. ↓A ‖ B Profit Analysis 2. Hold down the **<Ctrl>** key. 3. Click on the column E header. 4. Click Home→Font→Bold. Calibri — 1 **B** *I* **U** ▾ Font This was covered in: *Lesson 2-6: Select adjacent and non-adjacent rows and columns.*	1. Click in cell B7. 2. Click Home→Editing→ Autosum (Q4). Σ AutoSum ▾ ＡＺ ⚲ ↓ Fill ▾ ＺＡ Clear ▾ Sort & Find & Filter▾ Select▾ Editing OR Click Home→Editing→ Autosum→Average (Q5). Σ AutoSum ▾ Σ Sum Average Count Nu 3. Either press the **<Enter>** key or click the Autosum button again. This was covered in: *Lesson 2-3: Use AutoSum to quickly calculate totals.*	1. Type **Jan** into cell A4 and press the **<Enter>** key. 2. Click cell A4 once to make it the active cell. 3. Hover the mouse cursor over the bottom right corner of the cell until you see the black cross cursor shape. Jan ┼ 4. Click and drag down to cell A6. This was covered in: *Lesson 2-14: Use AutoFill for text and numeric series.*

If you have difficulty with the other questions, here are the lessons that cover the relevant skills:

1   Refer to: Lesson 2-2: Create a new workbook and view two workbooks at the same time.

3   Refer to: Lesson 2-1: Enter text and numbers into a worksheet.

6   Refer to: Lesson 2-15: Use AutoFill to adjust formulas.

7   Refer to: Lesson 2-15: Use AutoFill to adjust formulas.

9   Refer to: Lesson 2-6: Select adjacent and non-adjacent rows and columns.

11   Refer to: Lesson 2-18: Use the zoom control.

12   Refer to: Lesson 1-5: Save a workbook.

Session Three: Taking Your Skills to the Next Level

> One only gets to the top rung of the ladder by steadily climbing up one at a time, and suddenly all sorts of powers, all sorts of abilities which you thought never belonged to you – suddenly become within your own possibility.
>
> *Margaret Thatcher,*
> *Prime Minister of the United Kingdom from 1979-1990*

After mastering all of the techniques covered in session two, you're already able to do useful work with the world's most powerful business tool, but of course, you're only on the first rung of a very long ladder.

While you are now able to do the simple things well, there are a few more insights you need to really get Excel working.

Most of the skills covered in this session will take your powers beyond those of casual Excel users.

Session Objectives

By the end of this session you will be able to:

- Insert and delete rows and columns
- Use AutoComplete and fill data from adjacent cells
- Cut, copy and paste
- Cut, copy and paste using drag and drop
- Use Paste Values
- Increase/decrease decimal places displayed
- Transpose a range
- Use the multiple item clipboard
- Use Undo and Redo
- Insert, View and Print cell comments
- Understand absolute, relative and mixed cell references
- Create a template
- Use a template
- Freeze columns and rows
- Split the window into multiple panes
- Check spelling

Lesson 3-1: Insert and delete rows and columns

1   Open *The World's Fastest Cars* from your sample files folder.

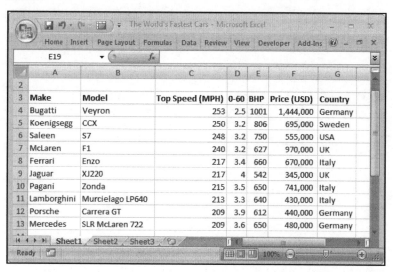

A worksheet opens showing some of the fastest cars in the world.

Until September 2007 the Bugatti Veyron was the fastest car in the world. Shelby has now stolen the crown with their SSC Ultimate Aero. There will probably be an even faster car by the time you read this book! We need to insert a row above row 4 to add the new car to the list.

2   Insert a blank row above row 4.

Right-click the row header button [4] and click *Insert* from the shortcut menu.

3   Add the following data to the new row:

3	Make	Model	Top Speed (MPH)	0-60	BHP	Price (USD)	Country
4	Shelby	SSC Ultimate Aero	257	2.7	1183	654,400	USA

4   If the text is bold faced restore it to normal.

This was covered in: *Lesson 1-11: Use the Mini Toolbar, Key Tips and keyboard shortcuts.*

5   Add a column to the left of column A.

Adding columns is just like adding rows. Right-click on the column header [A] and then click *Insert* from the short cut menu.

A blank column appears on the left hand side of the worksheet:

---

note

Other ways of inserting and deleting rows and columns

The right-click method, described in the text, is the fastest and most intuitive way to insert rows and columns but there are two additional methods.

To Insert rows or columns:

Click Home→Cells→Insert

OR

Press <Ctrl>+<Shift>+<+>

To delete rows or columns:

Click Home→Cells→Delete

OR

Press <Ctrl>+<->

The World's Fastest Cars

	A	B	C	D	E
1		The World's Fastest Cars			
2					
3		Make	Model	Top Speed (MPH)	0-60
4		Shelby	SSC Ultimate Aero	257	2.7
5		Bugatti	Veyron	253	2.5
6		Koenigsegg	CCX	250	3.2

6 Delete the newly-inserted Column A.

Deleting is just like adding. Right-click on the column header A but, this time, select *Delete* from the shortcut menu.

7 Insert four rows above row 3

Nearly every Excel user does this by inserting a single row four times until they learn the correct technique.

1. Select the four rows 3:6 by clicking and dragging across the row header buttons.

2. Right-Click anywhere in the selected area.

3. Click *Insert* from the shortcut menu.

Four blank rows are inserted.

8 Delete the newly-inserted four rows.

1. Select the four rows you want to delete (by dragging the mouse over row headers 3,4,5 and 6).

2. Right-click anywhere in the selected area.

3. Click *Delete* from the shortcut menu.

9 Save your work as: *The World's Fastest Cars-2.*

Lesson 3-2: Use AutoComplete and fill data from adjacent cells

1 Open *The World's Fastest Cars-2* from your sample files folder (if it isn't already open).

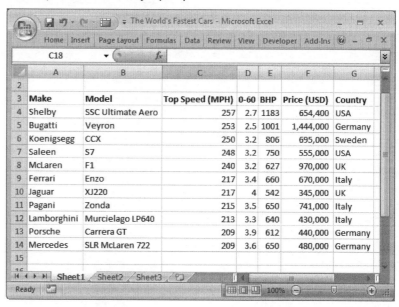

2 Type the letter **F** into cell A15.

Notice that Excel guesses that you want to type *Ferrari* into the cell. This is because the word Ferrari appears above it in the column.

If this doesn't happen somebody has switched AutoComplete off. See the sidebar to find out how to switch it back on.

3 Press the **<Tab>** key to accept the guess.

4 Enter **599 GTB** for the model and **205** for the top speed.

14	Mercedes	SLR McLaren 722		209	3.6	650
15	Ferrari	599GTB		205		
16						

5 Use the fill command to enter **3.6** into cell D15.

The Ferrari has the same 0-60 time as the McLaren SLR. Instead of typing **3.6** into the cell we can use the Fill command.

Click Home→Editing→Fill→Down.

The World's Fastest Cars-2

Notice that the Fill down hotkey combination of <Ctrl>+<D> is also revealed. This is an even faster way to fill down than using the mouse.

Notice also that there is a Right, Up and Left option. These can be used to copy any value to an adjacent cell.

6   Enter **620** for the BHP and **264,034** for the price.

7   Right-click in G15 and choose *Pick from Drop down list...* from the shortcut menu.

All unique countries that currently exist in column G are displayed as a list.

8   Click *Italy* to automatically enter the country.

9   Save your work as *The World's Fastest Cars-3*.

Lesson 3-3: Cut, copy and paste

trivia

The origins of cut and paste

The terms Cut, Copy and Paste remind us of the days when things weren't as easy as they are today.

Before the advent of computer technology, graphic artists would generate text for their work using a phototypesetting machine.

This machine used a photographic process to produce a strip of paper with high quality type printed upon it.

A layout artist would then cut the type into strips and paste it onto a sheet of paper.

When the work was finished it would be photographed to create a negative image ready to convert to a printing plate.

During the 1990's the layout business changed dramatically when graphic artists began to move to computer based desktop publishing.

Today most desktop publishing is done with one of the major software packages: Adobe PageMaker (which later was succeeded by Adobe InDesign), and QuarkXPress.

1 Open *The World's Fastest Cars-3* from your sample files folder (if it isn't already open).

2 Click cell A1 to make it the active cell.

3 Copy the text from cell A1 to the clipboard.

There are three ways to copy but these two are the quickest:

EITHER

- Right click and select Copy from the shortcut menu.

OR

- Press **<Ctrl>+<C>** on the keyboard.

The third method is to click Home→Clipboard→Copy.

The clipboard is a container for copied text and is common to all of Microsoft Office. When you ask Excel to copy it takes the value in cell A1 (in this case text) and places a copy of it onto the clipboard.

The clipboard is useful because we can later paste the clipboard's contents back into the worksheet (or into any other Office document such as a PowerPoint presentation, Word document or Email).

4 Click cell A17 to make it the active cell.

5 Paste the copied text into cell A17.

There are also three ways to paste but these two are the quickest:

EITHER

Right click cell A17 and then select Paste from the shortcut menu.

OR

Click cell A17 and then Press **<Ctrl>+<V>** on the keyboard.

The third (and slowest) method is to click:

Home→Clipboard→Paste

The text appears in cell A17.

14	Mercedes	SLR McLaren 722		209
15	Ferrari	599GTB		205
16				
17	**The World's Fastest Cars**			
18				

6 Edit the text to read: The World's Fastest Italian Cars.

This was covered in: *Lesson 2-1: Enter text and numbers into a worksheet.*

7 Select all of row 9 and copy it to the clipboard.

The World's Fastest Cars-3

Selecting an entire row was covered in: *Lesson 2-6: Select adjacent and non-adjacent rows and columns.*

8 Select all of row 19 and paste into it.

The contents of row 9 are copied to row 19.

17	The World's Fastest Italian Cars			
18				
19	Ferrari	Enzo	217	3.4

9 Select the range A11:G12.

These cells contain data for two more Italian cars.

10	Jaguar	XJ220	217	4	542	345,000	UK
11	Pagani	Zonda	215	3.5	650	741,000	Italy
12	Lamborghini	Murcielago LP640	213	3.3	640	430,000	Italy
13	Porsche	Carrera GT	209	3.9	612	440,000	Germany

10 Cut the text from A11:G12 to place it onto the clipboard.

There are three ways to cut but these two are the quickest:

EITHER

Right click and select Cut from the shortcut menu.

OR

Press **<Ctrl>+<X>**.

The third (and slowest) method is to click Home→Clipboard→Cut.

11 Click in cell A20 to make it the active cell.

12 Paste the cut range into the range beginning in cell A20.

The cut text appears with the top left hand corner in cell A20.

10	Jaguar	XJ220	217	4	542	345,000	UK
11							
12							
13	Porsche	Carrera GT	209	3.9	612	440,000	Germany
14	Mercedes	SLR McLaren 722	209	3.6	650	480,000	Germany
15	Ferrari	599GTB	205	3.6	620	264,034	Italy
16							
17	The World's Fastest Italian Cars						
18							
19	Ferrari	Enzo	217	3.4	660	670,000	Italy
20	Pagani	Zonda	215	3.5	650	741,000	Italy
21	Lamborghini	Murcielago LP640	213	3.3	640	430,000	Italy
22							

13 Save your work as *The World's Fastest Cars-4*.

Lesson 3-4: Cut, copy and paste using drag and drop

1 Open *The World's Fastest Cars-4* from your sample files folder (if it isn't already open).

2 Select cells A20:G21.

3 Hover the mouse cursor over the black border surrounding the range until you see a four-headed arrow.

19	Ferrari	Enzo	217	3.4	660	670,000	Italy
20	Pagani	Zonda	215	3.5	650	741,000	Italy
21	Lamborghini	Murcielago LP640	213	3.3	640	430,000	Italy
22							

It is very important that you see the four headed arrow and not the white cross or AutoFill cursor shape.

If you do not see a four headed arrow somebody may have switched the drag and drop facility off. See sidebar for how to bring it back.

note

If drag and drop doesn't work somebody has switched it off

It's almost certain that drag and drop will be enabled on any computer that you work on. It is such a useful feature that you'd never want to disable it.

If drag and drop doesn't work for you it's because somebody has switched it off.

Bring it back like this:

1. Click Office→ExcelOptions→ Advanced

2. In the first section (*Editing Options*) check *Enable fill handle and cell drag and drop*.

4 Click and drag the cells, dropping them to their previous location (beginning at cell A11).

You'll see a gray outline showing where the cells will be dropped. Move them to the location shown in the screen grab below.

10	Jaguar	XJ220	217	4	542	345,000	UK
11							
12							
13	Porsche	Carrera GT	A11:G12	3.9	612	440,000	Germany

When you release the mouse button the contents of the cells are moved back to A11:G12.

10	Jaguar	XJ220	217	4	542	345,000	UK
11	Pagani	Zonda	215	3.5	650	741,000	Italy
12	Lamborghini	Murcielago LP640	213	3.3	640	430,000	Italy
13	Porsche	Carrera GT	209	3.9	612	440,000	Germany

5 Select cells A11:G12.

6 Hover the mouse cursor over the black border surrounding the range until you see a four-headed arrow.

7 Right-click and drag the rectangle to rows 20 and 21.

When you release the mouse button several options are presented (see sidebar).

Move Here
Copy Here
Copy Here as Values Only
Copy Here as Formats Only
Link Here
Create Hyperlink Here
Shift Down and Copy
Shift Right and Copy
Shift Down and Move
Shift Right and Move
Cancel

The World's Fastest Cars-4

8 Click *Copy Here* from the shortcut menu.

This time the contents of the cells are copied rather than moved.

17	The World's Fastest Italian Cars						
18							
19	Ferrari	Enzo		217	3.4	660	670,000	Italy
20	Pagani	Zonda		215	3.5	650	741,000	Italy
21	Lamborghini	Murcielago LP640		213	3.3	640	430,000	Italy

9 Select all of row 15.

Selecting an entire row was covered in: *Lesson 2-6: Select adjacent and non-adjacent rows and columns.*

14	Mercedes	SLR McLaren 722		209	3.6	650	480,000	Germany
15	Ferrari	599 GTB		205	3.6	620	264,034	Italy
16								

10 Using drag and drop, copy the contents of row 15 to row 22.

17	The World's Fastest Italian Cars						
18							
19	Ferrari	Enzo		217	3.4	660	670,000	Italy
20	Pagani	Zonda		215	3.5	650	741,000	Italy
21	Lamborghini	Murcielago LP640		213	3.3	640	430,000	Italy
22	Ferrari	599GTB		205	3.6	620	264,034	Italy

11 Rename Sheet1 to World Cars and Sheet 2 to Italian Cars.

You learned how to re-name tabs in: *Lesson 1-7: View, add, rename, delete and navigate* worksheet tabs.

12 Select cells A17:G22 on the World Cars worksheet.

13 Cut the cells and paste them into cell A1 of the Italian Cars worksheet.

	A	B	C	D	E	F	G
1	The World's Fastest Italian Cars						
2							
3	Ferrari	Enzo	217	3.4	660	670,000	Italy
4	Pagani	Zonda	215	3.5	650	741,000	Italy
5	Lamborgh	Murcielag	213	3.3	640	430,000	Italy
6	Ferrari	599GTB	205	3.6	620	264,034	Italy

World Cars / **Italian Cars** / Sheet3

note

Other ways of copying cells via drag and drop

Hover over the border of the selected cells with the <Ctrl> key held down. You will see the mouse cursor shape change to a plus sign.

	215
LP640	213
	209

You can now drag and drop (holding the left mouse button down) to copy the cells to a new location.

14 Insert one blank row above row 3.

You learned how to do this in: *Lesson 3-1: Insert and delete rows and columns.*

15 Copy the titles from row 3 of the *World Cars* worksheet to row 3 of the *Italian Cars* worksheet.

1	The World's Fastest Italian Cars						
2							
3	Make	Model		Top Speed (MPH)	0-60	BHP	Price (USD)	Country
4	Ferrari	Enzo		217	3.4	660	670,000	Italy

16 Save your work as *The World's Fastest Cars-5*.

Lesson 3-5: Use Paste Values and increase/decrease decimal places displayed

1   Open *The World's Fastest Cars-5* from your sample files folder (if it isn't already open).

2   Add a new column to the left of column D on the World Cars worksheet.

Right click on the column D header and click *Insert* from the shortcut menu.

3   Rename cell C3 from *Top Speed (MPH)* to *MPH*.

4   Type **KM/H** into cell D3.

5   Re-size columns C and D so that they are just wide enough for their contents.

This skill was covered in: *Lesson 2-9: Re-size rows and columns.*

6   Given that one mile=1.609344 Km, enter a formula into cell D4 to convert MPH into KM/H.

This skill was covered in: *Lesson 2-12: Create your own formulas.*

The correct formula is: **=C4*1.609344.**

The Shelby's speed is now also displayed in Kilometers per hour.

	A	B	C	D	E	F
3	**Make**	**Model**	**MPH**	**KM/H**	**0-60**	**BHP**
4	Shelby	SSC Ultimate Aero	257	413.601408	2.7	1183

7   AutoFill the formula in Cell D4 down to (D15) the bottom of the list.

This skill was covered in: *Lesson 2-15: Use AutoFill to adjust formulas.*

	A	B	C	D	E	F
3	**Make**	**Model**	**MPH**	**KM/H**	**0-60**	**BHP**
4	Shelby	SSC Ultimate Aero	257	413.601408	2.7	1183
5	Bugatti	Veyron	253	407.164032	2.5	1001
6	Koenigsegg	CCX	250	402.336	3.2	806
7	Saleen	S7	248	399.117312	3.2	750
8	McLaren	F1	240	386.24256	3.2	627

The worksheet is giving the right answers but we're not really interested in seeing speeds to five decimal places. It would be nice to simply show whole numbers (also called integers) as we do for Miles per Hour.

8   Select cells D4:D15.

9   Use the *Decrease Decimal* button to format the values in column D to display as whole numbers.

Click the Home→Number→Decrease Decimal button six times.

	A	B	C	D	E	F
3	**Make**	**Model**	**MPH**	**KM/H**	**0-60**	**BHP**
4	Shelby	SSC Ultimate Aero	257	414	2.7	1183
5	Bugatti	Veyron	253	407	2.5	1001

10 Make column D narrower to make things neater.

This skill was covered in: *Lesson 2-9: Re-size rows and columns.*

	A	B	C	D	E	F
3	**Make**	**Model**	**MPH**	**KM/H**	**0-60**	**BHP**
4	Shelby	SSC Ultimate Aero	257	414	2.7	1183
5	Bugatti	Veyron	253	407	2.5	1001

11 Select the range D4:D15 and copy the cell values to the clipboard.

Select the cells, right-click anywhere in the selected range and then click *Copy* from the shortcut menu.

12 Paste the values into cells D17:D28.

Right-click cell D17 and click Paste from the shortcut menu.

Unexpectedly, all of the values are pasted as zeros.

	A	B	C	D	E
15	Ferrari	599 GTB	205	330	3.6
16					
17				0	

13 Examine the formula in cell D17.

Click cell D17 and look at the formula displayed in the Formula Bar at the top of the screen:

f_x =C17*1.609344

When you paste a formula Excel will, by default, adjust the formula in exactly the same way it does when you AutoFill.

14 Undo the previous paste.

Click the undo button on the quick access toolbar.

15 Paste again, this time using Paste Values.

Click in cell E17 to make it the active cell and then click Home→Clipboard→Paste→Paste Values.

This time the values within the cells (rather than the formulas used to calculate the values) are pasted.

	A	B	C	D	E	F
15	Ferrari	599GTB	205	330	3.6	620
16						
17				413.6		
18				407.2		
19				402.3		

16 Delete the values in cells E17:E28.

Select cells E17:E28 and press the **<Delete>** key.

17 Save your work as The World's Fastest Cars-6.

---

note

Other ways to paste values.

Using the Smart Tag

If you perform a regular *paste* and then suddenly realize that you really wanted to *paste values* you don't need to start again.

Notice that a Smart Tag is displayed at the bottom right corner of the pasted cells.

You can click the Smart Tag to change the paste to *Values Only*.

Using a right-click

If you right-click the destination cell and then click Paste Special… from the shortcut menu you will be able to choose *Values* from the Paste Special dialog.

Lesson 3-6: Transpose a range

Paste values is the most used special pasting option but there's another that is often very useful.

If a worksheet has many columns but few rows it may become impossible to print. In this case you may wish to reverse the arrangement so that the worksheet has many rows but few columns.

Transposing allows you to do this automatically.

1   Open *The World's Fastest Cars-6* from your sample files folder (if it isn't already open).

2   Rename Sheet3 to *Transposed.*

   This skill was covered in: *Lesson 1-7: View, add, rename, delete and navigate worksheet tabs.*

3   Select and copy the range A3:H15 on the *World Cars* worksheet.

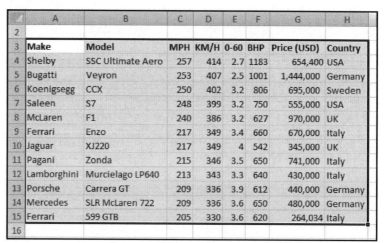

	A	B	C	D	E	F	G	H
2								
3	**Make**	**Model**	**MPH**	**KM/H**	**0-60**	**BHP**	**Price (USD)**	**Country**
4	Shelby	SSC Ultimate Aero	257	414	2.7	1183	654,400	USA
5	Bugatti	Veyron	253	407	2.5	1001	1,444,000	Germany
6	Koenigsegg	CCX	250	402	3.2	806	695,000	Sweden
7	Saleen	S7	248	399	3.2	750	555,000	USA
8	McLaren	F1	240	386	3.2	627	970,000	UK
9	Ferrari	Enzo	217	349	3.4	660	670,000	Italy
10	Jaguar	XJ220	217	349	4	542	345,000	UK
11	Pagani	Zonda	215	346	3.5	650	741,000	Italy
12	Lamborghini	Murcielago LP640	213	343	3.3	640	430,000	Italy
13	Porsche	Carrera GT	209	336	3.9	612	440,000	Germany
14	Mercedes	SLR McLaren 722	209	336	3.6	650	480,000	Germany
15	Ferrari	599 GTB	205	330	3.6	620	264,034	Italy
16								

4   Select cell A3 on the *Transposed* worksheet.

5   Click Home→Clipboard→Paste→Transpose.

The cells are copied in a rather interesting way. The columns have now become rows and the rows have become columns.

The World's Fastest Cars-6

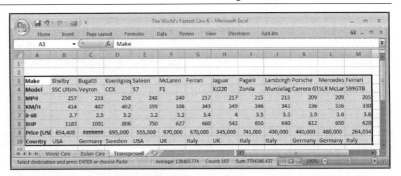

Notice also that the width of the columns have not been maintained. In the case of the (very expensive) Bugatti Veyron there isn't even enough space in the cell to display the price and a row of hashes is displayed instead.

(If you're used to calling the hash (#) a **pound sign** or **number sign** see the sidebar in: *Lesson 2-9: Re-size rows and columns* for an explanation).

6 Automatically size all columns in one operation.

1. Select every cell in the workbook by clicking the *select all* button in the top left corner of the worksheet:

2. Hover the muse cursor over the intersection of any two columns until you see the *re-size* cursor shape and then double-click.

Every column is perfectly sized.

	A	B	C	D	E
1					
2					
3	**Make**	Shelby	Bugatti	Koenigsegg	Saleen
4	**Model**	SSC Ultimate Aero	Veyron	CCX	S7
5	**MPH**	257	253	250	248

7 Save your work as The World's Fastest Cars-7.

Lesson 3-7: Use the Multiple Item Clipboard

When you copy items from any non-Office Windows application, the selected item is copied to the *Windows Clipboard*. You are then able to paste this item into any other Windows application.

While the *Windows Clipboard* can only contain one item, Office has its own clipboard that can contain up to 24 items.

Because all Office applications share the same *Office Clipboard*, it is possible to copy and paste up to 24 items between Excel, PowerPoint, Word, Access… and all other Office applications.

In this lesson we'll use the *Office Clipboard* to add contents to a new page in the workbook. The new page will contain details of the world's fastest *German* cars.

1   Open *The World's Fastest Cars-7* from your sample files folder (if it isn't already open).

2   Insert a new worksheet and name it *German Cars*.

This skill was covered in: *Lesson 1-7: View, add, rename, delete and navigate worksheet tabs.*

3   Click Home→Clipboard→Dialog Launcher.

This is our first experience of a dialog launcher button. The dialog launcher button is situated on the bottom right-hand corner of some dialogs.

The Clipboard task pane is displayed:

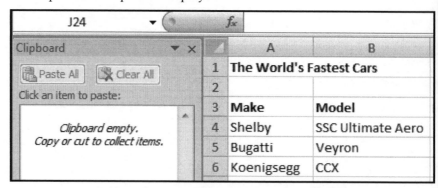

4   If any items are shown on the Clipboard click the Clear All button ![Clear All] to remove them.

5   Copy row 3 on the World Cars worksheet to the clipboard.

Right-click the row 3 row header and click *Copy* on the shortcut menu.

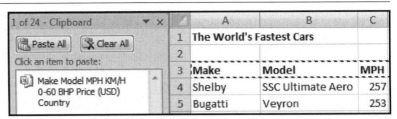

6   Copy row 5 in the World Cars worksheet to the clipboard.

7   Copy row 13 in the World Cars worksheet to the clipboard

8   Copy row 14 in the World Cars worksheet to the clipboard.

The header row along with details for the three German cars is now displayed on the clipboard (see sidebar).

9   Click the German Cars tab.

The blank German Cars worksheet is displayed.

10   Type **The World's Fastest German Cars** into cell A1 and bold face the text.

11   Click cell A3 to make it the Active Cell.

12   Complete the worksheet with a single click by clicking the Paste All button.

It would be possible to click once upon each of the four items on the Clipboard. Because we want the entire contents of the Clipboard four clicks are saved by using the *Paste All* button.

When you click the Paste All button, all of the items on the clipboard are pasted into adjacent rows:

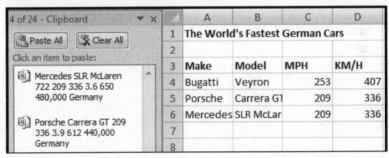

13   Automatically Re-size all of the columns so that the header row is visible.

This skill was covered in: *Lesson 3-6: Transpose a range.*

14   Close the clipboard.

Click the close button at the top right-hand corner of the clipboard.

15   Save your work as *The World's Fastest Cars-8.*

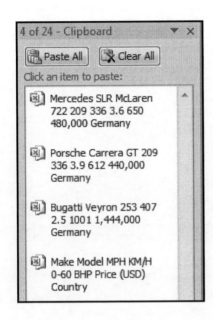

Lesson 3-8: Use Undo and Redo

Excel's undo feature is a lifesaver.

In previous versions of Excel it was only possible to undo the previous 16 operations, but in Excel 2007 you can now undo up to 100 actions.

Sometimes you may undo an action and then change your mind. Redo will step through the operations in reverse, in effect "undoing the undo"!

1   Open *The World's Fastest Cars-8* from your sample files folder (if it isn't already open) and select the World Cars worksheet.

2   Type USA Cars into cell A17 and bold face the text.

3   Copy row 3 into row 19.

4   Copy row 4 into row 20.

5   Copy row 7 into row 21.

The worksheet should now look like this:

	A	B	C	D	E	F	G	H
1	The World's Fastest Cars							
2								
3	Make	Model	MPH	KM/H	0-60	BHP	Price (USD)	Country
4	Shelby	SSC Ultimate Aero	257	414	2.7	1183	654,400	USA
5	Bugatti	Veyron	253	407	2.5	1001	1,444,000	Germany
6	Koenigsegg	CCX	250	402	3.2	806	695,000	Sweden
7	Saleen	S7	248	399	3.2	750	555,000	USA
8	McLaren	F1	240	386	3.2	627	970,000	UK
9	Ferrari		217	349	3.4	660	670,000	Italy
10	Jaguar	XJ220	217	349	4	542	345,000	UK
11	Pagani	Zonda	215	346	3.5	650	741,000	Italy
12	Lamborghini	Murcielago LP640	213	343	3.3	640	430,000	Italy
13	Porsche	Carrera GT	209	336	3.9	612	440,000	Germany
14	Mercedes	SLR McLaren 722	209	336	3.6	650	480,000	Germany
15	Ferrari	599GTB	205	330	3.6	620	264,034	Italy
16								
17	USA Cars							
18								
19	Make	Model	MPH	KM/H	0-60	BHP	Price (USD)	Country
20	Shelby	SSC Ultimate Aero	257	414	2.7	1183	654,400	USA
21	Saleen	S7	248	399	3.2	750	555,000	USA

World Cars / Italian Cars / Transposed / German Cars

6   Click the undo button on the quick access toolbar.

The Saleen details disappear from row 21.

7   Click the redo button on the quick access toolbar.

The Saleen details re-appear in row 21.

8   Click the drop-down arrow to the right of the undo button on the quick access toolbar.

---

note

Using the keyboard to undo and redo

It is well worth remembering the undo keyboard shortcut :

<Ctrl>+<Z>

I use it all of the time. It is also the undo shortcut for the other Office applications.

You'll use the Redo action far less, but for completeness it is:

<Ctrl>+<Y>

If you forget them, you'll see the keyboard shortcuts in the tooltip when you hover over the undo and redo buttons.

Undo Paste (Ctrl+Z)

The World's Fastest Cars-8

A drop-down menu appears showing all of the actions that have taken place (or the previous 100 actions if more than 100 actions have taken place) since the workbook was opened.

9   Click the Bold action to *Undo 4 Actions.*

Only the text *USA Cars* remains on the worksheet and it is no longer bold faced.

14	Mercedes	SLR McLaren 722	209	336
15	Ferrari	599GTB	205	330
16				
17	USA Cars			
18				

10   Click the drop-down arrow to the right of the redo button

on the quick access toolbar.

A drop-down menu appears showing all of the actions that have been undone and can be potentially re-done.

11   Click the last *Paste* action to redo four actions.

The worksheet reverts to its former state.

17	USA Cars								
18								
19	Make	Model	MPH	KM/H	0-60	BHP	Price (USD)	Country
20	Shelby	SSC Ultimate Aero	257	414	2.7	1183	654,400	USA
21	Saleen	S7	248	399	3.2	750	555,000	USA

12   Delete rows 17 to 21.

13   Save your work as The World's Fastest Cars-9.

Lesson 3-9: Insert cell comments

1   Open *The World's Fastest Cars-9* from your sample files folder (if it isn't already open) and select the *World Cars* worksheet.

2   Using Microsoft Word (not Excel), open *Car Descriptions* from your sample files folder.

     1.   Open Microsoft Word.

     2.   Click Office→Open and open *Car Descriptions* from your sample files folder.

3   Return to Excel.

You will notice two buttons on the Windows status bar at the bottom of the screen:

Click the button with the Excel logo to return to Excel.

note

Excel uses your log-in user name by default

If you don't set up your user name as described, Excel will use your Windows log-in user name instead.

This is the reason you'll often see cryptic user names (like JSmith93) in other people's worksheets.

note

Other ways to insert a comment

Click Review→Comments→ New Comment.

OR

Press <Shift>+<F2>

Car Descriptions

The World's Fastest Cars-9

4   Set up the name that will appear in the comment box.

Whenever you enter a comment your name is added to the top. This allows other users to identify the source of each comment if you later distribute the workbook.

Click Office→Excel Options→Popular.

In the category *Personalize your copy of Microsoft Office* type your name into the *User Name* box and then click the OK button.

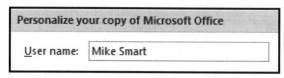

5   Copy the text for the Shelby SSC Ultimate Aero from the word document.

     1.   Return to Word.

     2.   Drag across the Shelby text with the mouse cursor.

     3.   Right-click within the selected text and click Copy from the shortcut menu.

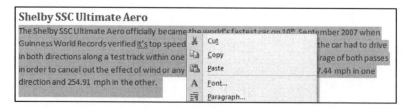

6   Add the comment text to the Shelby model cell (cell B4).

     1.   Return to Excel.

     2.   Right-click cell B4 and click *Insert Comment* on the shortcut menu.

A comment box with your name at the top is shown next to cell B4.

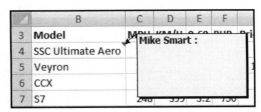

3. Paste into the comment box.

The text that you copied from the Word document appears in the box.

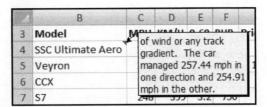

7 Enlarge the comment box, using the sizing handles, so that all text is visible.

The sizing handles are the small white dots that appear on the corners and edges of the comment box. When you hover over a sizing handle the cursor shape changes to a double headed arrow.

1. Hover carefully over the bottom-right sizing handle until you see the double-headed arrow.

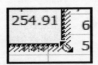

2. Click and drag to re-size the comment box.

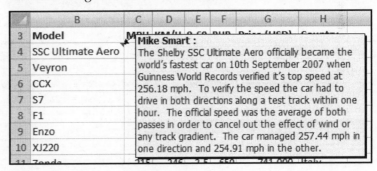

8 Click anywhere in the worksheet.

The comment disappears but a small red triangle has appeared in the top right corner of the cell.

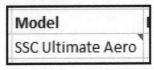

9 Add two more comments for the Saleen S7 and Pagani Zonda.

10 Save your work as The World's Fastest Cars-10.

Lesson 3-10: View cell comments

1 Open *The World's Fastest Cars-10* from your sample files folder (if it isn't already open) and select the *World Cars* worksheet.

Cells with comments show a small red triangle in the top right-hand corner.

2 View the comment behind a single cell.

Hover the mouse cursor over any of the cells with a red triangle. The cell comment is displayed.

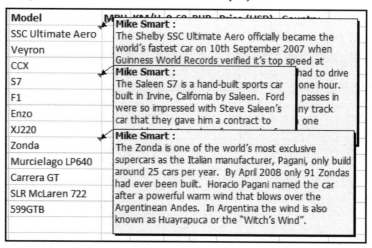

3 View all of the comments in a worksheet at the same time.

Click Review→Comments→Show All Comments.

Every comment on the worksheet is displayed.

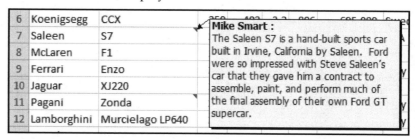

Unfortunately the comments overlap so you are unable to read them all at the same time. It is possible to view each comment by clicking it as this brings the window to the front but it isn't very elegant.

4 Move the comments so that they do not overlap.

Click a comment and then hover anywhere on the gray border *but not on a sizing handle* until you see a four headed arrow. When you see the four-headed arrow click and drag to move the comment.

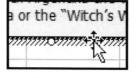

The World's Fastest Cars-10

	A	B	C	D	E	F	G	H	I
1	The World's Fastest Cars								
2									
3	**Make**	**Model**	**MPH**	**KM**					
4	Shelby	SSC Ultimate Aero	257						
5	Bugatti	Veyron	253						
6	Koenigsegg	CCX	250						
7	Saleen	S7	248						
8	McLaren	F1	240						
9	Ferrari	Enzo	217						
10	Jaguar	XJ220	217						
11	Pagani	Zonda	215						
12	Lamborghini	Murcielago LP640	213						
13	Porsche	Carrera GT	209						
14	Mercedes	SLR McLaren 722	209						
15	Ferrari	599GTB	205						

Mike Smart : The Shelby SSC Ultimate Aero officially became the world's fastest car on 10th September 2007 when Guinness World Records verified it's top speed at 256.18 mph. To verify the speed the car had to drive in both directions along a test track within one hour. The official speed was the average of both passes in order to cancel out the effect of wind or any track gradient. The car managed 257.44 mph in one direction and 254.91 mph in the other.

Mike Smart : The Saleen S7 is a hand-built sports car built in Irvine, California by Saleen. Ford were so impressed with Steve Saleen's car that they gave him a contract to assemble, paint, and perform much of the final assembly of their own Ford GT supercar.

Mike Smart : The Zonda is one of the world's most exclusive supercars as the Italian manufacturer, Pagani, only build around 25 cars per year. By April 2008 only 91 Zondas had ever been built. Horacio Pagani named the car after a powerful warm wind that blows over the Argentinean Andes. In Argentina the wind is also known as Huayrapuca or the "Witch's Wind".

> **note**
>
> **Other ways to show/hide comments**
>
> The right-click method is definitely the fastest but you can also show and hide comments using the Ribbon.
>
> To show or hide a comment:
>
> 1. Click cell B11 to make it the active cell.
>
> 2. Click:
>
> Review→Comments→ Show/Hide Comment

5 Hide all of the comments.

Click Review→Comments→Show All Comments.

The comments disappear.

6 Make the Zonda comment display all of the time.

Sometimes you will want to send somebody a worksheet and make sure that an important comment is on view when they open it.

Right click cell B11 and choose Show/Hide Comment from the shortcut menu.

The comment remains on display all of the time (even if you are not hovering over the comment cell).

7 Hide the Zonda comment.

Right click cell B11 and choose *Hide Comment* from the shortcut menu.

8 Save your work as *The World's Fastest Cars-11*.

Lesson 3-11: Print cell comments

One of the commonest requests asked by Excel users is: "how can I print a list of comments at the end of a worksheet".

Excel can do this but the feature is hidden away in the Page Setup dialog and missed by most users.

1   Open *The World's Fastest Cars-11* from your sample files folder (if it isn't already open) and select the *World Cars* worksheet.

2   Tell Excel to print comments at the end of the worksheet.

Here's how it's done.

1.   Click Page Layout→Page Setup→Dialog Launcher.

The *Page Setup* dialog is displayed.

2.   Click the *Sheet* tab and then choose the option *At end of sheet* from the *Comments* drop-down.

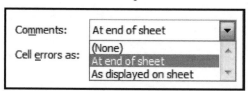

3   Click the *Print Preview* button to view the comments as they would print.

You can either click the *Print Preview* button on the *Page Setup* dialog or close the dialog and click: Office→Print→Print Preview.

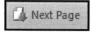

Click the *Next Page* button to view Page 2 of the preview. The comments are displayed exactly as they would print.

> **Cell:** B4
> **Comment:** Mike Smart :
> The Shelby SSC Ultimate Aero officially became the world's fastest car on 10th September 2007 when Guinness World Records verified it's top speed at 256.18 mph. To verify the speed the car had to drive in both directions along a test track within one hour. The official speed was the average of both passes in order to cancel out the effect of wind or any track gradient. The car managed 257.44 mph in one direction and 254.91 mph in the other.
>
> **Cell:** B7
> **Comment:** Mike Smart :
> The Saleen S7 is a hand-built sports car built in Irvine, California by Saleen. Ford were so impressed with Steve Saleen's car that they gave him a contract to assemble, paint, and perform much of the final assembly of their own Ford GT supercar.
>
> **Cell:** B11
> **Comment:** Mike Smart :
> The Zonda is one of the world's most exclusive supercars as the Italian manufacturer, Pagani, only build around 25 cars per year. By April 2008 only 91 Zondas had ever been built. Horacio Pagani named the car after a powerful warm wind that blows over the Argentinean Andes. In Argentina the wind is also known as Huayrapuca or the "Witch's Wind".

4   Close the print preview window.

The World's Fastest Cars-11

5   Make the Zonda comment display all of the time.

Right click cell B11 and choose Show/Hide Comments from the shortcut menu.

6   Move the Zonda comment so that it doesn't obscure the data in the worksheet.

This was covered in: *Lesson 3-10: View cell comments*.

7   Tell Excel to print comments exactly as they are displayed on the worksheet.

1. Click Page Layout→Page Setup→Dialog Launcher

The Page Setup dialog is displayed.

2. Click the Sheet tab and then choose the option *As displayed on sheet* from the Comments drop-down.

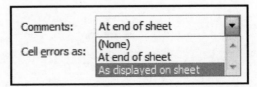

8   Click the *Print Preview* button to view the comment as it would print.

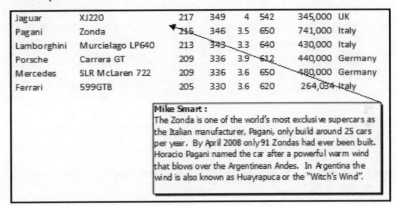

9   Close the print preview window.

10 Hide the comment.

Right click cell B11 and choose *Hide Comment* from the shortcut menu.

11 Save your work as: *The World's Fastest Cars-12*.

Lesson 3-12: Understand absolute and relative cell references

You've seen how useful Excel's AutoFill is when copying formulas. Most of the time things work perfectly, as you normally want to increment row and column references when you AutoFill across and down.

Sometimes AutoFill can be a little too helpful when it adjusts cell references that you would like to be left alone. This lesson will illustrate the type of worksheet that requires *absolute cell references* as we convert the USD (US Dollar) prices to GBP (Great Britain Pounds).

1 Open *The World's Fastest Cars-12* from your sample files folder (if it isn't already open) and select the *World Cars* worksheet.

2 Insert a column to the left of column H.

This skill was covered in: *Lesson 3-1: Insert and delete rows and columns.*

3 Type **Price (GBP)** into cell H3.

4 Type **USD/GBP** into cell G1.

5 Type **0.51195** into cell H1.

If you want more realism you can get the current exchange rate from www.oanda.com. If you are not in England or America it might be fun to change the exchange rates to match your own currency.

6 Place a formula in cell H4 that will calculate the price of a Shelby SSC Ultimate Aero in GBP (Great Britain Pounds).

Formulas were covered in: *Lesson 2-12: Create your own formulas.*

The correct formula is:

=**G4*H1**

We can now see that the Shelby costs £335.020. Surely a bargain!

	G	H	I
1	USD/GBP	0.51195	
2			
3	Price (USD)	Price (GBP)	Country
4	654,400	335,020	USA

7 Consider what will happen if we AutoFill this formula.

(AutoFill was covered in: *Lesson 2-15: Use AutoFill to adjust formulas*).

As the formula is AutoFilled downward the number part of each formula will be incremented like this:

	H
3	**Price (GBP)**
4	=G4*H1
5	=G5*H2
6	=G6*H3

Consider cell H5 (the price of the Bugatti Veyron). The formula in this cell is **=G5*H2**.

AutoFill has done a wonderful job with G5. It has changed the reference from the Shelby's price to the Bugatti and that's exactly what we wanted.

But AutoFill has seriously messed up with the H2 reference. The exchange rate is always in cell H1. It never moves.

To express this in "Excel-speak": G4 is a **relative reference** (ie we want AutoFill to adjust it) while H1 is an **absolute reference** (ie we want AutoFill to leave it alone).

8   Change the formula in cell H4 to make H1 into an absolute reference.

To make a reference absolute you simply add a dollar sign in front of both the letter and number.

So: H1 becomes $H$1.

Click cell H4 and then edit the formula (shown in the formula bar) so that it now reads.

=G4*$H$1

9   AutoFill the formula in cell H4 to the end of the list.

(AutoFill was covered in: *Lesson 2-15: Use AutoFill to adjust formulas*).

The price of each car is now displayed in both US Dollars and Great Britain Pounds.

	G	H	I
3	**Price (USD)**	**Price (GBP)**	**Country**
4	654,400	335,020	USA
5	1,444,000	739,256	Germany
6	695,000	355,805	Sweden

Click on each of the GBP prices and observe the formula shown in the formula bar at the top of the screen.

In every case Excel has adjusted the G4 part of the formula but left the H1 part of the formula alone.

H5				▼	*fx*	=G5*$H$1	

	C	D	E	F	G	H
3	**MPH**	**KM/H**	**0-60**	**BHP**	**Price (USD)**	**Price (GBP)**
4	257	414	2.7	1183	654,400	335,020
5	253	407	2.5	1001	1,444,000	739,256

10   Save your work as *The World's Fastest Cars-13*.

Lesson 3-13: Understand mixed cell references

Before we tackle mixed cell references I must warn you that this subject is a bit of a brain teaser. The skill is well worth mastering as you'll find it extremely useful in many types of real-world worksheets.

1   Open *International Price List* from your sample files folder.

This worksheet will calculate the price of each car for five more markets. The exchange rates are shown in row 4.

2   Add a formula to calculate the UK price of a Shelby SSC Ultimate Aero.

Formulas were covered in: *Lesson 2-12: Create your own formulas.*

The correct formula is:

=C6*D4

We can see that the Shelby costs £335.020.

	C	D	E	F	G	H
3		GBP	EUR	JPY	CAD	CHF
4		0.51195	0.64682	198.687	1.04422	1.05489
5	USA $	UK £	Euros €	Japan ¥	Canada $	Switzerland fr.
6	654,400	335,020				

3   Consider what will happen if we AutoFill this formula.

(AutoFill was covered in: *Lesson 2-15: Use AutoFill to adjust formulas*).

As the formula is AutoFilled downward the number part of each formula is incremented like this:

	C	D
6	654400	=C6*D4
7	1444000	=C7*D5
8	695000	=C8*D6

You may be thinking that this is just like the problem poised in: *Lesson 3-12: Understand absolute and relative cell references.*

Why not simply make D4 into an absolute reference? Like this:

	C	D	E
3		GBP	EUR
4		0.51195	0.64682
5	USA $	UK £	Euros €
6	654400	=C6*$D$4	

Think carefully about what will then happen when you AutoFill to the right.

International Price List

AutoFill knows that when you fill right you *usually* want the letter part of each formula incremented like this:

	C	D	E
3		GBP	EUR
4		0.51195	0.64682
5	USA $	UK £	Euros €
6	654400	=C6*$D$4	=D6*$D$4
7	1444000	=C7*$D$4	
8	695000	=C8*$D$4	

This is going to mess up the Euro price completely. The UK price will be fine but AutoFill has made two errors.

1. It is still using the GBP exchange rate for the EUR prices because we made that absolute.

2. It is referencing the UK price of the Shelby instead of the US dollar price because C6 is a relative reference.

Let's tackle each problem one at a time

1. We want the GBP exchange rate to adjust to the EUR exchange rate as the formula is filled to the right. In this case the D part of D4 should be relative but the 4 part should be absolute. This can be denoted by D$4 instead of $D$4.

2. We want the US Dollar price to always be used against the US Dollar Exchange rates in Row 4. Therefore we want the C part of C6 to be absolute. As AutoFill fills downward we need the price to be adjusted to the relevant car so the 6 part of C6 needs to be relative. This can be denoted by $C6 instead of $C$6.

4 Correct the formula so that it will AutoFill correctly.

Enter the formula =$C6*D$4 into cell D6.

This will AutoFill correctly like this:

	C	D	E
3		GBP	EUR
4		0.51195	0.64682
5	USA $	UK £	Euros €
6	654400	=$C6*D$4	=$C6*E$4
7	1444000	=$C7*D$4	=$C7*E$4
8	695000	=$C8*D$4	=$C8*E$4

5 AutoFill across to cell H6.

The correct Shelby prices are shown in five currencies.

6 AutoFill down to cell H17.

The correct prices are shown for all cars and all currencies.

7 Make the columns wide enough to display the prices.

8 Save your work as *International Price List-1*.

---

tip

A faster way to add dollar signs to create mixed references.

3. Click on the formula bar so that the cursor is touching the cell reference you want to convert to mixed:

4. Press the <F4> key repeatedly on the keyboard.

Each time you press <F4> Excel cycles through all possible absolute and mixed references:

Lesson 3-14: Create a template

What is a template?

You'll often find yourself making copies of older workbooks that are nearly the same as the one you need. You'll then delete the bits you don't need and add the bits that you do.

If you find this happening it's time to make a template.

The template is just a normal workbook that contains the starting point for a task that you often need to do. You can put anything into a template that you can put into a regular workbook.

Templates are a great time saver.

Microsoft has even provided you with a set of templates that you may find useful, and there are more available for free via the Internet.

1   Open *First Quarter Sales and Bonus* from your sample files folder.

2   Delete the contents of cells *C6:D14*.

3   Replace the text in cell A1 with the words: *Bonus Calculator*.

<table>
<tr><td></td><td>A</td><td>B</td><td>C</td><td>D</td><td>E</td></tr>
<tr><td>1</td><td colspan="5">**Bonus Calculator**</td></tr>
<tr><td>2</td><td></td><td></td><td></td><td></td><td></td></tr>
<tr><td>3</td><td>Sales</td><td></td><td></td><td></td><td></td></tr>
<tr><td>4</td><td></td><td></td><td></td><td></td><td></td></tr>
<tr><td>5</td><td>First Name</td><td>Last Name</td><td>Sales</td><td>Target</td><td>Target Sales</td></tr>
<tr><td>6</td><td>Andrew</td><td>Fuller</td><td></td><td></td><td>-</td></tr>
<tr><td>7</td><td>Anne</td><td>Dodsworth</td><td></td><td></td><td>-</td></tr>
<tr><td>8</td><td>Janet</td><td>Leverling</td><td></td><td></td><td>-</td></tr>
<tr><td>9</td><td>Laura</td><td>Callahan</td><td></td><td></td><td>-</td></tr>
<tr><td>10</td><td>Margaret</td><td>Peacock</td><td></td><td></td><td>-</td></tr>
<tr><td>11</td><td>Michael</td><td>Suyama</td><td></td><td></td><td>-</td></tr>
<tr><td>12</td><td>Nancy</td><td>Davolio</td><td></td><td></td><td>-</td></tr>
<tr><td>13</td><td>Robert</td><td>King</td><td></td><td></td><td>-</td></tr>
<tr><td>14</td><td>Steven</td><td>Buchanan</td><td></td><td></td><td>-</td></tr>
<tr><td>15</td><td></td><td>Total:</td><td>-</td><td></td><td></td></tr>
<tr><td>16</td><td></td><td></td><td></td><td></td><td></td></tr>
<tr><td>17</td><td>Bonus</td><td></td><td></td><td></td><td></td></tr>
<tr><td>18</td><td></td><td></td><td></td><td></td><td></td></tr>
<tr><td>19</td><td>First Name</td><td>Last Name</td><td>Salary</td><td>Bonus</td><td>Total</td></tr>
<tr><td>20</td><td>Andrew</td><td>Fuller</td><td>2,500</td><td>-</td><td>2,500.00</td></tr>
<tr><td>21</td><td>Anne</td><td>Dodsworth</td><td>2,000</td><td>-</td><td>2,000.00</td></tr>
<tr><td>22</td><td>Janet</td><td>Leverling</td><td>2,600</td><td>-</td><td>2,600.00</td></tr>
<tr><td>23</td><td>Laura</td><td>Callahan</td><td>2,800</td><td>-</td><td>2,800.00</td></tr>
<tr><td>24</td><td>Margaret</td><td>Peacock</td><td>3,000</td><td>-</td><td>3,000.00</td></tr>
<tr><td>25</td><td>Michael</td><td>Suyama</td><td>1,800</td><td>-</td><td>1,800.00</td></tr>
<tr><td>26</td><td>Nancy</td><td>Davolio</td><td>4,500</td><td>-</td><td>4,500.00</td></tr>
<tr><td>27</td><td>Robert</td><td>King</td><td>2,000</td><td>-</td><td>2,000.00</td></tr>
<tr><td>28</td><td>Steven</td><td>Buchanan</td><td>3,000</td><td>-</td><td>3,000.00</td></tr>
<tr><td>29</td><td></td><td>Total:</td><td>24,200</td><td>-</td><td>24,200.00</td></tr>
</table>

note

This worksheet looks flashy!

If you are wondering how to make your own worksheets look as flashy as this one you'll only need a little more patience.

You'll learn every skill you need to make your worksheets look as good, and even a lot better, than this one in the next session: *Session Four: Making Your Worksheets Look Professional.*

First Quarter Sales and Bonus

note

Changing the default template folder

If the template will only ever be used by you on this machine there's no problem with the default template location.

If you are part of a workgroup who want to share a common template library you'd want to place the template folder on a file server that everybody in the office had access to.

Excel's designers seem to have forgotten to include a template folder location option so you have to change it in rather an odd way.

Believe it or not, you have to go to Word and change the default template folder there. When you return to Excel you'll find that the default template folder has also changed.

To change the location of the Template folder you must open Word and click:

Office→Word Options→ Advanced

At the bottom of the *Advanced* options list there's a *File Locations* button.

Click this button and you'll be able to change the location of the default template folder for all Office applications.

This is exactly the type of workbook you'd probably want to make into a template. The bonus has to be calculated every quarter and it will save a lot of work.

4   Save your work as: *Bonus Calculator*.

5   Save the workbook as a template.

Every quarter you could simply load last quarter's spreadsheet, save it with a new name and then delete the cell values. But you'd have to do that every quarter and then, one day, you might forget the *save as* step and end up over writing the old file.

A much better solution is to save the empty workbook as a template.

1.   Click the Office button, choose *Save As* from the left of the dialog and *Other formats* from the right.

2.   Click the drop down list arrow labeled *Save as Type* at the bottom of the *Save As* dialog.

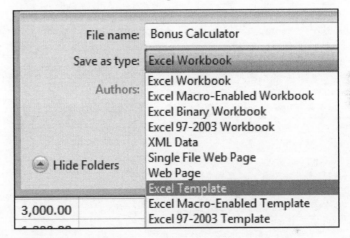

3.   For this workbook the best choice is *Excel Template*.

If this template needs to be used by users with older versions of Excel you'd choose *Excel 97-2003* template.

If the workbook contained macros (working with macros is an Expert level skill covered fully in the *Expert Skills* book in this series) you'd need to choose *Excel Macro-Enabled Template*.

4.   Click the Save button to save the template to the default template folder. The existing name: *Bonus Calculator* is fine.

The default template folder is

C:\Users\ user name \AppData\Roaming\Microsoft\Templates

If you want to change this location see the sidebar for instructions.

6   Close the template.

Lesson 3-15: Use a template

1 Click Office→New.

2 Click the *My templates...* list item on the left of the dialog.

note

Can I make my own templates appear in the Installed Templates group?

The installed templates are located in the folder:

C:\Program Files\Microsoft Office\Templates\Language ID Number

Language ID Number is a four digit code representing the language types that are currently installed.

The English (US) version of Office 2007 has the language code 1033 so you'll find installed templates in:

C:\Program Files\Microsoft Office\Templates\1033

If you save one of your own template files to this location you'll see it appear in the *Installed Templates* group along with Microsoft's own.

A dialog appears showing all of the templates in your personal templates folder:

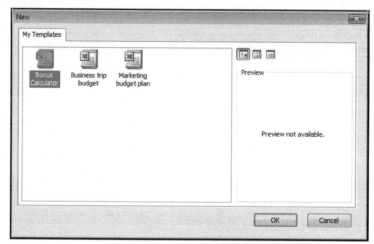

3 Either double-click *Bonus Calculator* (the template saved in the last lesson) or click *Bonus Calculator* once and then click the *OK* button.

A new workbook is created from the template.

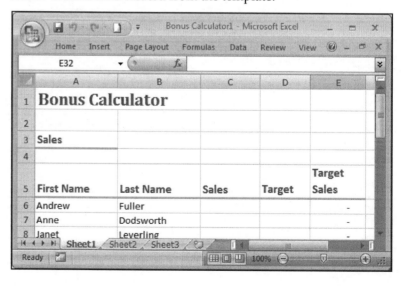

Notice that the workbook has been named *Bonus Calculator1*. You are not looking at the template but a new workbook created from the template.

4 Use an installed template.

Installed templates are a set of Microsoft templates that were created when you installed Excel.

Create a new workbook in exactly the same way as you did using the *Bonus Calculator* template but choose *Installed Templates* and then select one of Microsoft's templates.

Some of Microsoft's templates may seem a little overwhelming at the moment but they'll seem far less intimidating by the time you reach the end of this book!

5 Create a new workbook using an existing workbook as a template.

This is very similar to loading the existing workbook and then saving it with a different name.

Proceed as before but, this time, choose *New from existing…* instead of *My Templates*.

You are then able to navigate to any Excel workbook and copy it into a new workbook without altering the original.

6 Create a workbook from Microsoft's on-line library of templates.

The Internet is a wonderful thing. Microsoft have a huge library of templates that they add to all of the time and make available to you for free.

Proceed as before, but this time choose any of the categories from the *Microsoft Office Online* section.

Some of their templates are very interesting but do read the cautionary note in the sidebar before using any of them.

note

If you don't fully understand how a template works don't use it.

Many of Microsoft's templates contain program code written in a language called Visual Basic for Applications (VBA).

VBA programming is way beyond the skills of nearly all Excel users (I would estimate that far less than 1% of Excel users can hand-craft VBA code).

If you can use this type of template "as is", or if you have a VBA programmer on your staff who is also an Excel expert, you may find templates containing VBA code useful. Otherwise there's a danger that you may end up with a worksheet you don't understand and are unable to maintain.

For this reason I'd always advise you to create your own worksheets (and templates) from scratch so that you fully understand how they are built and are able to maintain them.

A Smart Method *Excel VBA* book will be available soon. This will be of interest to Excel Expert Level users who have very advanced requirements.

Lesson 3-16: Freeze columns and rows

1   Open *Sales First Quarter 2008* from your sample files folder.

Notice that it is easy to see which data is in each column when you are at the top of the worksheet and can see the header row:

	A	B	C	D
1	Date	First Name	Last Name	Company Name
2	01-Jan-08	Nancy	Davolio	Eastern Connection
3	01-Jan-08	Nancy	Davolio	Eastern Connection

But things get confusing when you scroll further down the list:

	A	B	C	D
128	17-Feb-08	Margaret	Peacock	Rancho grande
129	17-Feb-08	Margaret	Peacock	Rancho grande
130	18-Feb-08	Janet	Leverling	Blondel père et fils

It is no longer clear what information is contained in each column because the header row has disappeared.

2   Press **<Ctrl>+<Home>** to quickly move to Cell A1.

3   Click View→Window→Freeze Panes.

A rich menu is displayed

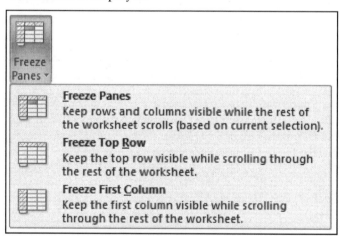

With Excel's new rich menus the meaning of each option is quite clear.

4   Click the *Freeze Top Row* list item.

A small black line appears beneath the first row.

5   Scroll down the list.

Notice that as you scroll down, the top row remains in place.

Sales First Quarter 2008

	A	B	C	D
1	Date	First Name	Last Name	Company Name
47	16-Jan-08	Margaret	Peacock	Simons bistro
48	16-Jan-08	Margaret	Peacock	Simons bistro
49	16-Jan-08	Margaret	Peacock	Simons bistro
50	17-Jan-08	Margaret	Peacock	QUICK-Stop

note

Another way to freeze the top row would be to convert the range into a table.

Excel automatically freezes column headers in tables.

Tables are covered extensively in the *Expert Skills* book in this series.

6   Unfreeze the top row.

Click: View→Window→Freeze Panes once more. The first choice has now changed to *Unfreeze Panes*. Click this menu item to put things back to normal.

7   Freeze the first column.

Do exactly as you did before but, this time, select *Freeze First Column* from the rich menu.

Notice that the date column is now locked into place. As you scroll to the right the date remains in the first column.

	A	F	G	H
1	Date	Country	Product Name	Quantity
2	01-Jan-08	UK	Thüringer Rostbratwurst	21
3	01-Jan-08	UK	Steeleye Stout	35

8   Unfreeze the panes.

9   Freeze the first two rows and the left most three columns.

Whilst a simple freezing of the top row or first column may sometimes be what you need, you'll often want to freeze columns *and* rows.

You'll sometimes also want to freeze more than one column and/or row.

1.   Click in cell D3 to make it the active cell. This is your way of telling Excel that you want to freeze all cells above, and to the left of, cell D3.

2.   Click: View→Window→Freeze Panes again but, this time, select the first option from the rich menu: *Freeze Panes*.

The first two rows and first three columns are frozen.

	A	B	C	D	
1	Date	First Name	Last Name	Company Name	
2	01-Jan-08	Nancy	Davolio	Eastern Connection	
3	01-Jan-08	Nancy	Davolio	Eastern Connection	
4	01-Jan-08	Nancy	Davolio	Eastern Connection	

10   Unfreeze the panes.

Lesson 3-17: Split the window into multiple panes

1   Open *Sales First Quarter 2008* from your sample files folder (if it isn't already open).

2   Press **<Ctrl>+<End>** to quickly move to the end of the worksheet (cell J242).

> This is quite a long list. Imagine that you need to compare sales for 3rd February to sales for 3rd March.
>
> This could involve a lot of scrolling unless you split the window into two panes.

3   Drag a horizontal split bar down to the center of the screen.

> The split bar is located at the top of the vertical scroll bar. Hover the mouse cursor over it until you see the following cursor shape.

> (If you can't see the split bar you probably forgot to unfreeze the panes at the end of the last session).
>
> When you see the shape, click and drag down to the center of the screen.
>
> The screen is split into two independently scrolling horizontal panes.

4   Scroll the lower pane so that the first sale on 3rd March 2008 is shown on the first line.

5   Scroll the upper pane so that the first sale on 3rd February 2008 is shown on the first line.

Sales First Quarter 2008

6   Remove the split window view by returning the split bar to its original location.

Drag the bar up to the top of the screen. It then disappears, returning the view to normal.

7   Drag a vertical split bar to the intersection of columns C and D.

The vertical split bar is located on the right hand side of the horizontal scroll bar. Hover the cursor over it until you see the following cursor shape.

When you see the shape, click and drag left until the gray indicator bar is at the intersection of columns C and D.

You can then release the mouse button to split the window into two independently scrolling vertical panes.

8   Remove the split window view by returning the split bar to its original location.

Drag the bar to the right-hand side of the screen. It then disappears returning the view to normal.

Lesson 3-18: Check spelling

Excel shares the same powerful spell checker included with Word and other Office applications.

Most European companies have a corporate standard for their spelling, often American English or British English. Excel also includes standard support for eighteen different dialects of English as well as other languages.

While most words are included in Excel's dictionary, you will often be warned that a correct spelling is misspelled. When this is the case you can add the word to the dictionary so that Excel doesn't keep nagging you about it in the future.

1   Open *Empire Car Sales Stock List* from your sample files folder.

	F	G
5	Colour	Selling points
6	Black	Can accelarate faster than most sports cars.
7	Topaz Blue	One concientous owner from new.
8	Yellow	Acheives nearly 50 miles to the gallon.
9	Silver	Particulaly clean example of this executive coupe.
10	Blue	Reconised as one of the safest cars on the road.
11	Brown	A collector's car strictly for connisseurs.

We'll have to hope that Empire's cars are better than their spelling!

You may find it fun to try to identify their spelling errors before we set the Spell Checker loose on the job. The *selling points* column contains many frequently incorrectly spelt words.

2   Check the spelling for the words in the range F5:G7.

If you select a range of cells before invoking the spell checker, only the selected range will be checked.

1.   Select the range F5:G7

2.   Click Review→Proofing→Spelling to start the spell checker.

If all of the words are spelt correctly the spell checker does not display. In this case there are errors so the Spell Check dialog is displayed.

note

Setting the default language.

Click Office→Excel Options→ Proofing.

You are then able to set the Excel default dictionary language.

note

Dictionaries for other languages.

The English version of Excel includes support for English, French and Spanish.

Microsoft also offer language packs for 35 other languages ranging from Chinese to Ukrainian. The packs can be ordered on line and are inexpensive ($25 US at time of writing).

In the example above note that the Dictionary Language was set to English (United States). The British spelling of the word *colour* does not appear in the American English dictionary because, in America, it is spelt: *color*.

If your dictionary is set to English (United Kingdom) you will not see this error because *colour* is the correct UK English spelling.

See the sidebar if you want to change your dictionary to a different language.

3   Click *Change* to accept Excel's suggested correction.

4   Click *Change* twice more to accept Excel's suggestions for *accelerate* and *conscientious*.

5   Spell check the single word *Particulaly* in cell G9.

Sometimes you'll spell a single word and be unsure that it is correctly spelt. You will want to be able to quickly check the single word.

1.   Click cell G9 and then select the word Particulaly in the formula bar at the top of the window.

2.   Click Review→Proofing→Spelling to start the spell checker.

3.   Chick Change to accept the correct spelling.

6   Spell check the entire worksheet.

Click in any cell on the worksheet. When you don't select a range, or a single word, the spell checker checks the entire worksheet.

If you didn't click cell A1, cells to the right and beneath the selected cells are checked first and then Excel asks: *Do you want to continue checking at the beginning of the sheet*?

7   Click *Change* to accept all changes until you are prompted for Alfasud.

Alfasud is a real word for a car (a model produced by Alfa Romeo between 1976 and 1989) but it isn't in the Excel dictionary. Perhaps Empire sells a lot of Alfasuds and don't want to be pulled up by the spell checker every time the word is used.

To prevent this happening, click *Add to Dictionary* so that Excel will recognize the word in the future.

When the spell check is completed a dialog will display.

8   Save your work as Empire Car Sales Stock List-1.

Session 3: Exercise

1   Open *The Best Selling Albums of All Time* from your sample files folder.

2   Insert one row above row 7, type *AC/DC* for the Artist and *Back in Black* for the Album.

3   Use AutoComplete to put the text *Rock* into cell C7 and type *42* for copies sold (millions).

4   Delete rows 10 and 11 to remove the *The Bee Gees* and *Pink Floyd* from the list.

5   Insert a formula in cell E6 to calculate how much revenue the album sales would have generated if sold at the Average Album Price shown in cell E3.

       Don't forget that the reference to cell E3 will have to be an absolute reference.

6   AutoFill the formula to the end of the list to see the estimated revenue for the top four selling albums.

7   Use AutoSum to add a value for total copies sold and total revenue to cells D10 and E10.

8   Remove decimal places displayed in cells E6:E10 so that the revenue is rounded to the nearest million.

9   Add a comment to cell B6 saying "Thriller was Michael Jackson's sixth studio album and was produced with a budget of $750,000".

10   Save your work as *The Best Selling Albums of All Time-1*.

	A	B	C	D	E
1	**Best Selling Albums of All Time**				
2					US$
3			Average Album Price		14.99
4					
5	**Artist**	**Album**	**Genre**	**Copies Sold (millions)**	**Revenue (Million USD)**
6	Michael Jackson	Thriller	Pop/R&B	108	1619
7	AC/DC	Back in Black	Rock	42	630
8	Whitney Houston	The Bodyguard	Pop/R&B	42	630
9	Eagles	Their Greates Hits (1971-1975)	Rock	41	615
10		Total:		233	3493
11					
12					
13					
14					
15					

Mike Smart :
Thriller was Michael Jackson's sixth studio album and was produced with a budget of $750,000.

The Best Selling Albums of All Time

If you need help slide the page to the left

Session 3 Exercise answers

These are the four questions that most students find the most difficult to remember:

Q 7	Q 5	Q 4	Q 2
1. Click in cell D10. 2. Click Home→Editing→AutoSum 3. Either press the **<Enter>** key or click: Home→Editing→AutoSum one more time. This was covered in: *Lesson 2-3: Use AutoSum to quickly calculate totals.*	1. Type the following formula into cell E6: =D6*$E$3 2. Press the **<Enter>** key. This was covered in: *Lesson 3-12: Understand absolute and relative cell references.*	1. Right-click on the row header for row 7. 2. Click *Delete* from the shortcut menu. This was covered in: *Lesson 3-1: Insert and delete rows and columns.*	1. Right-click on the row header for row 7. 2. Click *Insert* from the shortcut menu. This was covered in: *Lesson 3-1: Insert and delete rows and columns.*

If you have difficulty with the other questions, here are the lessons that cover the relevant skill:

1   Refer to: Lesson 1-4: Open and navigate a workbook.

3   Refer to: Lesson 3-2: Use AutoComplete and fill data from adjacent cells.

6   Refer to: Lesson 2-15: Use AutoFill to adjust formulas.

8   Refer to: Lesson 3-5: Use Paste Values and increase/decrease decimal places displayed.

9   Refer to: Lesson 3-9: Insert cell comments.

10   Refer to: Lesson 1-5: Save a workbook.

4

Session Four: Making Your Worksheets Look Professional

> It is only shallow people who do not judge by appearances.
>
> *Oscar Wilde (1854 - 1900)*

Never under-estimate the importance of presentation. In many areas of life it is valued more than content.

This session will enable you to make your worksheets get noticed.

By the end of this session everybody will be convinced that you are an Excel genius because your worksheets will be visually excellent.

Session Objectives

By the end of this session you will be able to:

- Format dates
- Understand date serial numbers
- Format numbers using built-in number formats
- Create custom number formats
- Horizontally and Vertically align the contents of cells
- Merge cells, wrap text and expand/collapse the formula bar
- Understand themes
- Use cell styles and change themes
- Add color and gradient effects to cells
- Add borders and lines
- Create your own custom theme
- Create your own custom cell styles
- Use a master style book and merge styles
- Use simple conditional formatting
- Manage multiple conditional formats using the rules manager
- Bring data alive with visualizations
- Create a formula driven conditional format
- Use the format painter
- Rotate text

Lesson 4-1: Format dates

You may notice that I've been very careful in using internationally safe date formats throughout this book.

A classic cause of errors when dealing with international worksheets is the use of a date such as the following:

10/03/2008

This means *10th March 2008* in some countries (such as the UK) and *3rd October 2008* in others (such as the USA).

If your work may be viewed by an international audience it is far better to use a date format that cannot possibly cause confusion.

In this lesson we'll re-format a date into the compact and universally readable format of: *10-Mar-08.*

1   Open *Sales Week Ended 14th March 2008* from your sample files folder.

Notice the hashes in the date column. This tells you that the column isn't wide enough to display the date.

	A	B	C	D
1	Invoice No	Date	Customer	Country
2	10918	##########	Bottom-Dol	Canada
3	10917	##########	Romero y to	Spain
4	10926	##########	Ana Trujillo	Mexico

If you're used to calling the hash (#) a **pound sign** or **number sign** see the sidebar in: *Lesson 2-9: Re-size rows and columns* for an explanation.

2   Auto-resize cells A1:G17 so that their contents are fully visible.

This was covered in: *Lesson 2-9: Re-size rows and columns.*

At present the dates are formatted with the month spelled out in full:

	A	B	C
1	Invoice No	Date	Customer
2	10918	10 March 2008	Bottom-Dollar Markets
3	10917	10 March 2008	Romero y tomillo
4	10926	10 March 2008	Ana Trujillo Emparedados y helados

We're going to re-format them to the shorter form: *10 Mar 08.*

3   Select cells B2:B17.

4   Right-click anywhere in the selected range and choose *Format Cells…* from the shortcut menu.

You can also do this from the Ribbon (see sidebar).

The *Format Cells* dialog appears.

5   Click the Number tab (if it isn't already selected) and then choose Date from the category list box.

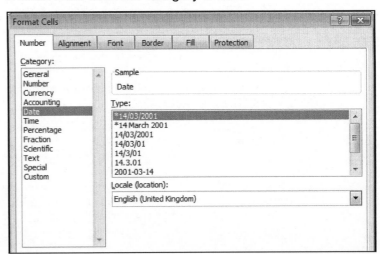

The dates you see may be different from those shown above (see sidebar).

I wanted the format 14-Mar-2008 but that isn't in the list. When you need a slightly special format it is worth checking the *Custom* category to see whether there is a pre-defined format available.

6   Click *Custom* in the category list box.

7   Apply a custom format so that the dates display in the format: 10-Mar-08.

Scroll through each of the entries in the *Type* list box, keeping your eye on the preview in the *Sample* frame.

When you reach the format *dd-mmm-yy* you will see *10-Mar-08* in the sample box. That's just what you need so click the OK button to accept.

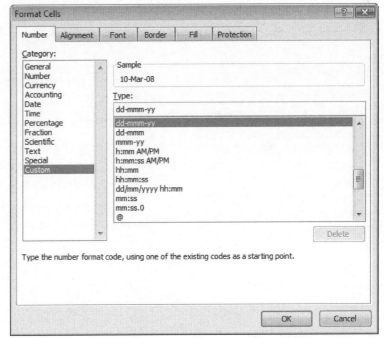

8   Save your work as Sales Week Ended 14th March 2008-1.

note

Why do I see different date formats in the *Format Cells* dialog?

The date formats shown in the *Format Cells* dialog may change based upon your default *Locale*.

You may have notice the *Locale* drop-down list at the bottom of the *Format Cells* dialog:

This defaults to the Locale (location) set in your Windows *Regional and Language Options*.

You can change your current location from the Windows control panel.

trivia

The Julian and Gregorian calendars

When you work with very old dates you can run into a problem with the Julian and Gregorian calendars.

In 1582 it was noticed that the seasons had drifted by 10 days because the Julian system had incorrectly miscalculated a year as being 365 ¼ days. It is actually slightly shorter than this.

Pope Gregory XIII decreed that, in order to put things right, the world had to lose 10 days to make up for all of those extra leap years.

The reformed Gregorian calendar also adopted a new leap year rule, skipping the leap year every millennium to keep things on track in future years.

It took nearly 200 years for everybody to get on board with the Gregorian calendar. The Catholic countries of Spain, Italy and Portugal went for it at once but England and parts of America didn't convert until September 14th 1752.

This means that in Spain the dates October 5th 1582 to October 14th 1582 never actually existed. In England it was the dates Sept 3rd 1752 to September 14th 1752.

The strangest case of all was Sweden who decided to "phase it in gradually" between 1700 and 1740 meaning that their calendar was out of step with the rest of the world for 40 years.

If you work with historical data from this era you have to be very careful indeed.

Lesson 4-2: Understand date serial numbers

Excel stores dates in a very clever way. Understanding Excel's date storage system empowers you to use date arithmetic. You can use date arithmetic to compute the difference between two dates (in days) or to shift date ranges by a given time interval.

How Excel stores dates

Dates are stored as simple numbers called *date serial numbers*. The serial number contains the number of days that have elapsed since 1st January 1900 (where 1st January 1900 is 1).

The world began in 1900

An interesting shortcoming of Excel is its inability to easily work with dates before 1900. Excel simply doesn't acknowledge that there were any dates before this time. If you work with older dates you will have to work-around this limitation.

In Excel every time is a date, and every date is a time

This one is an eye opener! We've already realized that 5th January 1900 is stored as the number 5. What would the number 5.5 mean? It would mean midday on 5th January 1900.

It is possible to format a date to show only the date, only the time, or both a time and a date.

When you enter a pure time into a cell, the time is stored as a number less than one. Excel regards this as having the non-existent date of 00 January 1900!

When you enter a pure date into a cell, the time is stored as midnight at the beginning of that day.

1 Create a new blank workbook and put the numbers 1 to 5 in cells A1:A5

2 Type the formula **=A1** into cell B1followed by the **<Enter>** key, and then AutoFill the formula to the end of the list.

AutoFill was covered in: *Lesson 2-14: Use AutoFill for text and numeric series.*

	A	B
1	1	1
2	2	2
3	3	3
4	4	4
5	5	5

trivia

The peculiar case of the Excel date bug and Lotus 1-2-3

Here's the Gregorian leap year rule © 1582 Pope Gregory XIII:

Every year that is exactly divisible by four is a leap year, except for years that are exactly divisible by 100; the centurial years that are exactly divisible by 400 are still leap years.

This means that the year 1900 wasn't a leap year but 2000 was (causing many millennium software bugs).

The designers of Lotus 1-2-3 weren't paying enough attention to the rules and didn't understand the centurial years rule. Their Date() function thus recognised the mythical date February 29th 1900.

Because Excel wanted to be compatible with Lotus 1-2-3 they had to replicate the Lotus bug when they designed Excel.

Try entering 29th Feb 1900 into a worksheet and it will gladly accept it.

This bug has the effect of introducing a one-day error into any date arithmetic you may do that includes a date before 29th February 1900.

note

Dates and the Apple Macintosh

There's a fundamental difference between *Excel for the Apple Macintosh* and *Excel for Windows* that can cause problems.

Apple serial numbers begin on January 2nd 1904 (serial number 1) while Windows serial numbers begin on January 1st 1900.

This can offset all of the dates when you import a Macintosh worksheet.

3   Apply a date format to column A that will show a four digit year.

This was covered in: *Lesson 4-1: Format dates.*

	A	B
1	01 January 1900	1
2	02 January 1900	2

This reveals that the numbers 1 to 5 represent the dates 1-Jan-1900 to 05-Jan-1900.

4   Change the date format in column A so that it shows both dates and times.

Setting a custom format was covered in: *Lesson 4-1: Format dates.*

Choose the custom format: **dd/mm/yyyy hh:mm.** (If it isn't shown in the list you will need to type it into the *Type* box).

Notice that when you enter a date without a time, the time is set to midnight at the beginning of that day.

	A	B
1	01/01/1900 00:00	1
2	02/01/1900 00:00	2
3	03/01/1900 00:00	3
4	04/01/1900 00:00	4
5	05/01/1900 00:00	5

5   Change the time in cell A2 to 12:00.

Notice that the number in cell B2 has altered to 2.5 showing that times are stored by Excel as the decimal part of a number.

	A	B
1	01/01/1900 00:00	1
2	02/01/1900 12:00	2.5

6   Compute the number of days that occurred between 01/01/1900 and 01/01/2000.

Now that you have a good grasp of Excel's serial numbers this task is easy.

1. Enter the two dates in cells A7 and A8, one beneath the other

2. Apply the comma style to cell A9

3. Subtract one date from the other by entering the formula: =A8-A7 into cell A9.

	A
7	01/01/1900 00:00
8	01/01/2000 00:00
9	36,525.00

You now know that 36,525 days occurred during the last millennium (actually 36,524 due to the Lotus 1-2-3 bug – see sidebar).

7   Close the workbook without saving.

Lesson 4-3: Format numbers using built-in number formats

Formatting fundamentals

When you format a number you never change its value. For example if you format the number:

> 483.45495

... so that it only displays two decimal places. The number displays like this:

> 483.45

It is important to realize that the actual value in the cell remains at the old value of 483.45495. All we have done is to change the way in which the value is presented to the user.

1   Open *Sales Week Ended 14th March 2008-1* from your sample files folder.

2   Apply the comma style to column E.

There is an extremely useful quick format button called the *comma style*. This is perfect for formatting monetary values with a single click. The comma style places a comma after thousands and displays exactly two decimal places.

1.   Select all of Column E.

2.   Click Home→Number→Comma Style.

All of the values in Column E now display correctly.

D	E	F	G
Country	Amount	Tax	Total
Canada	1,447.50	0.175	1700.8125
Spain	365.89	0.175	429.92075

Note that there is also a very similar *Accounting Number Format* style (I think that Microsoft should have more intuitively named it the Currency Style).

note

The Comma[0] and Currency[0] Styles.

With previous version of Excel I was forever applying the comma style and then losing the decimal places as a quick way to add the thousand separators. This used to take three clicks (comma style|decrease decimal|decrease decimal).

Excel 2007 saves a click with the Comma[0] and Currency[0] styles.

To apply these styles click:

Home→Styles→Cell Styles→Comma[0] or Currency[0]

We'll be learning a lot more about cell styles later in this session.

Sales Week Ended
14th March 2008-1

note

Solutions to the "penny rounding" problem

Formatting a floating point number to two decimal places often results in the *penny rounding problem* when you sum a column of numbers.

There are two solutions to the problem. One is a very good solution, the other can cause problems.

Best practice

The best solution to the problem is to address it when the column is first calculated.

In this lesson's example worksheet the formula used to calculate G2 is:

=E2*(F2+1)

Excel has a Round() function that can be used to round the number to two decimal places at the point of calculation.

The new formula would become:

=ROUND(E2*(F2+1),2)

Changing precision

Click Office→Excel Options→ Advanced

In the *When Calculating This Workbook* group click the *set precision as displayed* check box.

This alters the default behaviour of Excel so that each value in the worksheet is regarded as being precisely the same as its display value when performing calculations.

Using this option can cause data to become inaccurate as it is a global setting affecting the entire worksheet (and any other worksheets you may open before turning it off).

Use this feature with extreme caution!

This is very similar to the comma style but adds a leading currency symbol and an appropriate number of decimal places. The *More Accounting Formats…* option supports a vast number of international currency styles.

Try the currency style out to see how it works. I've found that the comma style is more appropriate for most of my work as I'm usually working in one country and one currency making the currency type obvious.

3   Apply the comma style to column G.

Column G has many decimal places in some cases as the sales tax calculation results in as many as six decimal places.

Apply the comma style to column G and notice how all of the values are displayed rounded to the nearest two decimal places.

It is a key concept (as discussed in the introduction to this lesson) to realize that the values in the cells have not changed. For example, if you add two cells containing the value 1.4, the result will be 1.4+1.4=2.8. If you then format the cells as whole numbers you'll see that 1+1=3 as each number is rounded up or down.

See the sidebar for potential solutions to this problem.

4   Apply the percentage style to column F.

The example sales tax rate is the UK's current 17.5%. When working with percentages it is useful to enter them so that you can calculate a percentage simply by multiplying by the cell.

Instead of 17.5 (more readable) the values are entered as 0.175 (easier to use). In order to make percentages both readable and useful Microsoft has created the percentage style. If you type 17.5% into a cell the actual value within the cell will be 0.175.

1.   Select column F.

2.   Click Home→Number→Percentage Style.

3.   Click Home→Number→Increase Decimal ⬚ once, to make the values in column F display more accurately.

D	E	F	G
Country	Amount	Tax	Total
Canada	1,447.50	17.5%	1,700.81
Spain	365.89	17.5%	429.92

5   Save your work as Sales Week Ended 14th March 2008-2.

Lesson 4-4: Create custom number formats

The built-in number formats are very quick and convenient but are also quite limited.

For example, there was a credit note on 11-Mar-08 for 637.49 plus tax. You could easily miss the little minus sign to the left of the amount.

Germany	500.00	17.5%	587.50
Italy	637.49	17.5%	749.05
Italy	- 637.49	17.5%	- 749.05

Old-school accountants like to show brackets around negative values. You just can't miss those brackets! Here's what we want to see:

Germany	500.00	17.5%	587.50
Italy	637.49	17.5%	749.05
Italy	(637.49)	17.5%	(749.05)

There's one little problem with this requirement. Excel 2007 doesn't support brackets in any of the built-in or pre-defined custom formats.

Fortunately it is possible to create your own custom format when none of the built-in styles fit your requirement.

Overview of custom formats

There's plenty of documentation in the help system and on the Internet about the rather cryptic formatting codes provided with Excel 2007. Just about everything is possible once you've got to grips with the basic concepts.

To communicate the custom format to Excel, you must construct a custom format string.

Zeros mean "Display significant zeros". You tell Excel how many you want within the format string. For example, 0.00 means *display one leading zero and two decimal places*. The following examples should make things clear:

Custom Format String	Value	Display
0	1234.56	1235
0.0	1234.56 1234.5	1234.6 1234.5
0.00	1234.56 1234.5	1234.56 1234.50
00.000	4.56	04.560
0.000	1234.56	1234.560

Sales Week Ended 14th March 2008-2

The hash symbol (#) is mainly used to add comma separators to thousands and millions.

Custom Format String	Value	Display
#	123.4500	123
#.##	123.45	123.45
	123.50	123.5
#,#	1234.56	1,235
#,#.##	1234.56	1,234.56
	1234.50	1,234.5
	12341234.56	12,341,234.56

Because the hash symbol can be used in conjunction with zeroes it is also possible to indicate that you want both thousand separators *and* a specific number of leading or trailing zeroes.

Custom Format String	Value	Display
#,#0.00	12341234.5	12,341,234.50

You can also specify two different format strings separated by a semicolon. The first provides formatting for positive values and the second for negative values. This information enables us to construct the custom format string required.

Custom format string	Value	Display
#,#0.00;(#,#0.00)	12341234.5	12,341,234.50
	-12341234.5	(12,341,234.50)

1   Open *Sales Week Ended 14th March 2008-2* from your sample files folder (if it isn't already open).

2   Select columns E and G.

This was covered in: *Lesson 2-6: Select adjacent and non-adjacent rows and columns.*

3   Right-click anywhere in column E or G and then select *Format Cells…* from the shortcut menu.

4   Select *Custom* from the *Category* list on the left of the dialog.

5   Type the custom format: **#,#0.00;(#,#0.00)** into the box labeled *Type* and click the OK button.

Type:
#,#0.00;(#,#0.00)

The negative values on the worksheet are now surrounded by brackets.

Italy	637.49	17.5%	749.05
Italy	(637.49)	17.5%	(749.05)

6   Save your work as Sales Week Ended 14th March 2008-3.

Lesson 4-5: Horizontally align the contents of cells

This table summarizes Excel's different horizontal alignment options.

Icon	Description	What it does	Example
General ▾	General (the default)	Aligns numbers and dates to the right and text to the left.	Canada 1,447.50 / Spain 365.89
▤	Align Left	Aligns cell contents left. If the cell contains text and the adjacent cell is empty, text spills to the right. If the cell contains text and the adjacent text isn't empty, text is truncated.	Bottom-Dollar Markets Bottom-Dollar Markets Bottom-Dollar M Canada
▤	Align Center	Aligns cell contents to the center. If the cell contains text and the adjacent cells are empty, text spills to the left and right. If the cell contains text and the adjacent cells are not empty, text is truncated.	Bottom-Dollar Markets Bottom-Dollar Markets 10-Mar-08 om-Dollar Mar Canada
▤	Align Right	Aligns cell contents to the right. If the cell contains text and the adjacent cell is empty, text spills to the left. If the cell contains text and the adjacent cell isn't empty, text is truncated.	Bottom-Dollar Markets Bottom-Dollar Markets 10-Mar-08 om-Dollar Markets C
▤	Justify	Text lines up to the left and right of the cell (like a newspaper)	to be or not to be, that is the question.
▤	Distributed	Words are distributed evenly across the cell.	City of London
No icon	Fill	Text is repeated until the cell is filled	CatCatCatCatCatCat

Sales Week Ended 14th March 2008-3

note

How to access the justified, distribute, and fill options.

The justify and distributed option are not on the Ribbon as most users wouldn't find a need for them.

If you find them useful you can add buttons to the Quick Access Toolbar. Refer to: *Lesson 1-10: Customize the Quick Access Toolbar and preview the printout.*

The Fill option doesn't even have a toolbar button. This needs to be accessed from the Format Cells dialog.

To access the Format Cells dialog right-click any cell and choose *Format Cells...* from the shortcut menu.

You'll then find a *Horizontal Alignment* drop-down list on the *Alignment* tab.

1 Open *Sales Week Ended 14th March 2008-3* from your sample files folder (if it isn't already open).

2 Notice that the text in row one doesn't align with the column contents.

Numerical and date values are, by default, right aligned.

Columns E, F and G contain numerical data but the text headings of their columns are left aligned.

You can see the problem more clearly if the columns are widened:

D	E	F	G
Country	Amount	Tax	Total
Canada	1,447.50	0.175	1,700.81
Spain	365.89	0.175	429.92

3 Right-align the column headers for columns E, F and G.

Select cells E1:G1 and then click:

Home→Alignment→Align Text Right

The column headers now look much better.

E	F	G
Amount	Tax	Total
1,447.50	1.75%	1,472.83

4 Right-align cell B1.

Column B also has a problem as the dates and column header do not align.

Select cell B1 and then click Home→Alignment→Align Text Right.

	B	C
1	Date	Customer
2	10-Mar-08	Bottom-Dollar Markets
3	10-Mar-08	Romero y tomillo

You will normally align column headers to the right for numeric/date columns, and to the left for text columns.

5 Bold-face row 1.

Select row 1 and then click Home→Font→Bold. **B**

	A	B	C
1	**Invoice No**	**Date**	**Customer**
2	10918	10-Mar-08	Bottom-Dollar Markets

6 Save your work as Sales Week Ended 14th March 2008-4.

Lesson 4-6: Merge cells, wrap text and expand/collapse the formula bar

1 Open *Sales Week Ended 14th March 2008-4* from your sample files folder (if it isn't already open).

2 Insert three blank rows above row 1.

   This was covered in: *Lesson 3-1: Insert and delete rows and columns.*

3 In cell A1 type: **Sales Week Ended 14th March 2008**.

4 Center the title across columns A to G.

   The title cell (A1) doesn't look bad but wouldn't it be nice to center it above the transactions listed beneath? You could simply copy and paste it into cell D1 but it still wouldn't be perfectly central.

   The solution is to merge cells A1:G1 so that they turn into one big cell. It will then be possible to center the text inside the merged cell. Excel provides a handy *Merge and Center* button to do this in one click.

   1. Select cells A1:G1.

   2. Click Home→Alignment→Merge & Center.

   The title appears at the center of the merged cell.

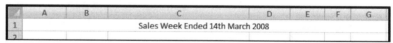

	A	B	C	D	E	F	G
1			Sales Week Ended 14th March 2008				

5 View the text in cell A22.

   There is a long description in cell A22. You probably can't see all of it on your screen.

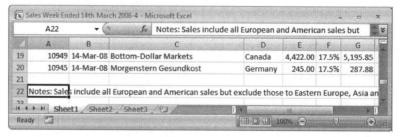

   Re-sizing the formula bar allows all of the text to be read.

   Click cell A22 and then click the Expand Formula Bar button.

   The text becomes visible in the enlarged formula bar:

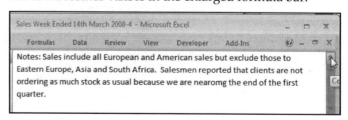

6 Re-size the formula bar.

Sometimes there isn't enough space in the expanded formula bar to view all of the text.

If this is the case hover the mouse over the bottom border of the formula bar until you see the double-headed arrow cursor shape.

When the double-headed arrow is visible, click and drag downward or upward to re-size the formula bar as required.

7   **Collapse the formula bar.**

When you have read the text there is no need to keep the formula bar expanded. Click the same button used to expand the formula bar ⬆ and the bar will collapse.

8   **Merge cells A22:G22.**

1.   Expanding the formula bar isn't a great solution. We will create a box at the bottom of the report to contain all of the text.

2.   Select cells A22:G22.

3.   Click Home→Alignment→Merge & Center Drop Down.

A drop-down menu is displayed.

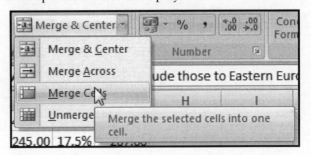

4.   Click Merge Cells to make all of the selected cells into one large cell.

9   **Make row 22 deep enough to accommodate all of the text.**

This was covered in: *Lesson 2-9: Re-size rows and columns.*

The cell is now deep enough to accommodate the text but you can still only see one line. This is because the text isn't *wrapping*.

10   **Wrap the text within the merged cells.**

Click Home→Alignment→Wrap Text.

The text now displays well except that it appears at the bottom of the cell. We'll discover how to fix this later, in: *Lesson 4-7: Vertically align the contents of cells.*

11   **Save your work as Sales Week Ended 14th March 2008-5.**

Lesson 4-7: Vertically align the contents of cells

This table summarizes Excel's different vertical alignment options.

Icon	Description	What it does	Example
General ▾	General (the default)	Aligns cell contents to the bottom of the cell.	Bottom-Dollar Markets
☰	Top Align	Aligns cell contents to the top of the cell	Bottom-Dollar Markets
☰	Middle Align	Aligns cell contents to the middle of the cell.	Bottom-Dollar Markets
☰	Bottom Align	Aligns cell contents to the bottom of the cell	Bottom-Dollar Markets
No icon	Justify	Lines of text are spread out so that the space between each is equal, the first line is at the top and the last line is at the bottom.	to be or not to be, that is the question.
No Icon	Distributed	The same as Justify!	to be or not to be, that is the question.

1   Open *Sales Week Ended 14ᵗʰ March 2008-5 from* your sample files folder (if it isn't already open).

2   Top align the contents of cell A22.

The contents of cell A22 are currently bottom aligned (the default).

> Notes: Sales include all European and American sales but exclude those to Eastern Europe, Asia and South Africa. Salesmen reported that clients are not ordering as much stock as usual
> 22 because we are nearing the end of the first quarter.

When you place a block of text into a cell in this way you will typically want it to be top-aligned.

Click Home→Alignment→Top Align to align the text at the top of the cell.

Sales Week Ended 14th March 2008-5

> Notes: Sales include all European and American sales but exclude those to Eastern Europe, Asia and South Africa. Salesmen reported that clients are not ordering as much stock as usual because we are nearing the end of the first quarter.

3 Increase the height of row 4 so that it is about twice its present height.

This was covered in: *Lesson 2-9: Re-size rows and columns.*

3			
4	Invoice No	Date	Customer
5	10918	10-Mar-08	Bottom-Dollar Markets

You can see why the default vertical alignment is *bottom align*. This alignment works really well for title rows.

4 Wrap the text in cell A4.

This was covered in: *Lesson 4-6: Merge cells, wrap text and expand/collapse the formula bar.*

5 Split the words *Invoice* and *No* so that they appear on separate lines.

1. Double-click cell A4 to enter Edit mode and then position the cursor to the left of the word *No*.

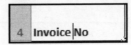

2. Press **<Alt>+<Enter>**.

3. Press the **<Enter>** key again to exit Edit mode.

The two words appear on separate lines.

6 Horizontally right-align the text in cell A4.

This was covered in: *Lesson 4-5: Horizontally align the contents of cells.*

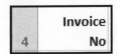

7 Automatically Re-size column A and row 4 so that each are just big enough for the cell contents.

This was covered in: *Lesson 2-9: Re-size rows and columns.*

	Invoice		
4	No	Date	
5	10918	10-Mar-08	

8 Save your work as Sales Week Ended 14th March 2008-6.

note

What are serifs?

They are the little lines at the edges of text that allow the eye to more easily scan words.

Serifs

Sans
Serif

note

Can I change the default theme?

Yes you can, along with any other Excel default settings.

Open a new empty Excel workbook and apply your chosen default theme.

Save the workbook as a template to the xlStart folder with the name: *book*.

There are two xlStart folders. One of them determines the settings when you are logged in to your computer and the other determines settings for all users of your computer.

If you are using Vista you'll find the xlStart folder at:

C:\Users\Username\AppData\Roaming\Microsoft\Excel

and C:\Program Files\Microsoft Office\Office 12 folders

Windows XP users will find them at:

C:\Documents and Settings\Username\Application Data\Microsoft\Excel

and C:\Program Files\Microsoft Office\Office 12

Lesson 4-8: Understand themes

A theme is simply a set of fonts, colors and effects that go very nicely together. It's a brand new feature for Office 2007.

Font sets

A font set consists of two complementary fonts that work well as a pair.

A golden rule of typesetting is to never have more than two fonts in a document. Old school typesetters would always use a serif font for the body text (also called the *Normal* text) and a sans-serif font for the titles (just as this book does). See sidebar for the difference between serif and sans-serif fonts.

There's a modern school of thought that suggests that breaking this rule is cool and Microsoft have done just that with their default set for Excel 2007 (called the *Office* set) by choosing a serif font (Cambria) for their titles and a sans-serif (Calibri) for normal text. To avoid upsetting purists they also include the *Office2* set that has them the conventional way around!

You can see all 23 pre-defined font sets by clicking:

Page Layout→Themes→Fonts.

You can also create your own font sets if you don't like any of the pre-defined ones.

Color sets

trivia

Times New Roman is probably the most widely used and successful serif typeface in the world.

This font was commissioned by the Times newspaper in 1931 and was used to print the Times until 1982 when it was replaced due to incompatibility with faster printing presses. It is still widely used in book publishing.

Times New Roman was the default font in Word for all versions right up to 2007 and is still available in Excel's *Office Classic* font set.

Helvetica is probably the most widely used and successful sans-serif font. It was designed in Switzerland in 1957. Windows doesn't include Helvetica but uses *Arial*, a very similar font that most non-experts cannot distinguish from Helvetica.

I used to advise my students that if they stuck to the "killer combination" of Arial/Times New Roman they would never go far wrong, because readers are very used to them and thus find them extremely easy to read

Microsoft has now changed all of the rules by introducing the Cambria/Calibri font pair.

Just as the Times newspaper designed their font to facilitate reading at small type sizes in newspapers, Cambria/Calibri were designed specifically to be easy to read on computer screens using Microsoft's *Clear Type* rendering technology.

Office 2007 is the first office version to have *Clear Type* rendering switched on by default. It works particularly well on LCD flat-panel displays.

Clear Type has saved me reams of paper because now, for the first time, I am able to proof read my books on-screen without causing eye strain. This has saved a lot of forests!

Color sets are a little more involved than font sets

The ten colors along the top row are the *theme colors*. The left most four are used for *text and background colors* and the other six are *Accent colors*. This set of colors has been selected by design professionals to work well together. There are actually twelve theme colors but you can only see ten of them. The two hidden theme colors are used for hyperlinks.

The *standard colors* are best avoided. They are colors that will remain the same no matter what theme is in use. If you use standard colors (or the More Colors… option) the worksheet may look odd if the theme needs to be changed in the future. You can see all 21 pre-defined color sets by clicking:

Page Layout→Themes→Colors.

Effects

You'll only notice a change in theme effects if you have graphic elements on your worksheet such as drawing shapes or chart objects. We'll see this working later in: *Lesson 5-5: Format 3-D elements and align text.*

Theme effects are applied to the outline and fill of shapes.

You can see all 21 pre-defined effects by clicking:

Page Layout→Themes→Effects.

Themes

Themes are simply a group of one *color* set, one *font* set and one *effects* set.

Because Microsoft have consistently named their Colors, Fonts, Effects and Themes the *Office* theme consists of the *Office* color set, the *Office* font set and the *Office* effects set.

Themes aren't just for Excel

The Themes feature is also included in Excel, Word, PowerPoint and Outlook. Choosing the same theme for your documents, spreadsheets, presentations and Emails can give all of your communications a consistent and professional appearance.

Lesson 4-9: Use cell styles and change themes

In order for themes to work their magic you must get into the habit of using cell styles to format cells based upon the options available in the current theme.

For many years expert Word users have used styles to quickly produce professional documents. Their mortal sin would be to apply a font size or color directly to a document.

Now that Excel 2007 also supports styles, professional users should adopt the same discipline.

1   Open *Sales Week Ended 14th March 2008-6* from your sample files folder (if it isn't already open).

2   Apply the Title style to cell A1.

Even though cell A1 now encompasses cells A1:G1 it retains the cell reference A1.

It would be possible to manually apply a font and color to cell A1 but we're going to do things the professional way and use the *Title* style.

1. Select cell A1.

2. Click Home→Styles→Cell Styles.

The styles gallery appears.

3. Click *Title* to apply the Title style to cell A1.

Cell A1 is formatted with the Title style.

3   Apply the Heading 3 style to cells A4:G4.

Select cells A4:G4 and then click:

Home→Styles→Cell Styles→Heading 3.

4   Apply the Note style to cell A22.

Select cell A22 and then click Home→Styles→Cell Styles→Note.

5   Apply the *20% - Accent 5* style to cells A5:D20.

Select cells A5:D20 and then click:

Conditional Formatting ▾ Format as Table ▾ Cell Style ▾

Styles

note

Removing a style from a cell.

All cells have the Normal style by default. Select a cell or range of cells and click:

Home→Styles→Cell Styles→Normal

You will then remove the cell style, and all other cell formatting such as bold face or underline, from the cell or range.

Sales Week Ended 14th March 2008-6

Home→Styles→Cell Styles→20% - Accent 5

6 Apply the *20% - Accent 6* style to cells E5:G20.

Select cells E5:G20 and then click:

Home→Styles→Cell Styles→20% - Accent 6

The worksheet now looks very different

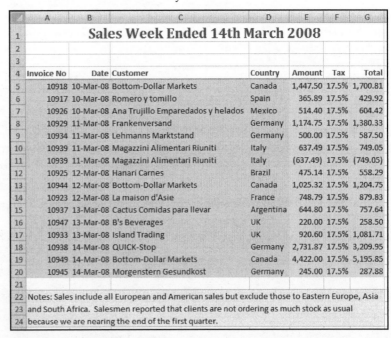

	A	B	C	D	E	F	G
1			Sales Week Ended 14th March 2008				
2							
3							
4	Invoice No	Date	Customer	Country	Amount	Tax	Total
5	10918	10-Mar-08	Bottom-Dollar Markets	Canada	1,447.50	17.5%	1,700.81
6	10917	10-Mar-08	Romero y tomillo	Spain	365.89	17.5%	429.92
7	10926	10-Mar-08	Ana Trujillo Emparedados y helados	Mexico	514.40	17.5%	604.42
8	10929	11-Mar-08	Frankenversand	Germany	1,174.75	17.5%	1,380.33
9	10934	11-Mar-08	Lehmanns Marktstand	Germany	500.00	17.5%	587.50
10	10939	11-Mar-08	Magazzini Alimentari Riuniti	Italy	637.49	17.5%	749.05
11	10939	11-Mar-08	Magazzini Alimentari Riuniti	Italy	(637.49)	17.5%	(749.05)
12	10925	12-Mar-08	Hanari Carnes	Brazil	475.14	17.5%	558.29
13	10944	12-Mar-08	Bottom-Dollar Markets	Canada	1,025.32	17.5%	1,204.75
14	10923	12-Mar-08	La maison d'Asie	France	748.79	17.5%	879.83
15	10937	13-Mar-08	Cactus Comidas para llevar	Argentina	644.80	17.5%	757.64
16	10947	13-Mar-08	B's Beverages	UK	220.00	17.5%	258.50
17	10933	13-Mar-08	Island Trading	UK	920.60	17.5%	1,081.71
18	10938	14-Mar-08	QUICK-Stop	Germany	2,731.87	17.5%	3,209.95
19	10949	14-Mar-08	Bottom-Dollar Markets	Canada	4,422.00	17.5%	5,195.85
20	10945	14-Mar-08	Morgenstern Gesundkost	Germany	245.00	17.5%	287.88
21							
22	Notes: Sales include all European and American sales but exclude those to Eastern Europe, Asia						
23	and South Africa. Salesmen reported that clients are not ordering as much stock as usual						
24	because we are nearing the end of the first quarter.						

7 Insert a row above row 21.

This was covered in: *Lesson 3-1: Insert and delete rows and columns.*

8 Use AutoSum to place a total in cell G21.

This was covered in: *Lesson 2-3: Use AutoSum to quickly calculate totals.*

9 Apply the Total style to cell G21.

Select cell G21 and then click Home→Styles→Cell Styles→Total.

The total cell is neatly formatted.

Canada	4,422.00	17.5%	5,195.85
Germany	245.00	17.5%	287.88
			18,137.37

10 Preview your finished work under different themes.

Because you did things the professional way, using styles instead of directly formatting cells, it is now possible to cycle through the themes. You may find one of the other themes more attractive.

1. Click Page Layout→Themes→Themes.

   The Themes gallery appears.

2. Hover over each theme in turn. You'll be amazed at how your work completely changes as each theme's style set is applied.

11 Save your work as Sales Week Ended 14th March 2008-7.

Lesson 4-10: Add color and gradient effects to cells

A brand new feature for Excel 2007 is the ability to add gradient effects (instead of solid colors) to cells.

Most of the time solid colors are all you need, but you may want to make data look more interesting for a PowerPoint presentation, or for publication in a newsletter or a web page.

When you add colors it is usually best to stay within those of the current theme. This enables you to quickly change the appearance of the worksheet to match that of a PowerPoint presentation or Word document that uses a different theme (see sidebar for an example of this in action).

In this lesson we'll add a gradient to the sharp transition between the orange (pink) totals section and the aqua transaction details section.

1   Open *Sales Week Ended 14th March 2008-7* from your sample files folder (if it isn't already open).

2   Check the colors that are currently being used for the transaction and totals section in your worksheet.

   1. Click anywhere in the blue area of your worksheet (cells A5:C21).

   2. Click the drop-down arrow next to Home→Font→Fill Color.

   Notice that one color has a small square around it. When you hover over this button you will see that the fill color for the left-hand side of the worksheet is *Aqua, Accent 5, Lighter 80%*.

   3. Do the same for the orange (pink) colored cells (in cells D5:G21). You'll find that they are *Orange, Accent 6, Lighter 80%*. The cells appear to be pink, of course, but they are really a 20% tint of orange that appears to be pink to the eye.

3   Set a gradient fill in column D.

   1. Select cells D5:D21.

   2. Right-click inside the selected range and click Format Cells... from the shortcut menu.

   3. Click the Fill Tab.

4. Click the Fill Effects… button.

5. In the Colors frame, choose *Aqua, Accent 5, Lighter 80%* for Color 1.

6. In the Colors frame, choose *Orange, Accent 6, Lighter 80%* for Color 2.

7. Select the Vertical shading style.

8. Select the top left variant.

9. Click OK and then OK again.

   A smooth gradient fill has been added to column D.

4 Save your work as Sales Week Ended 14th March 2008-8.

Lesson 4-11: Add borders and lines

1   Open *Sales Analysis* from your sample files folder.

We're going to use the powerful *borders and lines* feature to make this worksheet more readable.

Before	After

	A	B	C	D	E
1					
2			Total		
3		Analysis Type	Cash	Percent	
4		By Category			
5		Beverages	25,326	20%	
6		Meat/Poultry	65,780	52%	
7		Vegetables	35,679	28%	
8		Total	126,785		
9		By Month			
10		Oct	45,300	36%	
11		Nov	36,800	29%	
12		Dec	44,685	35%	
13		Total	126,785		
14		By Country			
15		UK	56,175	44%	
16		USA	42,368	33%	
17		Canada	28,242	22%	
18		Total	126,785		
19					

2   Add cell styles to rows 2,3,4,9 and 14.

1. Select cells B2:D3.

2. Click Home→Styles→Cell Styles→60% Accent 3.

3. Select Cells B4:D4, B9:D9 and B14:D14.

   This was covered in: *Lesson 2-7: Select non-contiguous cell ranges and view summary information.*

4. Click Home→Styles→Cell Styles→40% Accent 3.

5. Select cells B2:D3.

6. Click Home→Styles→Cell Styles→Heading 4.

3   Switch off the worksheet gridlines.

When you are working with borders it is always a good idea to switch off the gridlines so that you can have a better idea of how the worksheet will print.

This feature appears in two different places on the Ribbon. Uncheck either of the following check boxes:

View→Show/Hide→Gridlines

OR

Page Layout→Sheet Options→Gridlines→View

Sales Analysis

4   Add a solid border around the entire range.

1. Select cells B2:D18.

2. Click: Home→Font→Borders drop-down arrow→ Outside Borders.

5 Add solid borders inside cells C2:D3.

1. Select cells C2:D3.

2. Click Home→Font→Borders drop-down arrow→All Borders.

tip

Use the draw border line tool to quickly add complex borders.

The fastest way to quickly add borders is to simply draw them into place using the Draw Border tool.

Click:

Home→Font→Draw Border

You can then simply draw borders straight onto the grid. There's also an *Erase Border* tool available on the same menu.

6 Add top and bottom borders to *By Category, By Month* and *By Country*.

1. Select Cells B4:D4, B9:D9 and B14:D14.

2. Click Home→Font→Borders drop-down arrow→ Top and Bottom Border.

Top and Bottom Border

7 Add dotted underlines to the borders of cells B5:D8, B10:D13 and B15:D18.

1. Select cells B5:D8, B10:D13 and B15:D18.

2. Right-click any of the selected cells and click *Format Cells…* from the shortcut menu.

The Format Cells dialog appears.

3. Click the Border tab of the Format Cells dialog.

4. Click the *Dotted Line* style.

5. Click the Inside button.

note

Changing the border line or color from the drop-down menu.

The Format Cells dialog method of adding borders is more powerful than the menu method.

The ability to change line style and color from the menu (a new feature for Excel 2007) means you'll rarely have to resort to using the Format Cells dialog for borders.

To change line style or color from the Borders drop-down menu select Line Color or line Style.

The selected color and/or style will remain active until you close Excel. Next time you open Excel it will have returned to the default.

6. Click the OK button.
The dotted lines are displayed within the cells.

8 Add left and right borders to cells C5:C8, C10:C13 and C15:C18.

1. Select cells C5:C8, C10:C13 and C15:C18.

2. Click Home→Font→Borders→Left Border.

3. Click Home→Font→Borders→Right Border.

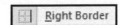

9 Save your work as Sales Analysis-1.

Lesson 4-12: Create your own Custom theme

If none of the 20 built-in themes suffice you can click:

Page Layout→Themes→More Themes at Microsoft Office Online.

The last time that I looked there were another 28 themes available for download.

Some clients have a defined corporate style and are extremely particular that colors, fonts and other layout items reinforce their corporate identity.

When individuality is important, you need your own custom theme.

1 Open *Sales Week Ended 14^(th) March 2008-8* from your sample files folder (if it isn't already open).

2 Select a different set of theme colors.

Click Page Layout→Themes→Colors.

All of the pre-defined sets of colors are displayed (see sidebar). Try hovering your mouse over them one at a time, to see how your worksheet would look if you changed the theme colors.

Choose a different set that you think look attractive.

3 Create a custom set of theme colors.

Click Page Layout→Themes→Colors→Create New Theme Colors.

The Create New Theme Colors dialog appears.

Click any of the colors on the left of the dialog and select a different color. Notice that, as you do, the Sample frame shows a preview of how your theme looks. Let your imagination run wild and create your own custom color theme.

When you change theme colors you will see a preview of the new color theme here.

Click here to change any of the theme colors.

Type **TSM Corporate** into the Name box and then click the Save button to create your own personalized set of custom colors.

4 Select a different set of fonts.

As discussed in: *Lesson 4-8: Understand themes,* a theme consists of a color set, a font set and an effects set.

note

Can I change the default theme?

If you've adopted a custom theme as your corporate standard you will probably want this to become the default.

To do this, refer to the sidebar in: *Lesson 4-8: Understand themes.*

Sales Week Ended 14^(th) March 2008-8

A font set consists of two fonts: a heading font and a body font.

Click Page Layout→Themes→Fonts

All of the pre-defined sets of fonts are displayed (see sidebar). Try hovering your mouse over them one at a time, to see how your worksheet would look if you changed the theme fonts.

Choose a different set that you think look attractive.

5   Create a custom set of theme fonts.

Click Page Layout→Themes→Fonts→Create New Theme Fonts.

The *Create New Theme Fonts* dialog appears.

Select two complimentary fonts. Ideally one should be a serif font and one should be a sans-serif font (this issue is discussed in the sidebar within: *Lesson 4-8: Understand themes*).

Type **TSM Corporate** into the *Name* box and then click the save button to create your own personalized set of custom fonts.

6   Select a different set of effects.

Unlike colors and fonts you can't create a custom set of effects. You have to choose from the pre-defined ones.

Effects change the appearance of drawing objects and we haven't yet covered these (they will make an appearance in: *Lesson 5-5: Format 3-D elements and align text*).

You can change the theme effects by clicking:

Page Layout→Themes→Effects

Choose a different set at random to see how this works.

7   Save the corporate theme.

1.   Click Page Layout→Themes→Themes→Save Current Theme.

2.   Enter the name *TSM Corporate* in the *File Name* text box.

3.   Click the save button.

8   Revert to the standard Office theme.

1.   Click Page Layout→Themes→Themes.

     Notice that your custom theme is listed at the top in the Custom group.

2.   Click the Office theme to put things back the way they were.

Lesson 4-13: Create your own Custom cell styles

Excel 2007 has a large number of pre-defined cell styles grouped into:

- Good, Bad and Neutral – to mark particularly good or bad results.

- Data and Model – usually used in a worksheet containing formulas to mark cells that require user input or contain formula results.

- Titles and Headings – for section titles and column headers.

- Themed Cell Styles - to color cells based upon the theme colors.

- Number Format – to quickly apply number formats, like the Comma[0] number format that is just like the comma style but with no decimal places.

Custom styles are only available in the workbook within which they were originally created. In order to use them in another workbook you need to use Excel's *merge styles* feature that will be covered in: *Lesson 4-14: Use a master style book to merge styles.*

1   Open *Sales Week Ended 14th March 2008-8* from your sample files folder (if it isn't already open).

2   Modify an existing cell style.

Click cell A23 to make it the active cell. This is the cell containing the Note text.

> Note: Sales include all European and American and South Africa. Salesmen reported that clien
> 23 because we are nearing the end of the first qua

1. Click Home→Styles→Cell Styles.

2. Right-click the Note style and click Modify from the shortcut menu.

3. The Style dialog appears (see sidebar).

4. Click the Format… button. The Format Cells dialog appears.

5. Click the Fill tab and select a light green background color:

6. Click the OK button and then the OK button once more.

7. If cell A23 isn't green click Home→Styles→Cell Styles and click once on the *Note* style.

Sales Week Ended 14th March 2008-8

Note that the background color of cell A23 (which has the *Note* style applied to it) has now turned light green.

You haven't permanently changed the *Office* theme's *Note* style. You've simply changed it for this workbook only. When you open another workbook that uses the *Office* theme the *Note* style will be light yellow once again.

3 Duplicate the *Note* built-in cell style.

1. Click Home→Styles→Cell Styles to display the Cell Styles gallery.

2. Right-click the *Note* cell style and then click *Duplicate* from the shortcut menu.

3. The Style dialog appears suggesting the name *Note 2* for your new cell style. Change this to *Blue Note* and click the OK button.

4. Click Home→Styles→Cell Styles to display the Cell Styles gallery once more. Notice that the *Blue Note* style is at the top of the gallery in the *Custom* section.

5. Change the background color of the new *Blue Note* style to light blue using the technique learned in: *Step 2-Modify an existing cell style*.

4 Create a custom cell style *By Example*.

This is the easiest way to create custom cell styles.

1. Select Cell A23.

2. Click Home→Font→Fill Color Drop-down and choose the *Purple, Accent 4, Lighter 80%* theme color.

3. Click Home→Styles→Cell Styles→New Cell Style.

The Style dialog appears but notice the words: *By Example.* This means that the style already contains all of the formatting information for cell A23.

4. Change the style name to **Purple Note** and click the OK button.

5 Save your work as Sales Week Ended 14th March 2008-9.

Lesson 4-14: Use a master style book to merge styles

When you create custom styles they are only available within the workbook in which they were created. Sometimes it is useful to have the same set of custom styles available across multiple workbooks.

In this lesson we'll cater for the following scenario at Empire Car Sales:

Syd Slater, the owner of Empire Car Sales, knows that you have to keep your stock turning over.

His salesmen are allowed to discount 10% of the sticker price on all cars. If the car has been on the forecourt for more than two weeks they are allowed to discount 15%, after three weeks 20%, and after four weeks the car goes back to auction.

Syd's salesmen need to know the maximum margin they can offer, but Syd doesn't want the customers to find this out, so they use a cunning system of color coding on the stock list:

10% Max Discount: Blue

15% Max Discount: Green

20% Max Discount: Red

The stock list is produced each week in Excel with three custom cell styles, one for each discount.

To avoid having to constantly re-create custom cell styles they are stored in a master style book called *Empire Styles* which Syd merges with his worksheets so that the three styles are always available.

1   Open a new blank workbook.

2   Create a custom style called 10% Max Discount with a background color of Light Blue.

> This was covered in: *Lesson 4-13: Create your own Custom cell styles.*

3   Create a custom style called 15% Max Discount with a background color of Light Green.

4   Create a custom style called 20% Max Discount with a background color of Light Red.

Because you have used theme colors for the custom styles their color will change if the theme is changed.

For example, if you change the theme to *Solstice,* the 10% Max Discount becomes orange, 15% becomes red and 20% becomes Yellow.

**Empire Car Sales
Stock List-1**

For this reason you could argue that it would be better to set the colors using the *More Colors* option so that the colors remained the same even if the theme was changed.

For the purposes of this lesson we will assume that Syd will not change from the Office theme and follow the normal rule of restricting color choice to theme colors. (See the sidebar in: *Lesson 4-10: Add color and gradient effects to cells* for an explanation of why this is best practice).

5   Save the workbook as *Empire Styles* but don't close it.

6   Open *Empire Car Sales Stock List-1* from your sample files folder.

7   Merge the styles from Empire Styles.

    1.   Click Home→Styles→Cell Styles→Merge Styles.

    2.   The Merge Styles dialog appears.

    3.   Select Empires Styles.xlsx and then click the OK button.

The three custom styles are now available within the current workbook.

8   Apply the 20% style to the Volkswagen and Mercedes.

9   Apply the 15% style to the BMW and Alfa Romeo.

10   Apply the 10% style to the Volvo and Ford.

Syd's salesmen are now ready to start selling!

11   Save your work as Empire Car Sales Stock List-2.

Lesson 4-15: Use simple conditional formatting

Simple conditional formatting applies a format to a cell based upon the value of the cell. In this lesson we'll change the cell background color to red if the cell has a value of less than 5,000 and to green if the value is over 30,000.

The same technique learned in this lesson can be used to apply conditional formats based upon text that begins with, ends with, or contains, specific characters.

You can also apply conditional formats to cells containing dates. For example, you can highlight dates such as today, tomorrow, in the last seven days, last week and this week. Conditional formatting will then cause the worksheet to change every time that you open it based upon the current date.

1   Open *Sales Report* from your sample files folder.

2   AutoFit cells A4:A26.

    1.   Select cells A4:A26.

    2.   Click: Home→Cells→Format→AutoFit Column Width.

3   AutoFit cells D4:D13.

4   Apply the comma style to column B and Column E.

This was covered in: *Lesson 4-3: Format numbers using built-in number formats.*

5   Merge cells A3:B3, D3:E3 and D18:E18.

This was covered in: *Lesson 4-6: Merge cells, wrap text and expand/collapse the formula bar.*

6   Apply the *Title* style to cell A1.

This was covered in: *Lesson 4-9: Use cell styles.*

7   Apply the *Heading 2* style to cells A3, D3 and D18.

8   Apply the *Heading 3* style to cells A4:B4, D4:E4 and D19:E19.

9   Apply the *Total* style to cells A26:B26, D13:E13 and D26:E26.

10   Change the theme to the *Flow* theme.

This was covered in: *Lesson 4-9: Use cell styles and change themes.*

The worksheet is now well formatted and has a professional appearance:

	A	B	C	D	E	F
1	Sales Report - 6 Months ended March 2008					
2						
3	Sales By Country			Sales by Category		
4	Country	Total Sales		Category	Total Sales	
5	Argentina	762.60		Beverages	70,168.10	
6	Austria	33,462.58		Condiments	24,938.06	

Sales Report

note

You can have as many conditional formats as you need

Previous versions of Excel were limited to three conditional formats per cell.

In Excel 2007 you can have an infinite number of conditional formats.

3	Sales By Country	
4	Country	Total Sales
5	Argentina	762.60
6	Austria	33,462.58
7	Belgium	6,109.48
8	Brazil	20,524.42
9	Canada	21,306.29
10	Denmark	16,658.80
11	Finland	5,525.00
12	France	26,155.54
13	Germany	28,361.38
14	Ireland	6,157.76
15	Italy	2,585.69
16	Mexico	3,524.30
17	Norway	1,058.40
18	Poland	459.00
19	Portugal	5,584.13

3	Sales By Country	
4	Country	Total Sales
5	Argentina	762.60
6	Austria	33,462.58
7	Belgium	6,109.48
8	Brazil	20,524.42
9	Canada	21,306.29
10	Denmark	16,658.80
11	Finland	5,525.00
12	France	26,155.54
13	Germany	28,361.38
14	Ireland	6,157.76
15	Italy	2,585.69

11 Select cells B5:B25.

12 Conditionally format the selected range so that any country with sales below 5,000 has a light red fill with dark red text.

1. Click Home→Styles→Conditional Formatting→ Highlight Cell Rules→Less Than…

   The Less Than dialog appears.

2. Type 5,000 in the text box and choose *Light Red Fill with Dark Red Text* for the font and fill color.

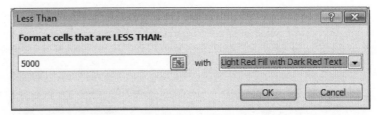

   Notice that as you type the value into the text box the worksheet adjusts in the background to preview what will happen with this conditional format.

   Note also that there's a Custom Format… option which enables you to choose effects such as underlines and theme colors. The advantage of restricting color choice to theme colors is discussed in: *Lesson 4-14: Use a master style book to merge styles (sidebar)*.

3. Click the OK button

   Cells that have a value of less than 5,000 are now highlighted in red (see sidebar).

13 Add another conditional format to the selected range so that any country with sales above 30,000 has a green fill with dark green text.

   Both conditional formats now display with the two sales values over 30,000 displayed in green (see sidebar).

14 Remove both conditional formats.

1. Select cells B5:B25.

2. Click Home→Styles→Conditional Formatting→ Clear Rules→Clear Rules from Selected Cells.

   The conditional formats are removed.

15 Save your work as Sales Report-1.

Lesson 4-16: Manage multiple conditional formats using the Rules Manager

The conditional formats applied in the last lesson depended upon the value of a single cell.

Often you will want a cell to be formatted based upon its relationship to other cells in a range.

In this lesson we'll color the top 25% of sales green, the middle 50% yellow and the bottom 25% red.

This lesson also introduces the *Rules Manager* that allows you to edit conditional format rules and to specify the order in which conditional formats are applied.

1   Open *Sales Report-1 from* your sample files folder (if it isn't already open).

2   Select cells B5:B25.

3   Conditionally format the selected range so that any country whose sales are in the top 25% has a green fill with dark green text.

    1.   Click Home→Styles→Conditional Formatting→ Top/Bottom Rules→Top 10%.

       The Top 10% dialog appears.

    2.   Change the value to 25% and choose Green fill with Dark Green Text for the fill.

Top 10%	? ✕
Format cells that rank in the TOP:	
25 ▲▼ % with Green Fill with Dark Green Text ▼	
	OK Cancel

    3.   Click the OK button.

4   Conditionally format the selected range so that any country whose sales are in the bottom 25% has a light red fill with dark red text.

Bottom 10%	? ✕
Format cells that rank in the BOTTOM:	
25 ▲▼ % with Light Red Fill with Dark Red Text ▼	
	OK Cancel

The top and bottom 25% of sales are now highlighted as specified in the conditional formats (see sidebar).

3	Sales By Country	
4	Country	Total Sales
5	Argentina	762.60
6	Austria	33,462.58
7	Belgium	6,109.48
8	Brazil	20,524.42
9	Canada	21,306.29
10	Denmark	16,658.80
11	Finland	5,525.00
12	France	26,155.54
13	Germany	28,361.38
14	Ireland	6,157.76
15	Italy	2,585.69

Sales Report-1

5 Add another conditional format so that any country with sales greater than zero has a yellow fill with dark yellow text.

Remember that the specification was to color the middle 50% of sales yellow?

Unfortunately all sales are now yellow because the yellow cells are over-writing the red and green cells.

6 Use the *Rules Manager* to control the order in which conditional formats are applied.

1. Select cells B5:B25.

2. Click Home→Styles→Conditional Formatting→Manage Rules.

   The Conditional Formatting Rules Manager dialog is displayed.

3. Click the first rule (the Cell Value > 0 rule).

4. Use the Move Down button [image] to move the rule to the bottom of the list (if you don't see the Move Down button it is because you haven't selected the rule).

5. Click the OK button.

   The red, green and yellow formatting rules are now applied as required. This works because of the conflict resolution rules (see sidebar).

7 Use the *Rules Manager* to edit the rules so that the top and bottom 30% values are now highlighted.

1. Select cells B5:B25.

2. Click Home→Styles→Conditional Formatting→Manage Rules.

3. Select the *Bottom 25%* rule.

4. Click the Edit Rule… button and change the criteria to: *30%*.

5. Edit the *Top 25%* rule in the same way so that it will show the top 30% values.

8 Remove all three conditional formats.

   This was covered in: *Lesson 4-15: Use simple conditional formatting.*

---

note

Conflict resolution rules.

In this lesson we applied three different conditional formats to the selected range.

Sometimes there will be a conflict between different conditional formatting rules.

Consider this specification:

- Format every value over 50 as blue underlined and bold.

- Format every value over 75 as red and italic.

The rules manager has a dilemma with a value of 80. Should it be blue or red, bold, italic, underlined or all three?

To resolve the conflict, rules are applied in the order listed in the rules manager. Attributes are applied only if an earlier conditional format has not set a conflicting condition.

1. The value is over 50 so apply blue, underlined, bold-face.

2. The value is over 75. Can't format red because the earlier condition has made the cell blue.

3. The value is over 75. Apply italics.

Lesson 4-17: Bring data alive with visualizations

Visualizations are a fantastic new feature for Excel 2007.

Visualizations are a half-way house between tables and charts. With a few clicks of the mouse they allow you to express numbers in a visual manner.

1 Open *Sales Report-1* from your sample files folder (if it isn't already open).

2 Add a data bar visualization to the *Sales by Country* figures.

1. Select cells B5:B25.

2. Click Home→Styles→Conditional Formatting→ Data Bars→Red Data Bar.

The visualization is applied (see sidebar).

Visualizations do not give a strictly accurate depiction of the values in the cells. The shortest bar is sized to ten percent of the value range in order to ensure that the lowest value bar doesn't disappear entirely.

3 Add a color scale visualization to the *Sales by Category* figures.

1. Select cells E5:E12.

2. Click Home→Styles→Conditional Formatting→ Color Scales→Green/Yellow Color Scale.

The visualization is applied (see sidebar).

4 Add an icon set visualization to the *Sales by Month* figures.

1. Select cells E20:E25.

2. Click Home→Styles→Conditional Formatting→Icon Sets→ 3 Flags.

3. Re-size column E so that it is wide enough to display the values.

The visualization is applied (see sidebar).

When the icon set contains three icons, Excel assigns the relative icons to the top third, middle third, and bottom third of the value range.

You will often need to change these arbitrary values.

5 Use the Rules Manager to modify the Sales by Month visualization so that three green flags are shown.

The Sales by Month visualization may discourage our salesmen because only one month is flagged as green with four months flagged red. We'll adjust the criteria for flag allocation so that three months are shown as green.

1. Select cells E20:E25.

2. Click Home→Styles→Conditional Formatting→Manage Rules.

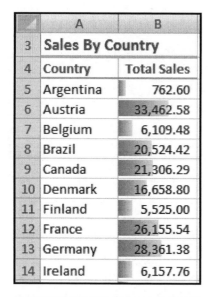

	A	B
3	**Sales By Country**	
4	Country	Total Sales
5	Argentina	762.60
6	Austria	33,462.58
7	Belgium	6,109.48
8	Brazil	20,524.42
9	Canada	21,306.29
10	Denmark	16,658.80
11	Finland	5,525.00
12	France	26,155.54
13	Germany	28,361.38
14	Ireland	6,157.76

	D	E
3	**Sales by Category**	
4	Category	Total Sales
5	Beverages	70,168.10
6	Condiments	24,938.06
7	Confections	31,883.54
8	Dairy Products	49,902.95
9	Grains/Cereals	19,570.36

	D	E
18	**Sales by Month**	
19	Date	Total Sales
20	Oct	37,515.73
21	Nov	45,600.05
22	Dec	45,239.63
23	Jan	61,258.07
24	Feb	38,483.64

Sales Report-1

© 2008 The Smart Method Ltd

tip

Use the *Show Bar Only* feature to create quick charts.

To create a "quick chart" for cells E5:E12:

1. Type the formula =E5 into cell F5.

2. AutoFill cell F5 down to F12.

3. Create a bar visualization for cells F5:F12 with the *Show Bar Only* option checked.

4. Widen column F to display a "quick chart".

Total Sales	
70,168.10	
24,938.06	
31,883.54	
49,902.95	

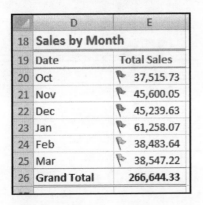

	D	E
18	**Sales by Month**	
19	Date	Total Sales
20	Oct	37,515.73
21	Nov	45,600.05
22	Dec	45,239.63
23	Jan	61,258.07
24	Feb	38,483.64
25	Mar	38,547.22
26	**Grand Total**	**266,644.33**

	A	B
3	**Sales By Country**	
4	Country	Total Sales
5	Argentina	
6	Austria	
7	Belgium	
8	Brazil	
9	Canada	
10	Denmark	

The Rules Manager dialog is displayed.

3. Click the Edit Rule button. **Edit Rule…**

4. Change the criteria so that values over 45,000 are green, values over 38,000 are yellow and values under 38,000 are red.

The flags are displayed as required, with three green flags (see sidebar).

6 Use the Rules Manager to show the visualizations for *Sales by Country* without the underlying data.

1. Select cells B5:B25.

2. Click Home→Styles→Conditional Formatting→Manage Rules.

The Rules Manager dialog is displayed.

3. Click the Edit Rule button. **Edit Rule…**

4. Check the Show Bar Only check box.

The bars are shown without the values (see sidebar).

5. Click the OK button on each dialog to close them.

7 Use the Rules Manager to bring back the values for *Sales by Country*.

Follow the same procedure as in the previous step to uncheck the *Show Bar Only* check box.

8 Save your work as Sales Report-2.

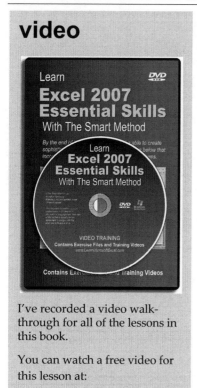
Lesson 4-18: Create a formula driven conditional format

While the built-in conditional format options are very powerful, you will occasionally have a conditional format requirement that is not catered for.

For example, I've lost count of the number of times I have been asked if it is possible to highlight an entire row, rather than a single cell within a row, based upon the value in one of the row's cells.

This lesson will show you how to achieve this using a formula-driven conditional format.

1 Open *Sales Summary First Quarter 2008* from your sample files folder.

Our challenge will be to highlight the entire row when the Country column contains the value: *USA*.

2 Apply a conditional format to Column C to change the background color to light Red when the text contains the text: USA.

1. Select column C and apply the following conditional formatting rule selecting Custom Format as the fill color:

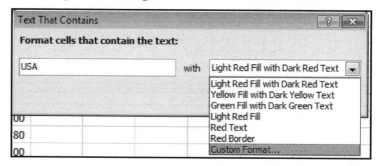

This was covered in: *Lesson 4-15: Use simple conditional formatting.*

2. Click the Fill tab and select a light red color for the conditional fill

3. Click the OK Button.

Every instance of USA in the worksheet now has the cell in column C highlighted.

	B	C	D
40	Familia Arquibaldo	Brazil	100.00
41	Hungry Coyote Import Store	USA	62.40
42	Hungry Coyote Import Store	USA	40.00
43	Wartian Herkku	Finland	146.00

Sales Summary First Quarter 2008

3   Apply a formula-driven conditional format to column B so that the same rows are highlighted.

This is a lot more difficult than the simple conditional format applied to column C.

1. Select column B.

2. Click Home→Styles→Conditional Formatting→New Rule…

   The New Formatting Rule dialog appears.

3. Select *Use a formula to determine which cells to format* from the *Select a Rule Type* list.

4. Type the formula **=C1="USA"** into the formula text box.

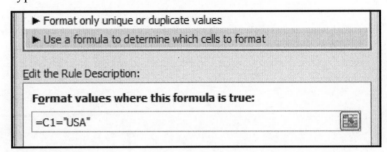

See sidebar for a discussion of this formula.

5. Click the Format button, then the Fill tab and apply the same light red fill color.

6. Click the OK button once, and then again, to close both dialogs.

Both columns now have a light red fill when the country is USA.

	A	B	C	D
40	14-Jan-08	Familia Arquibaldo	Brazil	100.00
41	15-Jan-08	Hungry Coyote Import Store	USA	62.40
42	15-Jan-08	Hungry Coyote Import Store	USA	40.00
43	16-Jan-08	Wartian Herkku	Finland	146.00

4   Apply the same formula-driven conditional format to columns A and D so that the whole row is highlighted.

	A	B	C	D
40	14-Jan-08	Familia Arquibaldo	Brazil	100.00
41	15-Jan-08	Hungry Coyote Import Store	USA	62.40
42	15-Jan-08	Hungry Coyote Import Store	USA	40.00
43	16-Jan-08	Wartian Herkku	Finland	146.00

5   Save your work as Sales Summary First Quarter 2008-1.

---

tip

Why does the formula relate to cell C1?

At first it seems rather odd that we refer to cell C1 in the conditional formatting formula.

C1 is in the title row so how can this be right?

The answer is to be found in Excel's treatment of absolute and relative cell references (originally explained in: *Lesson 3-12: Understand absolute and relative cell references*).

Excel regards the cell reference to be relative to the first row in the selected range.

Since we selected an entire column, row 1 is the reference row used to adjust the formula for every other row within the column.

In other words, Excel will look at cell C2 when applying row 2 conditional formatting, C3 when applying row 3… and so on.

This is exactly what we want to happen.

Lesson 4-19: Use the Format Painter

The format painter is one of the most useful tools in Microsoft Office.

You can use the format painter in PowerPoint, Word and all other Office products.

I find that at least half of the experienced Excel users who attend classroom courses have never discovered the format painter. I love it when they gasp in amazement at the enormous amount of time and effort they will save in future when using this tool.

In this lesson we're going to take a worksheet that is partially formatted and use the format painter to quickly copy formatting information (as opposed to values) from one cell to another.

1   Open *Sales Report-FP from* your sample files folder.

This worksheet has been partially formatted.

	A	B	C	D	E
1	Sales Report - 6 Months ended March 2008				
2					
3	Sales By Country			Sales by Category	
4	Country	Total Sales		Category	Total Sales
5	Argentina	762.6		Beverages	70168.1
6	Austria	33462.58		Condiments	24938.055
7	Belgium	6109.48		Confections	31883.54
8	Brazil	20524.42		Dairy Products	49902.95
9	Canada	21306.29		Grains/Cereals	19570.36
10	Denmark	16658.8		Meat/Poultry	35767.63
11	Finland	5525		Produce	17109.18
12	France	26155.54		Seafood	17304.51
13	Germany	28361.38		Grand Total	266644.325
14	Ireland	6157.755			

2   Apply the comma style to all of the values in column B.

This was covered in: *Lesson 4-3: Format numbers using built-in number formats.*

Values are now formatted with two decimal places and a thousand comma separator.

	A	B
9	Canada	21,306.29
10	Denmark	16,658.80
11	Finland	5,525.00

3   Click any value in column B and then click

Home→Clipboard→Format Painter.

The cursor shape changes to a paint brush.

Sales Report-FP

4   Click and drag across cells E5:E13.

The format of cells E5:E13 changes to match those of the values in column B.

	D	E
4	Category	Total Sales
5	Beverages	70,168.10
6	Condiments	24,938.06

5   Do the same for cells E20:E26.

Repeat exactly the same steps.

1. Click on any value in column B (this is the source).

2. Click Home→Clipboard→Format Painter.

3. Drag across cells E20:E26 (this is the target).

All values in this worksheet are now formatted with the comma style.

6   Use the format painter to copy formatting from cell A3 to cells D3 and D18.

This time we will use the format painter in a slightly different way.

If you double-click the format painter icon a *sticky format painter* results. This will stay switched on until you once again click the format painter icon to switch it off.

1. Click on cell A3 to make it the active (source) cell.

2. Double-click Home→Clipboard→Format Painter.

       ✦ Format Painter

3. The cursor shape changes to a paint brush. 🖑

4. Click cell D3. The format now matches cell A3 but the cursor remains the same. 🖑

5. Click cell D4. The format now matches cell A3 but the cursor remains the same. 🖑

6. Click Home→Clipboard→Format Painter ✦ Format Painter to switch off the format painter. The cursor reverts to the normal shape.

7   Copy formatting from cell A4 to cells D4:E4 and D19:E19 using the format painter.

8   Apply the Total style to cell B26.

This was covered in: *Lesson 4-9: Use cell styles and change themes.*

9   Copy the total style from cell B26 to cells E13 and E26 using the format painter.

10   Save your work as Sales Report-FP-1.

Lesson 4-20: Rotate text

1   Open *Top 20 Films from* your sample files folder.

2   Insert a new column to the left of column A.

> This was covered in: *Lesson 3-1: Insert and delete rows and columns.*

3   Cut and paste the contents of cell B1 to cell A1.

> This was covered in: *Lesson 3-3: Cut, copy and paste.*

4   Apply the *Title* style to cell A1, the *Heading 2* style to cells A3:E3 and the *Heading 4* style to cell D25.

> This was covered in: *Lesson 4-9: Use cell styles and change themes.*

5   Type: **Over 400M** into cell A4, **Over 350M** into cell A12 and **Over 300M** into cell A17.

6   Select cells A4:A11.

3		Title	Year
4	Over 400M	Titanic	1997
5		The Dark Knight	2008
6		Star Wars	1977
7		Shrek 2	2004
8		E.T.: The Extra-Terrestrial	1982
9		Star Wars: Episode I - The Phantom Menace	1999
10		Pirates of the Caribbean: Dead Man's Chest	2006
11		Spider-Man	2002
12	Over 350M	Star Wars: Episode III - Revenge of the Sith	2005

7   Merge the selected cells.

> This was covered in: *Lesson 4-6: Merge cells, wrap text and expand/collapse the formula bar.*

8   Rotate the text through ninety degrees.

    1.   Click Home→Alignment→Orientation.

    2.   Select *Rotate Text Up* from the drop-down list.

note

Other ways to rotate text

You can also rotate text using the *Format Cells* dialog though you'll nearly always find the Ribbon method faster and more convenient.

The format cells dialog is slightly more powerful as it allows you to rotate text by any angle.

1. Right-click a cell or range and click *Format Cells* from the shortcut menu.

2. Click the *Alignment* tab.

3. In the *Orientation* pane either type in the number of degrees of rotation or click and drag the red triangle to set it visually.

Top 20 Films

3		Title
4		Titanic
5		The Dark Knight
6		Star Wars
7		Shrek 2
8		E.T.: The Extra-T
9	Over 400M	Star Wars: Episo
10		Pirates of the Ca
11		Spider-Man
12		Star Wars: Episo
13		The Lord of the
14	Over 350M	Spider-Man 2
15		The Passion of t
16		Jurassic Park
17		The Lord of the
18		Finding Nemo
19		Spider-Man 3
20		Forrest Gump
21	Over 300M	The Lion King
22		Shrek the Third
23		Transformers

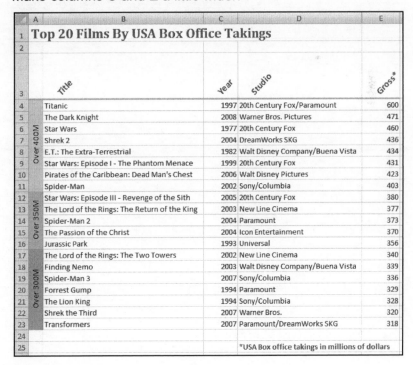

9 Merge and rotate the text in cells A12:A16 and A17:A23.

Your worksheet should now look like the sidebar.

10 Select cells A4:A17 and set the horizontal alignment to center and the vertical alignment to middle.

This was covered in: *Lesson 4-5: Horizontally align the contents of cells* and *Lesson 4-7: Vertically align the contents of cells.*

11 Apply the *Heading 4* style to cells A4:A17.

12 AutoFit cells A4:A17 so that they are just wide enough for the text.

This was covered in: *Lesson 2-9: Re-size rows and columns.*

13 Apply the *40% Accent 3* style to cell A4.

This was covered in: *Lesson 4-9: Use cell styles and change themes.*

Note that the cell reference for the old range A4:A11 is now the single cell reference A4.

14 Apply the *40% Accent 6* style to cell A12.

15 Apply the *40% Accent 2* style to cell A17.

16 Widen row 3 so that it is about three times the normal height.

17 Rotate the text in row 3 through 45 degrees.

Select row 3 and click Home→Alignment→Orientation→ Angle Counter Clockwise.

18 Make columns C and E a little wider.

	A	B	C	D	E
1		Top 20 Films By USA Box Office Takings			
2					
3		Title	Year	Studio	Gross*
4		Titanic	1997	20th Century Fox/Paramount	600
5		The Dark Knight	2008	Warner Bros. Pictures	471
6	Over 400M	Star Wars	1977	20th Century Fox	460
7		Shrek 2	2004	DreamWorks SKG	436
8		E.T.: The Extra-Terrestrial	1982	Walt Disney Company/Buena Vista	434
9		Star Wars: Episode I - The Phantom Menace	1999	20th Century Fox	431
10		Pirates of the Caribbean: Dead Man's Chest	2006	Walt Disney Pictures	423
11		Spider-Man	2002	Sony/Columbia	403
12		Star Wars: Episode III - Revenge of the Sith	2005	20th Century Fox	380
13	Over 350M	The Lord of the Rings: The Return of the King	2003	New Line Cinema	377
14		Spider-Man 2	2004	Paramount	373
15		The Passion of the Christ	2004	Icon Entertainment	370
16		Jurassic Park	1993	Universal	356
17		The Lord of the Rings: The Two Towers	2002	New Line Cinema	340
18		Finding Nemo	2003	Walt Disney Company/Buena Vista	339
19	Over 300M	Spider-Man 3	2007	Sony/Columbia	336
20		Forrest Gump	1994	Paramount	329
21		The Lion King	1994	Sony/Columbia	328
22		Shrek the Third	2007	Warner Bros.	320
23		Transformers	2007	Paramount/DreamWorks SKG	318
24					
25				*USA Box office takings in millions of dollars	

19 Save your work as Top 20 Films-1.

Session 4: Exercise

1   Open *House Mortgage* from your sample files folder.

2   Merge and center cells B3:J3.

3   Apply the Title style to cell A1, the Heading 1 style to cell B3, the Heading 3 style to cells A4:J4 and the Heading 3 style to cells A10:C10.

4   Apply the Heading 4 style to cells A5:A8 and cells A11:A15.

5   Apply the percentage style to cells B4:J4.

6   Apply the comma style to cells B5:J8.

7   Apply the percentage style to cells B11:C15 and then increase decimals to one place.

8   Type the word *Average* into cell A16 and use the Format Painter to match the formatting to that of the cell above (A15).

9   Horizontally right-align the text in cell A16.

10   Use AutoSum to place an average function into cells B16 and C16.

11   Place a thin black border beneath cells A15:C15.

12   Apply a 20% Accent 1 cell style to cells B4:J4 and B10:C10.

13   Change the theme to Foundry and adjust the width of column A so that all text is displayed.

14   Save your work as House Mortgage-1.

	A	B	C	D	E	F	G	H	I	J
1	House Mortgage Monthly Payments - 25 year term									
2										
3					interest rate					
4	House Value	2%	3%	4%	5%	6%	7%	8%	9%	10%
5	50000	211.93	237.11	263.92	292.30	322.15	353.39	385.91	419.60	454.35
6	100000	423.85	474.21	527.84	584.59	644.30	706.78	771.82	839.20	908.70
7	150000	635.78	711.32	791.76	876.89	966.45	1,060.17	1,157.72	1,258.79	1,363.05
8	200000	847.71	948.42	1,055.67	1,169.18	1,288.60	1,413.56	1,543.63	1,678.39	1,817.40
9										
10	Historical Base/Prime Rates	UK	USA							
11	1990	14.8%	7.3%							
12	1995	6.7%	5.5%							
13	2000	6.0%	5.5%							
14	2005	4.7%	2.3%							
15	2008	5.0%	2.0%							
16	Average	7.4%	4.5%							

House Mortgage

If you need help slide the page to the left

Session 4: Exercise answers

These are the four questions that most students find the most difficult to remember:

Q 13	Q 11	Q 10	Q 8
1. Click Page Layout→Themes→Themes→Foundry. 2. Select cells A4:A16. 3. Click Home→Cells→Format→AutoFit Column Width. This was covered in: *Lesson 2-9: Re-size rows and columns.*	1. Select cells A15:C15. 2. Click Home→Font→Borders→Bottom Border. This was covered in: *Lesson 4-11: Add borders and lines.*	1. Select cells B16:C16. 2. Click Home→Editing→Autosum→Average. 3. Either press the <Enter> key or click the Autosum button again. This was covered in: *Lesson 2-11: Use AutoSum to quickly calculate averages.*	1. Click in cell A15. 2. Click Home→Clipboard→Format Painter. 3. Click in cell A16. This was covered in: *Lesson 4-19: Use the Format Painter.*

If you have difficulty with the other questions, here are the lessons that cover the relevant skills:

1 Refer to: Lesson 1-4: Open and navigate a workbook.

2 Refer to: Lesson 4-6: Merge cells, wrap text and expand/collapse the formula bar.

3 Refer to: Lesson 4-9: Use cell styles and change themes.

4 Refer to: Lesson 4-9: Use cell styles and change themes.

5 Refer to: Lesson 4-3: Format numbers using built-in number formats.

6 Refer to: Lesson 4-3: Format numbers using built-in number formats.

7 Refer to: Lesson 4-3: Format numbers using built-in number formats.

9 Refer to: Lesson 4-5: Horizontally align the contents of cells.

12 Refer to: Lesson 4-9: Use cell styles and change themes.

14 Refer to: Lesson 1-5: Save a workbook.

5

Session Five: Charts and Graphics

A picture is worth a thousand words.

Frederick R. Barnard in "Printers' Ink", 8th Dec 1921.

Charts (also called graphs) are one of Excel's most powerful features.

While very numerate readers may be able to reach conclusions by scanning a table of numbers, most will find a chart a lot more intuitive.

PowerPoint presentations that are packed with numbers will send your audience to sleep, while hard-hitting graphical representations of your data will maintain interest and attention.

In this session you'll learn to present your data in a chart. You'll also learn some valuable "tricks of the trade" to present your data in the most effective way.

Charts never lie but they can give the truth scope!

Session Objectives

By the end of this session you will be able to:

- Create a simple chart with two clicks
- Move, re-size, copy and delete a chart
- Change the chart layout and add a data table
- Format chart element fills and borders
- Format 3-D elements and align text
- Move, re-size, add and delete chart elements
- Change a chart's source data
- Create a chart with numerical axis
- Deal with empty data points
- Add data labels to a chart
- Highlight specific data points with color and annotations
- Add gridlines and scale axis
- Emphasize data by manipulating pie charts
- Create a chart with two vertical axis
- Create a combination chart containing different chart types
- Add a trend line
- Switch chart rows/columns
- Add a gradient fill
- Create your own chart templates

Lesson 5-1: Create a simple chart with two clicks

note

Create a chart with the <F11> key.

If you click inside a range and then press the <F11> key Excel will instantly create a new chart on a new worksheet.

tip

You can create a chart without selecting any data.

When you want to chart an entire range (as is the case in this lesson) you don't need to select the data.

If you simply click anywhere within the range and then click Insert→Charts→Column, Excel will assume that you want to chart the entire range and select it for you.

important

Charts are dynamic

If the data underpinning a chart changes, the chart will instantly change to represent the new data values.

1 Open *World Sales from* your sample files folder.

This is a very simple worksheet showing January, February and March sales figures for three regions.

	A	B	C	D
1	Month	USA	Europe	Other
2	Jan	21,600	19,200	10,800
3	Feb	25,400	21,400	12,200
4	Mar	22,800	23,600	9,600

2 Select all of the data and all of the labels.

When Excel creates a chart it must know what each data element means. For this reason you must always select the labels *as well as* the values before you create your chart.

Missing the labels is one of the commonest errors in my classroom courses.

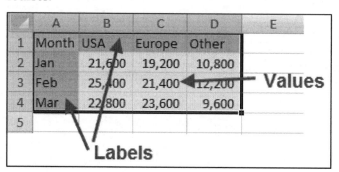

3 Click Insert→Charts→Column and hover the mouse pointer over some of the charts in the gallery.

As you hover the mouse button over each chart type Excel provides a ScreenTip describing the chart.

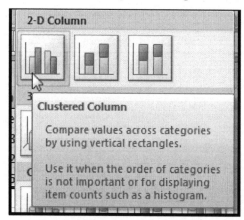

4 Click the left-most 2-D Column chart (the Clustered column Chart).

World Sales

In just two clicks we have created a very presentable chart. Excel uses the default layout and colors from the current workbook's theme.

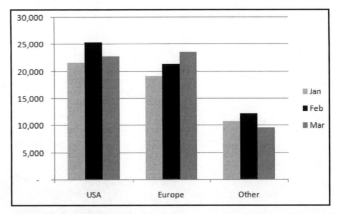

Notice that three new tabs have appeared on the Ribbon below a group called *Chart Tools*.

If you don't see this it is because you haven't activated the chart (see sidebar).

5   Change the chart style.

1.   Click Chart Tools→ Design→Chart Styles→ Chart Styles Gallery.

When you click the gallery button you are able to choose a new chart style from 48 pre-defined options. Each chart style uses theme colors so the appearance will change if you later change the workbook's theme.

2.   Click a new chart style to change the appearance of your chart.

6   Save your work as World Sales-1.

Lesson 5-2: Move, re-size, copy and delete a chart

1   Open *World Sales-1* from your sample files folder (if it isn't already open).

2   Move the chart to a different position on screen.

   1.   Hover with the mouse just inside the border of the selected chart until you see the four headed arrow cursor shape.

   2.   Click and drag the chart to the required position.

3   Re-size the chart.

   1.   Click just inside the border of the chart to activate it. When the chart is activated you will see a frame and corner handles around it. Excel also displays the Chart Tools group of Ribbon tabs.

   2.   Hover over one of the corner or side sizing handles on the edges of the chart until you see the two-headed arrow cursor shape.

   3.   When you see the two-headed arrow cursor shape, click and drag to re-size the chart. If you hold down the **<Shift>** key as you click-and drag one of the corners of the chart, the perspective will remain constant (ie the chart will get proportionately wider as it gets taller).

4   Create a duplicate chart by copy and paste.

   1.   Click just inside the border of the chart to activate it.

   2.   Right-click, on the border of the activated chart (just inside the border works too) and click Copy from the shortcut menu.

   3.   Right-click anywhere on the worksheet and click Paste from the shortcut menu to create the duplicate chart.

World Sales-1

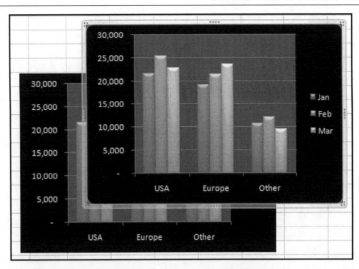

Note that even though the new chart is a duplicate it is not linked to the original chart in any way. You can freely change any part of either chart and it will never affect the other.

You can also use this technique to move a chart to a different worksheet (covered later in this lesson). The chart will still be linked to the data in the original worksheet.

5   Delete one of the charts.

    1.   Click just inside the border of either of the charts to activate it.

    2.   Press the **<Delete>** key on the keyboard.

6   Move the chart to its own worksheet.

Sometimes it is better to keep charts and data separate by placing a chart in its own chart worksheet. A chart worksheet is a special worksheet without any cells that can only contain a single chart.

    1.   Right-click just inside the border of the chart to activate it and then click *Move Chart...* from the shortcut menu.

    2.   Click the *New Sheet* option button, name the new sheet *Sales Summary Chart* and click the OK button.

The chart is now displayed within its own dedicated worksheet.

7   Move the chart back to its original location.

    1.   Right-click just inside the border of the chart and click *Move Chart...* from the shortcut menu.

    2.   Click the *Object in* option button and Choose *Sheet1* from the drop down list.

8   Save your work as World Sales-2.

Lesson 5-3: Change the chart layout and add a data table

1   Open *World Sales-2* from your sample files folder (if it isn't already open).

2   Click the chart to activate it.

3   Change the chart style back to the default style.

      1.   Click Chart Tools→Design→Chart Styles Gallery.

      2.   Click the second chart style from the left on the first row (the default style).

4   Click Chart Tools→Design→Chart Layouts Gallery.

The gallery contains eleven pre-defined chart layouts.

The main differences between the layouts are:

- Some layouts have a *Chart Title* across the top of the chart.
- Some layouts have a *Legend* which can be situated at the top, bottom, or right of the screen.
- Some layouts have *Axis Titles* on the horizontal axis, vertical axis, or both.
- Some layouts include a *Data Table*.

World Sales-2

5 Choose Layout 9. This layout includes a *Chart Title* element. a *Legend* element and two *Axis Title* elements.

6 Click the *Chart Title* element and type the title: **Sales First Quarter** followed by the **<Enter>** key.

7 Click the *Vertical Axis Title* element and type the title: **Sales** followed by the **<Enter>** key.

8 Click the *Horizontal Axis Title* element and type the title: **Region** followed by the **<Enter>** key.

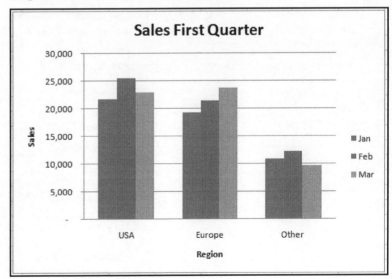

9 Save your work as: *World Sales-3.*

Lesson 5-4: Format chart element fills and borders

Up until now we've selected pre defined chart layouts from the gallery.

To unleash the real power of Excel charts we need to think of a chart as a collection of graphic elements (sometimes also called objects), each of which can be individually formatted.

Once you have the hang of how to format one graphic element it becomes easy to work with any other element, because the options are broadly the same.

In this lesson we'll learn some of the formatting options for the *Chart Title* element.

1   Open *World Sales-3* from your sample files folder (if it isn't already open).

2   Click the chart to activate it.

3   Click the Chart Title element to select it.

A frame appears.

4   Right-Click the Chart Title element and click *Format Chart Title* from the shortcut menu.

The *Format Chart Title* dialog appears.

5   Apply a *Blue Accent 1* fill (background color) to the Chart Title element.

1.   Click the Solid Fill option.

2.   Click the color button and choose the *Blue, Accent 1* fill color.

3.   Drag the slider to the right to set the transparency to about 80%.

---

note

Chart titles can display the contents of a specific cell.

Normally you will simply type the text that you need directly into the *Chart Title* element.

It is also possible to link the Chart Title to a worksheet cell so that it displays whatever text is in the specified cell.

Here's how it is done:

1.   Click the Chart Title.

2.   Type **=A1** (or any other cell reference.

The contents of cell A1 are then displayed in the Chart Title and will change whenever the text in cell A1 changes.

World Sales-3

Notice that the background color of the Chart Title element becomes lighter as you drag to the right, and darker as you drag to the left.

6   Click *Border Color* from the category list on the left of the dialog.

7   Click the *Solid Line* option button.

8   Choose a solid black color.

9   Click *Border Styles* from the category list on the left of the dialog.

Change the width to *1 pt*.

10   Click *Close* to apply a 1 point black border to the *Chart Title* element.

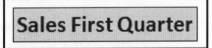

11   Save your work as World Sales-4.

Lesson 5-5: Format 3-D elements and align text

Shadows and 3-D formats are a brand new feature for Excel 2007.

The use of subtle shadows and 3-D formats will add a professional sheen to your work that was only previously possible with high-end graphics applications such as Adobe Photoshop.

1   Open *World Sales-4* from your sample files folder (if it isn't already open) and click the chart to activate it.

2   Click Chart Tools→Layout→Current Selection→ Chart Elements Drop Down →Chart Title.

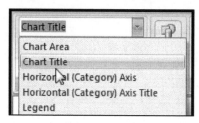

This is an alternative way to select chart elements. The drop-down shows every element in the currently selected chart.

We've already encountered Chart Title, Horizontal Axis Title, Legend and Vertical Axis Title in: *Lesson 5-3: Change the chart layout.* Here's what the other elements mean (see sidebar for more on data series):

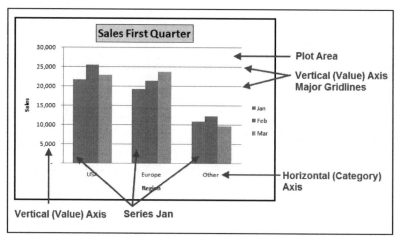

note

More about data series.

A data series is a group of data that is associated with a specific category.

For example, the *Series Jan* data series is a group of values, one for each of the categories USA, Europe and Other.

In this example there are three data series containing numerical data for each category.

If you do a lot of work with charts it is well worth adding the Chart Elements Drop-Down list to the Quick Access Toolbar (this was covered in: *Lesson 1-10: Customize the Quick Access Toolbar and preview the printout).*

3   Click Chart Tools→Layout→Current Selection→ Format Selection.

World Sales-4

This is an alternative way to bring up the Format dialog. The right-click method is usually faster but there are some chart elements that can be difficult to select with the mouse.

Notice the *Reset to Match Style* option in the *Current Selection* group. This allows you to reset the formatting back to the default when you've messed things up and want to start again!

4   Select *Shadow* from the category list on the left of the dialog.

5   Apply an *Offset Diagonal Bottom Right* shadow to the Chart Title.

While you can create your own shadows using the Transparency, Size, Blur, Angle and Distance sliders you'll probably find that the presets will suffice. Presets will also maintain uniformity between different chart elements.

There are plenty of shadows to choose from (see sidebar).

1.   Click the *Shadow Presets* drop-down arrow.

2.   Select the *Offset Diagonal Bottom Right* shadow (the top left shadow in the *Outer* group.

Notice that when you click, the effect is applied to the chart even before you've closed the dialog.

Sales First Quarter

6   Select *3-D Format* from the category list on the left of the dialog.

7   Apply a Circle top bevel to the Chart Title.

Just like shadows, you'll probably find what you need in the 3-D presets rather than creating your own custom 3-D effects.

Click the Top Bevel preset button to display a top bevel gallery and choose a Circle top bevel.

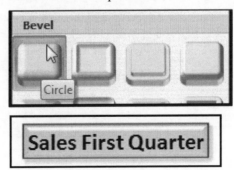

Sales First Quarter

8   Click the Close Button.

9   Save your work as World Sales-5.

Lesson 5-6: Move, re-size, add and delete chart elements

Several elements such as the Chart Title, Legend and Horizontal/Vertical titles can be moved by drag and drop.

In this lesson we'll see how to move these, and how to re-instate them to their pixel-perfect locations if you change your mind.

We'll also remove and add chart elements. Once you've got the hang of this you'll be able to custom design charts for any specific requirement.

1   Open *World Sales-5* from your sample files folder (if it isn't already open) and click the chart to activate it.

2   Click and drag the Chart Title to the left hand side of the chart.

1.   Click the Chart Title element to select it.

2.   Hover with the mouse over the border of the Chart Title element until you see a four headed arrow.

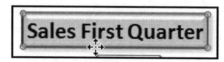

3.   When you see the four headed arrow, click and drag to move the element to the top left corner of the chart.

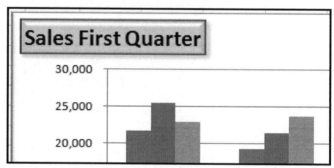

3   Move the Chart Title back so that it is above the chart at dead center.

You couldn't get this pixel-perfect using the mouse.

Click Chart Tools→Layout→Labels→Chart Title→Above Chart.

The title is restored to dead center.

4   Delete the legend.

1.   Click the legend element to select it

2.   Press the **<Delete>** key.

World Sales-5

5 Display the legend at the bottom of the screen.

With the chart activated, click Chart Tools→Layout→ Labels→Legend→Show Legend at Bottom.

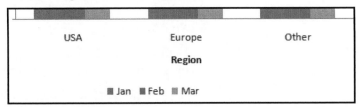

6 Add a thin black border to the legend.

This was covered in: *Lesson 5-4: Format chart element fills and borders.*

7 Re-size the legend so that it spans the entire width of the plot area.

1. Click the legend to select it. Notice the sizing handles on each corner and edge.

2. Hover over the square sizing handle on the right-hand edge of the element. Notice that the cursor shape changes to a two headed arrow.

3. When you see the two-headed arrow click and drag to re-size the legend so that it is the same width as the plot area. (You'll have to first size the right side and then the left).

8 Increase the size of the font within the legend.

1. Click the legend to select it.

2. Click Home→Font→Font Size Drop-down. Hover the mouse cursor over each font size and note that *Live Preview* allows you to see the effect of your choice.

3. Select 14 points for the new text size.

You'll often want to increase text sizes when you create charts for PowerPoint slides.

9 Save your work as World Sales-6.

Lesson 5-7: Change a chart's source data

You'll often need to change the data that the chart is depicting.

In this lesson you will change the chart so that it depicts sales for the USA only rather than the USA, Europe and Other territories.

1   Open *World Sales-6* from your sample files folder (if it isn't already open) and click just inside the border of the chart to select it.

2   Right-click in the plot area of the chart and click *Select Data* from the shortcut menu.

The *Select Data Source* dialog appears.

Notice the *Chart data range* shown at the top of the dialog. For the moment this is all that I want you to concentrate upon.

The range is shown as Sheet1!$A$1:$D$4.

This means the absolute range A1:D4 on the Sheet1 worksheet.

(Absolute cell references were covered in: *Lesson 3-12: Understand absolute and relative cell references*).

3   Change the *Chart data range* so that only USA sales are charted.

The current range is A1:D4.

	A	B	C	D
1	Month	USA	Europe	Other
2	Jan	21,600	19,200	10,800
3	Feb	25,400	21,400	12,200
4	Mar	22,800	23,600	9,600
5				

If we change the range to A1:B4 the other two regions will be removed.

You could simply type the new reference into the *Chart Data Range* text box but it is less error prone if you visually select the data with the mouse.

Click and drag with the mouse across cells A1:B4.

The data range displays in both the Select Data Source dialog and as a marquee on the worksheet.

It is very easy to mess up the data range in the text box. If you get an obscure error message simply delete all of the contents of the *Chart data range* text box and re-select.

Notice that, in the background, the chart has changed to reflect the new data range.

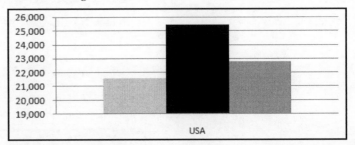

note

If your chart doesn't look like the screen grab in step 5.

In: **Error! Reference source not found.** you checked your program version and learned a little about *Service Packs*.

The original version of this book was created using *Service Pack 1*. Microsoft subsequently released *Service Pack 2* (and by the time you read this book they may be on an even later revision).

Service Pack 2 changed the way in which the chart switches the rows and columns when a new data range is selected.

If you see the *Months* at the bottom of the chart and the *Regions* underneath the chart columns you need to switch the rows and columns so that they match the screen grab at the bottom of this page.

To do this click the *Switch Row/Column* button in the *Select Data Source* dialog.

The *Switch Row/Column* button will be covered in depth in: *Lesson 5-20: Switch chart rows/columns and add a gradient fill.*

4   Change the data range to A1:C4 to chart sales for the USA and Europe.

5   Click OK to view the new chart.

If your chart doesn't look like the following screen grab see sidebar for an explanation, and a further step to correct it.

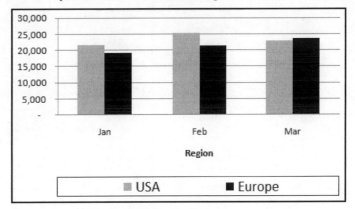

6   Save your work as *World Sales-7*.

Lesson 5-8: Assign non-contiguous source data by click and drag

In the previous lesson it was easy to select the source data because it comprised of a single block (we use the word: *contiguous* for this type of range).

In this lesson we'll take things a little further by selecting data that isn't in a single block (ie non-contiguous data) to show sales for the *USA* and *Other* categories.

1   Open *World Sales-7* from your sample files folder (if it isn't already open) and click the chart to activate it.

2   Right-click in the plot area of the chart and click *Select Data* from the shortcut menu.

The *Select Data Source* dialog appears.

3   Select the range A1:B4,D1:D4.

    1.   Select the range A1:B4.

    2.   Hold down the **<Ctrl>** key.

    3.   Select the range D1:D4.

Selecting non-contiguous ranges was covered extensively in: *Lesson 2-7: Select non-contiguous cell ranges and view summary information.*

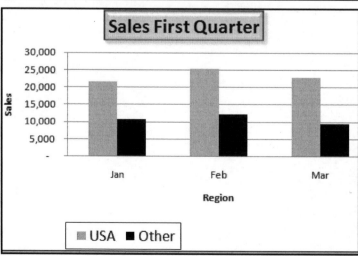

World Sales-7

4   Display totals in column E.

Type the word: **Total** into cell E1 and then use AutoSum to place the total for all regions into cells E2:E4.

Autosum was covered in: *Lesson 2-3: Use AutoSum to quickly calculate totals.*

	A	B	C	D	E
1	Month	USA	Europe	Other	Total
2	Jan	21,600	19,200	10,800	51,600
3	Feb	25,400	21,400	12,200	59,000
4	Mar	22,800	23,600	9,600	56,000

5   Change the source data so that only totals are charted.

Set the source data to cells A1:A4, E1:E4.

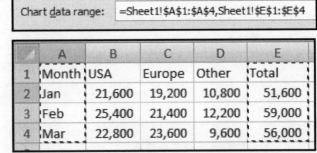

Chart data range: =Sheet1!$A$1:$A$4,Sheet1!$E$1:$E$4

	A	B	C	D	E
1	Month	USA	Europe	Other	Total
2	Jan	21,600	19,200	10,800	51,600
3	Feb	25,400	21,400	12,200	59,000
4	Mar	22,800	23,600	9,600	56,000

6   Click OK to close the Select Data Source dialog.

7   Save your work as *World Sales-8.*

note

An alternative method for selecting source data.

The Select Source Data dialog is by far the best way to set and modify source data for charts.

An alternative way is to copy a data range, activate the chart, and then click:

Home→Clipboard→Paste→ Paste Special...

A Paste Special dialog is then displayed that is specifically designed for charts:

Lesson 5-9: Change source data using the *Select Data Source* dialog tools

In previous versions of Excel it was only possible to define source data using the *Chart data range* text box. The dialog box in Excel 2007 now provides a better way of defining source data and axis labels at the same time.

1   Open *World Sales-8* from your sample files folder (if it isn't already open) and click the chart to activate it.

2   Right-click in the plot area of the chart and click *Select Data* from the shortcut menu.

The *Select Data Source* dialog appears.

3   Add a USA data series.

Click the Add button 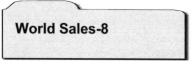 in the *Legend Entries (Series)* pane.

1.   Type **USA** for the series name.

2.   Delete the old series values from the text box.

3.   Select the range B2:B4 for the series values.

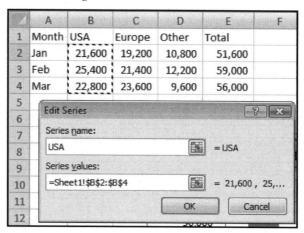

4.   Click OK.

The series is added to the dialog.

4   Delete the Total data series.

1. Click the total series to select it.

2. Click the Remove button.

5   Add the Europe and Other series.

The graph still isn't quite right because 1, 2 and 3 are showing as *Horizontal (Category) Axis Labels* instead of Jan/Feb/Mar.

6   Change the *Horizontal (Category) Axis Labels* to Jan/Feb/Mar.

1. Click the Edit button at the top of the *Horizontal (Category) Axis Labels* pane. ☑ Edi̲t

2. Select cells A2:A4 (the cells containing the text Jan/Feb/Mar).

> A̲xis label range:
> =Sheet1!$A$2:$A$4   = Jan, Feb, Mar

3. Click OK and OK again to dismiss both dialogs.

7   Save your work as World Sales-9.

Lesson 5-10: Chart non-contiguous source data by hiding rows and columns

In this lesson we'll look at an alternative method of charting a non-contiguous range simply by hiding the data elements we don't want to chart.

Excel allows you to hide rows and columns in a worksheet by effectively setting their width to zero. The default behavior of charts is to ignore these hidden rows and columns.

It is also possible to over-ride the default behavior and instruct Excel to chart hidden rows and columns.

1   Open *World Sales-9 from* your sample files folder (if it isn't already open) and click the chart to activate it.

2   Remove the Europe series from the chart by hiding column C.

Right-click on the button at the top of column C and then click *Hide* from the shortcut menu.

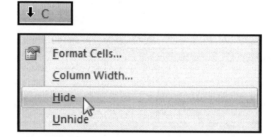

The European sales data is no longer shown on the chart.

3   Remove the February data from the chart by hiding row 3.

Right-click on the button on the left of row 3 and click Hide from the shortcut menu.

February data is no longer shown on the chart.

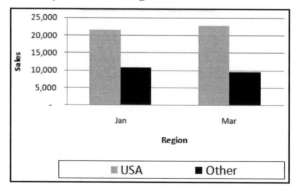

4   Display the hidden data in the chart.

Excel allows you to chart hidden data if you want to.

1.   Right-click in the plot area of the chart and click Select Data from the shortcut menu.

World Sales-9

The *Select Data Source* dialog appears.

2. Click the Hidden and Empty Cells button on the bottom left corner of the dialog.

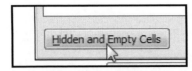

The Hidden and Empty Cells dialog appears.

3. Check the *Show data in hidden rows and columns* check box and click the OK button.

4. Click the OK button to dismiss the dialog.

The previously hidden chart data re-appears.

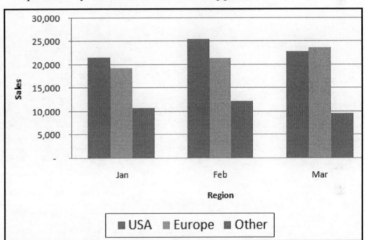

5 Unhide the hidden rows and columns.

1. Click any cell in the worksheet to de-activate the chart.

2. Click the Select All button at the top left corner of the worksheet to select every cell.

3. Click Home→Cells→Format→Hide & Unhide→Unhide Rows.

4. Click Home→Cells→Format→Hide & Unhide→Unhide Columns.

6 Save your work as World Sales-10.

Lesson 5-11: Create a chart with numerical axis

Sometimes Excel gets a little confused when it attempts to automatically generate a chart.

Problems usually occur when you need to plot numerical information along the horizontal axis. Excel sees the numerical labels and assumes that they are a series.

In this example we'll use such a worksheet to confuse Excel and then fix things up manually using the Select Data Source dialog.

1   Open *Annual Sales Summary* from your sample files folder.

2   Display the range as a clustered column chart.

    1.   Click anywhere inside the range.

       Note that it isn't necessary to select the range when you want to chart all of it.

       If you simply click any cell inside the range Excel will automatically select the entire range for the chart's source data.

    2.   Click Insert→Charts→Column→Clustered Column.

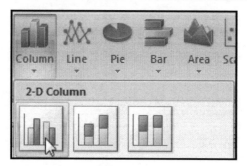

       The range is displayed as a chart but there's a problem. Excel has assumed that the numbers in the *Year* column are a data series.

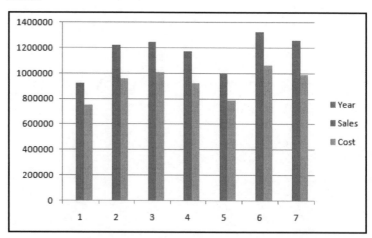

3   Right-click just inside the plot area of the chart and click *Select Data* from the shortcut menu.

The Select Data Source dialog is displayed.

Annual Sales Summary

The problem is immediately apparent. Excel has wrongly identified the year as series data rather than as axis labels.

4 Remove the Year *data series* and add the Year data as *Horizontal (Category) Axis Labels*.

1. Click *Year* in the left hand pane of the dialog and then click the Remove button.

2. Click the Edit button on the right hand pane (the pane showing *Horizontal (Category) Axis labels*.

3. Select cells A2:A8 for the Axis label range (the year data but not the column header).

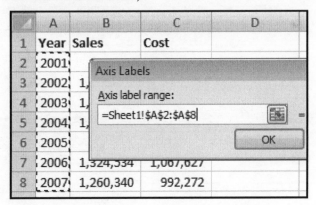

4. Click the OK button twice to close both dialogs.

5. The graph now displays correctly.

5 Save your work as Annual Sales Summary-1.

Lesson 5-12: Deal with empty data points

Sometimes you'll only have partial data for a series.

In the worksheet used for this lesson I'll share a secret with you. I weigh myself every day and keep a chart on my bathroom wall to make sure I'm staying at a healthy weight.

Sometimes I'm away travelling and can't weigh in as usual. When I get back I need to fill in the gaps.

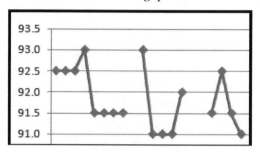

I use a line chart for my weight so the best solution is to simply draw a line connecting the last data point recorded before I went away with the first recorded upon my return.

For a bar chart the best solution would be to show no bars for the missing days. In other words, there would be gaps for each date when there was a missing bar.

1   Open *Weight 2008* from your sample files folder.

This is a simple worksheet showing my weight in kilograms for each date in July 2008. Notice that there are missing days when I was away from home.

2   Display the range as a *Line with Markers* chart.

1. Click on any of the date values within the range.

2. Click Insert→Charts→Line→Line with Markers.

The chart displays but there are gaps for the missing entries.

Weight 2008

3   Tell Excel to connect the gaps in the chart with a line.

   1.   Right-click just inside the plot area of the chart and click *Select Data* from the shortcut menu.

      The *Select Data Source* dialog is displayed.

   2.   Click the *Hidden and Empty Cells* button at the bottom left corner of the dialog.

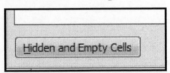

      The *Hidden and Empty Cells* dialog appears.

   3.   Click the *Connect data points with line* option button.

   4.   Click the OK button and OK again to dismiss both dialogs

      All data points are now connected with a line.

4   Save your work as Weight 2008-1.

Lesson 5-13: Add data labels to a chart

It is possible to approximate the values that are displayed in a chart by looking at the vertical axis.

Sometimes you will need to convey the precise values that are being charted. There are three ways of doing this:

- Embed the chart in the worksheet containing the source data so that the user can see both the chart and data.

- Add data labels to each point on the chart.

- Add a table to the bottom of the chart.

1 Open *Annual Sales Summary-1* from your sample files folder.

2 Change the source data so that only sales (not costs) for 2004 to 2007 are charted.

This will allow you to test your understanding of the skills learned in: *Lesson 5-8: Assign non-contiguous source data by click and drag, Lesson 5-9: Change source data using the Select Data Source dialog tools.* and
Lesson 5-11: Create a chart with numerical axis.

1. Select this data range:

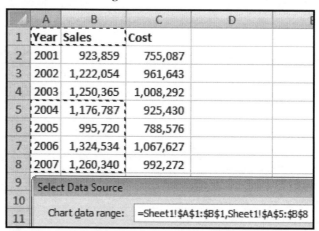

2. Set the data range for the Horizontal (Category) Axis Labels.

3. Delete the Year item from the Legend Entries (Series).

The Select Data Source dialog should then look like this:

... Resulting in the following chart:

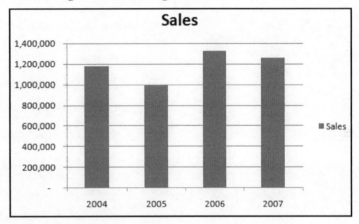

tip

Data labels can be moved and formatted just like any other element.

When preparing a chart for a PowerPoint presentation the data labels are often too small to be visible at the back of the room.

You may also want to fine-tune the positioning of data labels.

For most formatting options, right-click a data label to select the entire series and then click *Format Data Labels* from the shortcut menu.

If you need to change the font size select the series of data labels and then click:

Home→Font→Font Size

If you need to re-position or format a single data label, click once to select the data label series and then a second time to select the individual label you want to work with.

3 Add data labels to each bar.

Activate the chart and then click Chart Tools→Layout→ Labels→Data Labels→Outside End (see sidebar).

Data labels are now displayed at the center top of each bar.

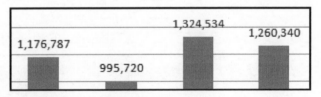

4 Switch off the data labels.

Activate the chart and then click:

Chart Tools→Layout→Labels→Data Labels→None.

5 Add a table to the bottom of the chart.

Activate the chart and then click:

Chart Tools→Layout→Labels→Data Table→Show Data Table

A table is displayed below the chart.

-	2004	2005	2006	2007
Sales	1,176,787	995,720	1,324,534	1,260,340

6 Save your work as Annual Sales Summary-2.

tip

Text boxes are more flexible than the built-in *Chart Title* elements.

Elements such as *Chart Title* and *Horizontal (Category) Axis Title* appear to have sizing handles but you cannot, in fact, re-size them. The only way to make them wider is to type in more text or change the font.

Text boxes have no such restrictions. For this reason you may sometimes find that it is preferable to substitute a text box for a Chart Title element.

Lesson 5-14: Highlight specific data points with color and annotations

Sometimes you will want to emphasize a specific data point in a series. For example, you may want to color a single column differently to its neighbors to emphasize some special attribute of the data point.

Color alone cannot convey why the data point is special. You will normally want to add a text box to the chart to qualify the reason for its different color.

In this session we'll imagine that the company is a hotel, and that 2005 was the centenary year for a special event in the resort leading to increased sales. To mark this we'll color the 2005 bar red and add an annotation saying *Centenary Year* to the bar.

1   Open *Annual Sales Summary-2 from* your sample files folder (if it isn't already open).

2   Change the color of the 2005 bar to red.

1.   Click the 2005 bar once. Notice that the entire data series is selected.

2.   Click the 2005 bar once more. This time only the 2005 bar is selected.

3.   Click Chart Tools→Format→Shape Fill→Red.

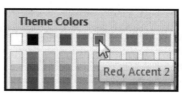

4.   The 2005 bar is now colored red. The legend has also changed to give a further visual prompt that the red bar relates to 2005.

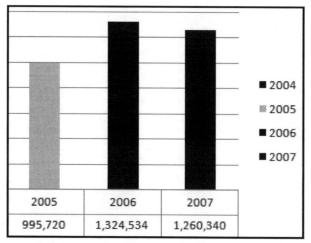

	2005	2006	2007
	995,720	1,324,534	1,260,340

3   Add a text box above, and to the right of, the red bar containing the text: **Centenary Year**.

1.   Click the chart to activate it.

Annual Sales
Summary-2

2. Click Chart Tools→Layout→Insert→Text Box.

3. Click on the chart, above and to the right of the red 2005 bar, and type **Centenary,** then press **<Shift>+<Enter>** and then type **Year.** (The **<Shift>+<Enter>** key combination moves you to the next line in a text box).

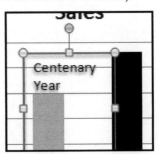

4 Add a border and fill to the text box.

Click the text box to select it and then click:

Drawing Tools→Format→Shape Styles→
Visual Style Gallery Drop-Down→Subtle Effect-Accent 1

This effect is the second on row four (see sidebar).

5 Re-size the text box.

Click the text box once to select and then drag the sizing handles to re-size so that the text fills the box.

6 Move the text box.

Click the text box once to select and then hover over any part of the border that is not a sizing handle. You will see the four-headed arrow cursor shape. When you see the four-headed arrow, click and drag to move the text box to an ideal position.

7 Add an arrow pointing from the text box to the red 2005 bar.

1. Click the chart to activate it. (Make sure that you click the chart and not the text box. The Chart Tools tab will not be displayed when only the text box is selected).

2. Click Chart Tools→Layout→Insert→Shapes→Arrow (see sidebar).

3. Click and drag to draw an arrow pointing from the text box to the red bar.

4. With the arrow selected, click Drawing Tools→Format→ Shape Styles→Gallery drop-down.

5. Choose an attractive style for the arrow.

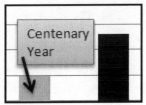

8 Save your work as Annual Sales Summary-3.

Lesson 5-15: Add gridlines and scale axes

As mentioned in this session's introduction, charts never lie but they can give the truth scope!

In this session we'll manipulate the vertical axis of a sales chart to give two entirely different views of a company's sales. Each chart emphasizes one of the following true statements.

- It is true that sales are increasing every month.

- It is true that sales are almost completely flat.

You'll see how we can manipulate a column chart to visually convey each of these "truths" to an audience. After this session you'll never look at a chart again without paying close attention to the vertical axis!

1   Open *Sales First Quarter* from your sample files folder.

	A	B
1	Month	Sales
2	Jan	80,010
3	Feb	80,040
4	Mar	80,080

This worksheet shows sales that are almost completely flat. Sales increased by 0.04% in February and by 0.05% in March.

A twentieth of a percent increase isn't anything at all.

2   Create a chart that illustrates flat sales.

Imagine you are the sales director of the company and need to have a pep talk with your salespeople. You want to show them a chart that demonstrates the lack of sales growth in order to motivate them to do better in April!

1.   Click inside the data range.

2.   Click Insert→Charts→Column→Clustered Column.

The following chart is automatically generated:

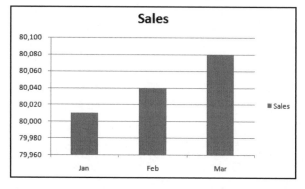

This isn't the chart you want at all. Sales look rather good!

The reason that the chart isn't as honest as it should be is because the vertical axis begins at 79,960. We're looking at the tips of bars that are very long.

Sales First Quarter

To fix things up we need a more honest vertical axis, one that begins at zero.

3. Right-click the vertical axis and select Format Axis... from the shortcut menu.

4. Change the minimum value to zero.

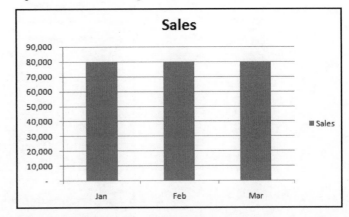

5. Click the Close button. The chart now depicts a more honest representation of flat growth.

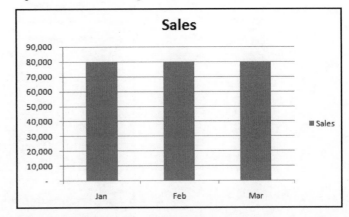

6. Right-click the vertical axis and select Format Axis... from the shortcut menu.

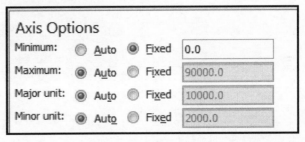

Notice how Excel has automatically managed the other settings. Major units for gridlines (the interval between numbers on the vertical axis) have now changed to 10,000.

7. Change the minor gridline value to 5000 (without the comma as Excel has a problem with commas in this dialog). We will enable the display of minor gridlines in a moment and will expect to see one minor gridline between each major gridline.

8. Click the Close button.

3 Enable minor gridlines.

Select the chart and then click:

Chart Tools→Layout→Axes→Gridlines→
Primary Horizontal Gridlines→Major & Minor Gridlines.

Minor gridlines are now displayed on the chart (see sidebar).

4 Save your work as Sales First Quarter-1.

tip

Use gridlines sparingly.

Too many gridlines can make a chart difficult to read. This lesson's Sales chart looks cluttered with minor gridlines and would look cleaner without any gridlines at all.

When you do use gridlines always choose a light color to focus attention upon foreground elements.

Lesson 5-16: Emphasize data by manipulating pie charts

In the last session we saw how a column chart could visually re-enforce different characteristics of the same data.

Pie charts also offer several techniques to present data in a way that will best convey your objectives. Designers of pie charts often use the presentational methods described in this lesson to make one value in a series seem bigger or smaller in relation to its neighbors.

1 Open *Competitor Analysis* from your sample files folder (if it isn't already open).

	A	B	C
1	Splendid Supplies Competitor Analysis		
2			
3	Competitor	Annual Sales (Millions)	Market Share
4	Cheapo discount stores	22.2	28%
5	Budget supplies	16.3	21%
6	Lo Cost warehouse	24.5	31%
7	Splendid Supplies	16.2	20%

This worksheet has been compiled by Splendid Supplies to monitor the activity of their three competitors. Splendid aren't doing so well, in fact, they have the lowest market share of the four.

There's a big investor meeting coming up and Splendid would like to make their market share seem a little more impressive!

2 Create a 3-D pie chart for the range A3:B7.

1. Select the range A3:B7.

2. Click Insert→Charts→Pie→Pie In 3-D (see sidebar).

A pie chart is displayed illustrating the market share of the four companies.

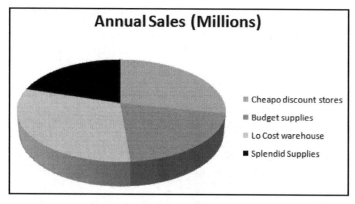

Splendid supplies don't look very impressive on this chart. Let's use our first presentational technique to make things seem a little better.

Competitor Analysis

3   Rotate the pie chart so that Splendid Supplies sales are at the front.

Because of the perspective of a 3-D pie, the slice at the front always seems the biggest (especially if you keep the perspective angle high).

1. Activate the chart.

2. Click Chart Tools→Layout→Background→3-D Rotation.

   The Format Chart Area dialog is displayed.

3. Use the *Rotation X* spin buttons to bring the Splendid Supplies slice to the front (about 220 degrees).

4. Change the Perspective to 35 degrees.

You'd never guess now that Splendid Supplies have the lowest market share.

4   Pull the Splendid Supplies slice slightly out of the pie.

A very common pie chart presentational technique is to pull the slice that you want to emphasize away from the pie chart. This slice then appears to be larger in relation to the other slices.

1. Activate the chart.

2. Click one of the slices on the chart once to select the entire pie.

3. Click the Splendid Supplies slice once to select it.

4. Click and drag the slice slightly out of the pie.

   Splendid Supplies now appears to be doing even better.

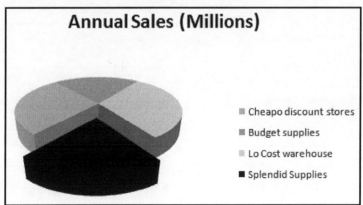

5   Save your work as Competitor Analysis-1.

Lesson 5-17: Create a chart with two vertical axis

Sometimes you'll have two data series that are very different in magnitude but you still want to show them on the same chart.

The examples used in this lesson are *UK Average House Prices* and *Bank Base Rates*. Analysts have noticed that when interest rates come down, house prices go up. To test this theory we will create a chart showing UK bank base rates against average house prices for the twelve years to 2008.

During the twelve year period house prices ranged from 68,788 to 199,021 while base rates fluctuated between 3.5% and 6.75%. We need two different vertical axes to make this chart work.

1   Open *UK House Prices* from your sample files folder.

2   Create a default *Line with Markers* chart from the range.

Click anywhere within the data and then click:

Insert→Charts→Line→Line with Markers

The default chart is displayed.

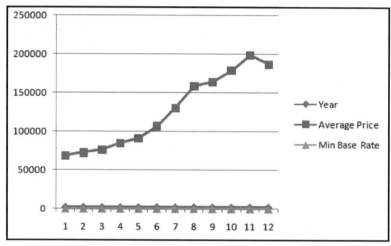

3   Remove Year from the legend and show the years 1997 to 2008 along the horizontal axis.

We covered this in: *Lesson 5-11: Create a chart with numerical axis.*

4   Select the *Min Base Rate* series.

Because the *Min Base Rate* series is in almost the same place as the horizontal axis this can be difficult with the mouse (though it is possible).

UK House Prices

You may find it easier to select the chart and then click *Series "Min Base Rate"* from:

Chart Tools→Layout→Current Selection→
Chart Elements drop down

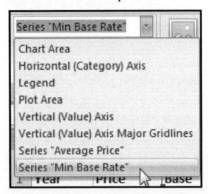

5   Move the *Min Base Rate* series to a secondary axis.

1. With the Min Base Rate series selected click
    Chart Tools→Layout→Current Selection→Format Selection

    The Format Data Series dialog is displayed.

2. Click the Secondary Axis option button and then click Close.

The chart is displayed with two vertical axes and Excel even auto-scales the new axis for you.

note

The secondary axis always appears on top of the primary axis.

You can see in the example chart that when the *Min Base Rate* series (the green line) crosses the *Average Price* series (the red line), the green line is on top.

There's no way to change the stacking order of the two lines.

6   Save your work as UK House Prices-1.

Lesson 5-18: Create a combination chart containing different chart types

Excel allows you to allocate a different chart type to each data series. This opens up many interesting possibilities such as superimposing a line chart on top of a Column chart.

In this lesson we'll re-cast the UK House Prices chart as a combination Column/Line chart with columns for house prices and a line for base interest rates.

1   Open *UK House Prices-1* from your sample files folder (if it isn't already open).

2   Select the *Average Price* data series.

   This was covered in: *Lesson 5-17: Create a chart with two vertical axis.*

3   Click Chart Tools→Design→Type→ Change Chart Type→Column→Clustered Column, and then click the OK button.

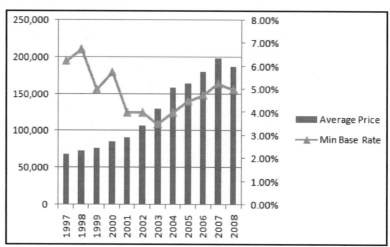

4   Adjust the Min Base Rate axis to move the series line as high as possible on the chart.

   The chart looks a little untidy as the line crosses the bars. Let's try to avoid this happening by adjusting the *Min Base Rate* series axis.

   1.   Right-click the Interest Rate's vertical axis and then select *Format Axis…* from the shortcut menu.

   2.   Click the Fixed option button next to *Maximum*.

   3.   Type **0.0675** into the text box followed by the **<Enter>** key.

   This will ensure that the line touches the top of the chart because the maximum base rate was 6.75%.

UK House Prices-1

This is very nearly the chart we need:

We can't do anything more to the *Min Base Rate* series to lift it higher.

The answer will be to adjust the *Average Price* series axis.

5　Adjust the *Average Price* axis to reduce the height of the bars.

The bars will shrink in size if we change the minimum value to 50,000 but retain the maximum value of 250,000. They would shrink even more if we also adjusted the maximum value to a figure above 250,000.

1.　Right Click the *Average Price* vertical axis and click *Format Axis...* from the shortcut menu.

2.　Click the *Fixed* option button next to *Maximum* to prevent Excel from automatically adjusting the maximum value to a lower number.

3.　Click the *Fixed* option button next to *Minimum*.

4.　Type **50000** (without a comma) into the *Minimum* text box followed by the **<Enter>** key. For some reason Excel won't recognize the number if you include a comma.

The chart now displays as intended.

6　Save your work as UK House Prices-2.

Lesson 5-19: Add a trend line

It is impossible to demonstrate empirically that a cause produces an effect. Just because the sun has risen every day since the beginning of the Earth does not mean that it will rise again tomorrow. However; it is impossible to go about one's life without assuming such connections, and the best that we can do is to maintain an open mind and never presume that we know any laws of causality for certain.

David Hume (1711-1776),
Scottish philosopher, economist, and historian.
From "An Enquiry Concerning Human Understanding".

Trend analysis applies the science of mathematics to the art of fortune telling.

If a value has been increasing for a long time, trend analysis would suggest that it will go on increasing. Some would say that the reverse is true, but Excel remains healthily optimistic that we can predict the future from the past!

Excel provides several different types of trend analysis. We're going to use a linear trend line and a two-period moving average to decide whether it is a good idea to buy a house this year!

1   Open *UK House Prices-2* from your sample files folder (if it isn't already open).

2   Remove the *Min Base Rate* data series.

   This was covered in: *Lesson 5-9: Change source data using the Select Data Source dialog tools.*

3   Change the chart type from *Clustered Column* to *Line with Markers*.

   Activate the chart and then click

   Chart Tools→Design→Type→Change Chart Type→
   Line with Markers

4   Add a linear trend line to forecast where property prices will be in the year 2012.

   1.   Click the chart to activate it.

   2.   Click Chart Tools→Layout→Analysis→Trendline→
        More Trendline Options…

        The Format Trendline dialog is displayed.

   3.   As 2012 is 4 periods after 2008 enter 4 in the *Forecast Forward* text box and then click the Close button.

Forecast		
Forward:	4.0	periods
Backward:	0.0	periods

UK House Prices-2

Excel confidently predicts that that the house you buy for 187K this year will bring you back a cool quarter of a million in four years time (though David Hume would advise you not to bet on it).

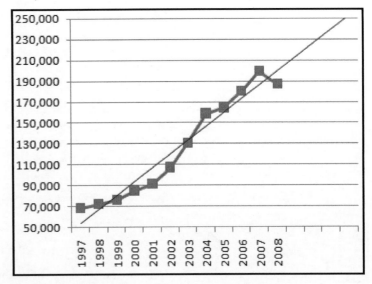

5   Remove the trend line.

Activate the chart and click:

Chart Tools→Layout→Analysis→Trendline→None.

6   Add a two period moving average.

Moving averages are one of the most loved instruments of speculators who predict the future values of shares, currencies and commodities based entirely upon charts. The theory is that when the moving average crosses the price line it is time to get out.

1.   Activate the chart.

2.   Click: Chart Tools→Layout→Analysis→Trendline→ Two Period Moving Average.

This time the analysis shows that, for the first time in ten years, it is time to sell up because the price has crossed the moving average!

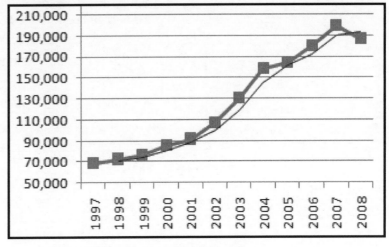

7   Save your work as UK House Prices-3.

Lesson 5-20: Switch chart rows/columns and add a gradient fill.

When a chart plots several data series it is possible to show the chart in two different ways. Transposing the rows and columns allows you to choose between these views.

When you prepare a chart for a PowerPoint presentation, or for inclusion in a high quality color publication, you want the chart to look professional and interesting. A Gradient background fill will put the finishing touch to your chart so that it looks like it was produced by a professional graphic artist.

1 Open *World Sales* from your sample files folder.

2 Create a Clustered Column chart from the entire range.

Click anywhere in the range and then click:

Insert→Charts→Column→2-D Column→Clustered Column.

The chart is created.

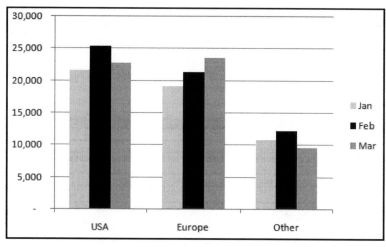

Notice that the regions (USA, Europe and Other) are situated along the horizontal axis and the months (Jan, Feb and Mar) are listed in the legend.

3 Switch Rows/Columns to transpose the Legend and Regions.

Activate the chart and then click:

Chart Tools→Design→Data→Switch Row/Column

The regions are now listed in the legend and the months are shown along the horizontal axis.

World Sales

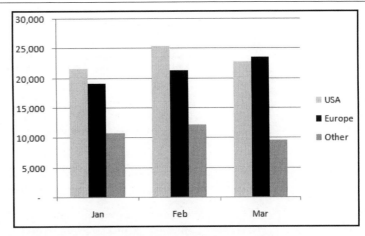

4 Add a gradient fill to the chart background.

1. Select the Chart Area element and then click:

   Chart Tools→Format→Current Selection→Format Selection

   (You could also have done this more quickly by right-clicking the Chart Area and selecting Format Chart Area… from the shortcut menu).

2. Click the Gradient Fill option button.

3. Choose one of the preset colors (I chose Parchment). As you click each fill color, notice that Live Preview displays your fill on the chart.

4. Explore the Type/Direction/Angle/Transparency and other settings until you are happy with the fill.

5. Click the Close button.

5 Set the Plot Area background to No Fill.

The chart doesn't look so good with a white plot area.

1. Select the plot area element and then click:

   Chart Tools→Format→Current Selection→Format Selection

2. Click the *No fill* option.

The chart now looks very professional with a gradient fill across the entire chart area.

6 Save your work as Gradient Fill.

Lesson 5-21: Create your own chart templates

If you use charts a lot you may find yourself applying the same fonts, fills, layouts and other attributes over and over again. If you find this happening it is time to create a chart template.

Templates can be used just like the built-in gallery charts. You can use templates to create a unique, personal, or corporate chart style that will enable you to produce consistently styled work.

In this lesson we'll develop a useful chart template with larger fonts to enable them to be more readable when incorporated into a PowerPoint presentation. We can then use this template in future for any chart that is destined to be used in a presentation.

1 Open *Gradient Fill* from your sample files folder (if it isn't already open).

2 Add a Chart Title element to the chart.

   Activate the chart and then click Chart Tools→Design→ Chart Layouts Gallery→Layout 1.

3 Increase the font size of the Chart Title element to 28 Points.

   Select the Chart Title element and then click Home→Font→Font Size Drop-Down to set the font to 28 points.

4 Increase the font size of the Vertical (Value) Axis, Horizontal (Category) Axis and Legend elements to 14 points.

   Select each element in turn and set the font in the same way as in the previous step.

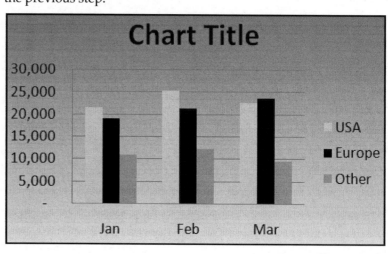

Gradient Fill

The chart now has labels that will be readable by viewers at the back of the room when projected onto a screen.

5   Save the chart design as a template.

1. Select the chart and then click:

   Chart Tools→Design→Type→Save As Template

2. Type **PowerPoint Clustered Column with Title and Gradient Fill** as the File Name.

3. Click the Save button.

6   Delete the chart.

Click once, just inside the border of the chart, to select it and then press the **<Delete>** key.

7   Create a new chart from the template.

1. Click anywhere inside the data range A1:D4.

2. Click Insert→Charts→Dialog Launcher.

The Insert Chart dialog is displayed.

3. Click the Templates category on the left of the dialog and hover the mouse cursor over the single icon displayed on the right hand side of the dialog. Notice that the tip text displays the name of the template you have just saved.

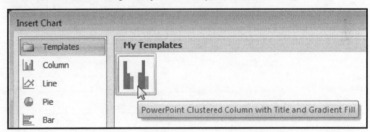

4. Either double-click the template icon, or click it once to select and then click the OK button. A chart is displayed with all of the attributes of your template.

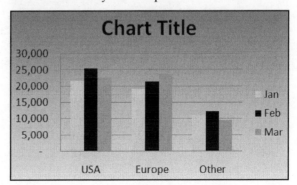

8   Save your work as PowerPoint Template.

Session 5: Exercise

1   Open the Exercise 5 file from your sample files folder.

2   Create a 2-D Clustered Column chart showing all data in the range.

       The chart will look strange at first because Excel isn't capable of automatically charting this data.

3   Switch rows and columns so that the European country names are shown in the legend.

4   Use the Select Data Source dialog to remove the year series and place the years along the Horizontal (Category) axis.

5   Change the scale of the vertical axis so that it has a minimum value of 15 and a maximum value of 50.

6   Format the legend so that a solid line black border appears around it.

7   Use the Select Data Source dialog to only show sales for the UK, Spain and Italy.

8   Increase the font size of the legend to 12 points.

9   Add a Chart Title by changing the layout of the chart to *Layout 1.*

10   Change the Chart Title text to: *European Sales.*

11   Add a gradient fill to the *Chart Area* element using the *Daybreak* preset colors.

12   Format the *Plot Area* element so that it has no fill.

13   Save your work as Exercise 5-1.

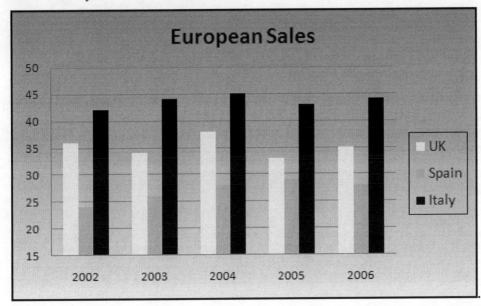

Exercise 5

If you need help slide the page to the left

Session 5: Exercise answers

These are the four questions that most students find the most difficult to remember:

Q 11	Q 7	Q 5	Q 4
1. Right-click just inside the border of the chart and click *Format Chart Area...* from the shortcut menu. 2. Click the Gradient Fill option button. 3. Choose the Daybreak preset color from the colors gallery. 5. Click the close button. This was covered in: *Lesson 5-20: Switch chart rows/columns and add a gradient fill.*	1. Right-click just inside the border of the chart and click Select Data... from the shortcut menu. 2. Click the France item in the *Legend Entries (Series)* list and then click the Remove button. 3. Click the Germany item in the *Legend Entries (Series)* list and then click the Remove button. 4. Click the OK button. This was covered in: *Lesson 5-9: Change source data using the Select Data Source dialog tools.*	1. Click the vertical axis to select it. 2. Right-Click the vertical axis and click Format Axis... from the shortcut menu. 3. Click the Fixed option buttons for the maximum and minimum values. 4. Type the value 15 in the minimum value text box and make sure that 50 is shown in the maximum value text box. 5. Click the close button. This was covered in: *Lesson 5-15: Add gridlines and scale axes.*	1. Right-click just inside the border of the chart and click *Select Data...* from the shortcut menu. 2. Click the *Year* item in the *Legend Entries (Series)* list and then click the Remove button. 3. Click the Edit button on top of the *Horizontal (Category) Axis Labels list.* 4. Select cells A4:A8. 5. Click the OK button on each dialog. This was covered in: *Lesson 5-11: Create a chart with numerical axis.*

If you have difficulty with the other questions, here are the lessons that cover the relevant skills:

1   **Refer to:** *Lesson 1-4: Open and navigate a workbook.*

2   **Refer to:** *Lesson 5-1: Create a simple chart with two clicks.*

3   **Activate the chart and then click Chart Tools→Design→Data→Switch Row/Column.**

6   **Refer to:** *Lesson 5-4: Format chart element fills and borders.*

8   **Refer to:** *Lesson 5-21: Create your own chart templates.*

9   **Refer to:** *Lesson 5-3: Change the chart layout and add a data table.*

10   **Refer to:** *Lesson 5-3: Change the chart layout and add a data table.*

12   **Refer to:** *Lesson 5-20: Switch chart rows/columns and add a gradient fill.*

13   **Refer to:** *Lesson 1-5: Save a workbook.*

Session Six: Working With Multiple Worksheets and Workbooks

> There are no big problems; there are just a lot of little problems.
>
> *Henry Ford (1863-1947)*
> *American industrialist and pioneer of assembly-line production*

Henry Ford knew that big problems are really just a lot of little problems bundled together.

Often you will find that a worksheet is getting over-complicated and difficult to work with. This session will give you the skills needed to quickly break one, very complex, worksheet into many smaller, and easier to manage, worksheets.

This session will also show you how to view different parts of large worksheets at the same time and how to create cross-worksheet formulas that summarize data from several different worksheets.

Session Objectives

By the end of this session you will be able to:

- View the same workbook in different windows
- View two windows side by side and perform synchronous scrolling
- Duplicate worksheets within a workbook
- Move and copy worksheets from one workbook to another
- Hide and unhide a worksheet
- Create cross-worksheet formulas
- Understand worksheet groups
- Use find and replace

Lesson 6-1: View the same workbook in different windows

Excel allows you to view the same worksheet in two separate worksheet windows. This is useful when you need to compare different areas of the same worksheet.

1   Close any Excel workbooks that are currently open.

2   Open *Sales First Quarter 2008* from your sample files folder.

This workbook has only one worksheet containing 242 rows of data.

3   Open a new window to see February 2008 and January 2008 sales at the same time.

Click View→Window→New Window.

Nothing seems to have happened except that the Title bar now reads: *Sales First Quarter 2008:2*

Two views of the same workbook are now open at the same time but you can only view one at a time which isn't very useful.

4   View both windows at the same time.

Click View→Window→Arrange All.

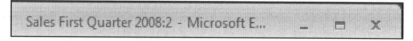

The *Arrange Windows* dialog appears:

5   Select the Horizontal option and then click the OK button.

Both windows are displayed in the window, one below the other. You are able to freely scroll to any position in either window.

Sales First Quarter 2008

In the screen grab below I've scrolled the bottom window down to see February sales:

It's important to realize that we are not looking at two different worksheets, but two different views of the same worksheet.

If you change a value in one of the views, you'll immediately see the changed value in the other.

You will now appreciate the importance of closing any open workbooks in step 1. If you had several workbooks open, you would now be viewing all of them in multiple windows.

6 Close the *Sales First Quarter 2008:2* view and maximize the *Sales First Quarter 2008:1* worksheet.

1. Click in the Sales First Quarter 2008:2 window. Notice how the title bar changes color to indicate that this is now the active window.

2. Click the close button in the top right hand corner of the worksheet.

3. Click the Maximize button in the top right-hand corner of the Sales First Quarter 2008 worksheet.

Lesson 6-2: View two windows side by side and perform synchronous scrolling

When only two workbooks are open, the *Arrange All* method covered in the previous lesson will work just fine.

It is more likely that you will have many workbooks (or views of the same workbook) open and will want to see two specific workbooks on screen at the same time.

You may sometimes be given a workbook that somebody else has changed and need to identify what has been altered. We'll use Excel's synchronous scrolling feature to make this task easier.

1   Close any Excel workbooks that are currently open.

2   Open *Exercise 6* from your sample files folder.

3   Open *Sales First Quarter 2008 Revised* from your sample files folder.

4   Open *Sales First Quarter 2008* from your sample files folder.

Only the last workbook opened: *Sales First Quarter 2008* is visible on screen:

5   Click View→Window→View Side By Side.

The Compare Side By Side dialog is displayed:

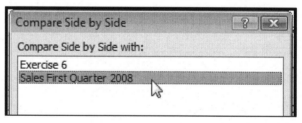

6   Select *Sales First Quarter 2008 Revised* as the workbook you want to view with the current workbook and then click the **<OK>** button.

The workbooks should display one above the other.

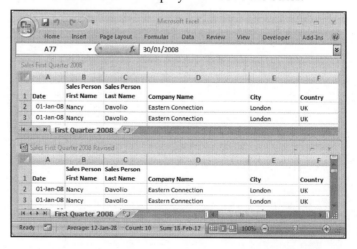

Sales First Quarter 2008

Sales First Quarter 2008 Revised

Exercise 6

If you don't see this, click:

View→Window→Reset Window Position

This is often needed when the workbooks are not maximized within the Excel application window.

You also need to do this after re-sizing the Excel application window.

7   Unlock the windows so that they no longer scroll together.

1.   Click View→Window→Synchronous Scrolling to switch synchronous scrolling off. You are now able to freely scroll each window independently.

2.   Scroll each window to the top (so that row 1 is at the top of each window).

3.   Click View→Window→Synchronous Scrolling to switch synchronous scrolling back on so that both windows automatically scroll together.

8   Identify differences between the two workbooks.

1.   Scroll one of the windows and notice that both windows now scroll together.

2.   Scroll down so that you can see row 77. Notice that row 78 has gone out of synchronization because one of the 29-Jan-08 sales to Hungry Owl has been deleted from the *Revised* workbook.

9   Re-synchronize the windows.

1.   Click View→Window→Synchronous Scrolling to switch Synchronous Scrolling off.

2.   Scroll so that the first transaction on 30th Jan 2008 is on the first row in both windows.

3.   Click View→Window→Synchronous Scrolling to switch Synchronous Scrolling back on.

10   Close all open workbooks without saving.

Lesson 6-3: Duplicate worksheets within a workbook

In this lesson we're going to disassemble a large worksheet and make it into three smaller worksheets.

You'll often find that data is easier to work with if you divide it into logically separated sections.

1   Open *Sales First Quarter 2008* from your sample files folder.

This workbook shows all sales completed in January, February and March 2008. Our task will be to split them into separate months.

2   Create a new worksheet and name it *January*.

This skill was covered in *Lesson 1-7: View, add, rename, delete and navigate worksheet tabs*.

3   Select every cell in the *First Quarter 2008* worksheet.

1.   Click the *First Quarter 2008* worksheet tab.

There's a special button at the top left corner of every worksheet called the *Select All* button.

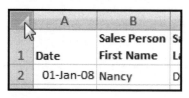

2.   Click the *Select All* button to select every cell in the worksheet.

4   Copy all selected cells.

The easiest way to do this is to right-click within the selected range and then select Copy from the shortcut menu.

5   Paste the copied cells into the January worksheet beginning at cell A1.

Click the January tab, right-click in cell A1 and select Paste from the shortcut menu.

6   Create another copy of the worksheet using *Move or Copy*.

Excel provides a simpler way to duplicate a worksheet.

1.   Right-click the First Quarter 2008 worksheet tab and choose *Move or Copy* from the shortcut menu.

The Move or Copy dialog appears.

2.   Select *(move to end)* in the *Before sheet* list.

3.   Check the *Create a copy* check box.

4.   Click the *OK* button.

Note

Other ways to select all cells.

Select All is a very common requirement and it is well worth remembering the keyboard shortcut:

<Ctrl>+<A>

It's a shortcut I use every day!

Sales First Quarter 2008

Notice that Excel has named the new worksheet: *First Quarter 2008 (2)*.

7 Change the name of the new worksheet to *February*.

This skill was covered in *Lesson 1-7: View, add, rename, delete and navigate worksheet tabs*.

8 Create another copy of the worksheet using *drag and drop*.

There's an even quicker way to create a duplicate worksheet.

1. Click once on the First Quarter 2008 tab to select it.

2. Hold down the **<Ctrl>** key.

3. Click and hold the mouse button on the *First Quarter 2008* tab.

The cursor changes shape to a page with a plus sign:

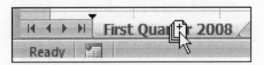

4. Drag to the right until you see a black insertion arrow to the right of the February tab.

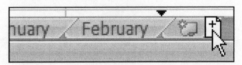

When you release the mouse button another copy of the worksheet is created.

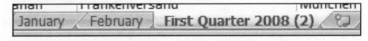

9 Change the name of the new worksheet to *March*.

10 Remove rows from the January, February and March workbooks so that only the named month's transactions remain.

This was covered in: *Lesson 3-1: Insert and delete rows and columns*.

11 Save your work as Sales First Quarter 2008-1.

Lesson 6-4: Move and copy worksheets from one workbook to another

In *Lesson 6-3: Duplicate worksheets within a workbook* we worked with a single workbook.

It is also possible to move and copy worksheets between workbooks using the same technique.

1   Close any workbooks that are currently open.

2   Open *Sales First Quarter 2008-1* from your sample files folder (if it isn't already open).

3   Open *First Quarter Sales and Bonus* from your sample files folder.

4   Click View→Window→ Arrange All to arrange the windows horizontally in the Excel window.

> This was covered in: *Lesson 2-2: Create a new workbook and view two workbooks at the same time.*

The two workbooks are now shown together.

First Quarter Sales and Bonus

Sales First Quarter 2008-1

5   Rename *Sheet1* in the *First Quarter Sales and Bonus* workbook to *Bonus*.

> This was covered in: *Lesson 1-7: View, add, rename, delete and navigate worksheet tabs.*

6   Hold down the **<Ctrl>** key and drag and drop the *Bonus* sheet from the *First Quarter Sales and Bonus* workbook to the *Sales First Quarter 2008-1* workbook.

A copy of the *Bonus* worksheet is created in the *Sales First Quarter 2008-1* workbook.

7   Drag and drop the *Sheet3* worksheet from the *First Quarter Sales and Bonus* workbook to the *Sales First Quarter 2008-1* workbook.

You will have to click the *First Quarter Sales and Bonus* workbook once to activate it before you can drag and drop the sheet tab.

This time, because you didn't hold the **<Ctrl>** key down, the worksheet is moved rather than copied.

8   Change the name of the moved worksheet to *Summary*.

This skill was covered in: *Lesson 1-7: View, add, rename, delete and navigate worksheet tabs.*

9   If necessary, move the worksheet tabs in the *Sales First Quarter 2008-1* workbook so that they appear in the following order:

This skill was covered in: *Lesson 1-7: View, add, rename, delete and navigate worksheet tabs.*

| First Quarter 2008 | January | February | March | **Summary** | Bonus |

10   Maximize the Sales First Quarter 2008-1 workbook window.

This was covered in: *Lesson 1-3: Understand the Application and Workbook windows.*

11   Save your work as Sales First Quarter 2008-2.

Lesson 6-5: Hide and unhide a worksheet

Sometimes you'll want to prevent users from viewing and changing one or more worksheets.

In this case you will want to hide the worksheet.

A hidden worksheet becomes invisible to the user but is still there. You can bring back hidden worksheets by unhiding them.

1   Open *Sales First Quarter 2008-2* from your sample files folder (if it isn't already open).

In this workbook you may not want viewers to see the *First Quarter 2008* worksheet as the information is already contained in the *January/February/March* worksheets.

You might also want to hide the Bonus worksheet as it contains confidential information.

2   Select the *First Quarter 2008* and *Bonus* worksheets.

1. Click on the *First Quarter 2008* worksheet tab.

2. Hold down the **<Ctrl>** key.

3. Click on the *Bonus* worksheet tab.

Both worksheet tabs should now appear slightly lighter than the others:

First Quarter 2008 / January / February / March / Summary / Bonus /

3   Hide the *First Quarter 2008* and *Bonus* worksheets.

The easiest way to do this is to right click either of the selected tabs and then click *Hide* from the shortcut menu.

The worksheets vanish.

January / February / March / Summary /

It's also possible to do this from the Ribbon less efficiently (see sidebar).

Sales First Quarter 2008-2

note

Hiding and unhiding a worksheet using the Ribbon

The right-click method is far faster than using the Ribbon but here's how it can be done:

To hide a worksheet:

Click Home→Cells→
Format→
Hide & Unhide→
Hide Sheet

To Unhide a worksheet:

Click Home→Cells→
Format→
Hide & Unhide→
Unhide Sheet

Then select the sheet you want to hide/unhide from the dialog and click the OK button.

important

Don't rely on hidden worksheets for security.

There is no password associated with hiding and unhiding a worksheet. A knowledgeable user can easily unhide any hidden worksheets.

It is possible to protect the structure before distributing a workbook. When this is done it isn't possible to unhide and view the worksheet unless you know the password.

This topic is fully covered in the *Expert Skills* book in this series in which a whole session is dedicated to security.

4   Unhide the bonus worksheet.

Excel will never allow you to hide all worksheets so this method will always work.

1.   Right-click on any of the visible worksheet tabs.

2.   Click *Unhide* from the shortcut menu.

The Unhide dialog is displayed:

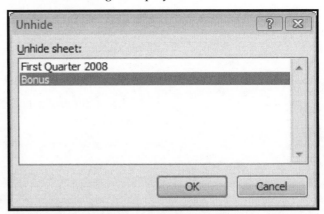

3.   Click *Bonus* and then click the OK button

You can also unhide the worksheets less efficiently using the Ribbon (see sidebar).

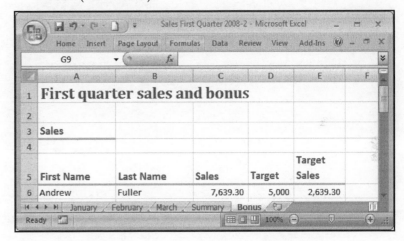

5   Save your work as Sales First Quarter 2008-3.

Lesson 6-6: Create cross worksheet formulas

You'll often want to summarize information from multiple worksheets within a workbook.

This can be done by simply prefixing the cell reference with the worksheet name followed by an exclamation mark.

1   Open *Sales First Quarter 2008-3* from your sample files folder (if it isn't already open).

2   Select the January tab and scroll to the bottom of the range.

3   Type the word **Total:** into the first empty cell in column G (cell G87).

4   Right-Align the cell.

This was covered in: *Lesson 4-5: Horizontally align the contents of cells.*

5   Bold-face row 87.

This was covered in: *Lesson 1-11: Use the Mini Toolbar, Key Tips and keyboard shortcuts.*

6   Use AutoSum to add totals to columns H and J.

This was covered in: *Lesson 2-3: Use AutoSum to quickly calculate totals.*

	G	H	I	J
85	Gumbär Gummibärchen	10	24.90	249.00
86	Tourtière	40	5.90	236.00
87	Total:	**2,401**		**66,692.80**

7   Add similar totals to the February and March worksheets.

8   Select the Summary tab.

9   Type the text: **First Quarter Summary** into cell A1 and apply the *Title* cell style.

This was covered in: *Lesson 4-9: Use cell styles and change themes.*

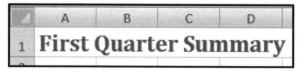

10   Type **Month**, **Units** and **Price** into cells A3, B3 and C3.

11   Type **Jan** into cell A4 and then AutoFill down two cells to add Feb and Mar.

This was covered in: *Lesson 2-14: Use AutoFill for text and numeric series.*

12   Apply the *Heading 2* style to cells A3:C3.

Sales First Quarter 2008-3

13 Apply the *Heading 4* style to cells A4:A6.

	A	B	C	D
1	**First Quarter Summary**			
2				
3	**Month**	**Units**	**Price**	
4	Jan			
5	Feb			
6	Mar			

14 Add a formula to cell B4 to display the total units sold in January.

1. Click cell B4.

2. Press the equals key on your keyboard (**=**) to begin a formula.

3. Click on the January tab.

4. Scroll to the bottom of the screen using the scroll bars or arrow keys being careful not to click on any cell.

5. Click on cell H87 (the cell with the total in it).

6. Press the **<Enter>** key on the keyboard.

The total is shown on the summary sheet.

	Month	Units	Price
3	**Month**	**Units**	**Price**
4	Jan	2401	

15 Use the same technique to add summary totals to **Units** and **Price** for all three months.

	Month	Units	Price
3	**Month**	**Units**	**Price**
4	Jan	2401	66,692.80
5	Feb	2132	41,207.20
6	Mar	1770	39,979.90

16 Note the formulas that Excel has created.

Click cell B4 and then look at the formula bar at the top of the screen. Note that the formula is:

		f_x	=January!H87	
	A	B	C	
3	**Month**	**Units**	**Price**	
4	Jan	2401	66,692.80	

The formula is simply the worksheet name, followed by an exclamation mark, followed by the cell reference.

Note the important sidebar information regarding worksheet names that contain spaces.

17 Save your work as Sales First Quarter 2008-4.

---

important

You must use quotation marks if a worksheet name contains spaces.

The example worksheet names used in this session do not contain any spaces.

If you had a worksheet called *January Sales* you would have to construct your formula like this:

='January Sales'!K22

Because worksheet names with spaces are more difficult to work with, many Excel users prefer to name their sheets without spaces by capitalizing the first letter of every word.

Example:

JanuarySales
EuropeIncludingSouthAfrica

---

note

Selecting non-contiguous worksheets

Non-contiguous simply means *not next to each other*.

When the worksheet tabs aren't next to each other, hold down the **<Ctrl>** key and click each in turn. If you make a mistake you can **<Ctrl>+<Click>** a second time to de-select one tab.

You can be even cleverer and use a combination of **<Shift>+<Click>** and **<Ctrl>+<Click>** when some of the tabs are next to each other and others are not.

Widget Supplies Price List

Lesson 6-7: Understand worksheet groups

A very interesting (and little known) feature of Excel is its ability to group worksheets into a three-dimensional array of worksheet cells.

When worksheets are grouped, it is possible to perform a single operation upon all of the worksheets in the group. This can be very useful when you need to:

- Print out all of the worksheets in the group.

- Enter data into the same cell for all worksheets in the group.

- Apply formatting to the same cell or range for all worksheets in the group.

1   Open *Widget Supplies Price List* from your sample files folder.

The formatting of this workbook leaves a lot to be desired. It consists of three worksheets all showing the same information but lacking any style.

	A	B	C	D	E	F	G
1	Price List						
2	Prices Effe	20th March 2008					
3	When calculating prices the following exchange rates will be used						
4							
5		USD	GBP	EUR	JPY		
6	USD	1	1.8383	1.4708	0.00911		
7							
8	Descriptic	Dollars	Pounds	Euros	Yen		
9	Standard \	3.75	2.039928	2.549633	411.6356		
10	Premium	5.5	2.991895	3.739462	603.7322		
11	De-luxe g	7.95	4.324648	5.405222	872.6674		
12							

We're going to use the magic of grouping to format all three worksheets at the same time.

2   Select all three worksheets to create a worksheet group.

1.   Click the Widgets worksheet tab.

2.   Hold down the **<Shift>** key and click the Sprockets worksheet tab.

All three tabs now have a white background to show that they are selected.

| ▶| | **Widgets** | Grommets | Sprockets |

Something else has also happened. The bar at the top of the screen now indicates that the worksheets form a worksheet group.

3   Apply formatting to the Sprockets worksheet to make it look attractive.

When you have grouped every worksheet in a workbook, you have a little problem. You can't switch between worksheets and still keep the group selected. As soon as you click a selected sheet the other two are de-selected.

To work-around this we'll have to insert a new blank worksheet. The sheet's only purpose is to allow you to switch between sheets in the selected group.

1. Add a worksheet called *dummy*.

2. Select the Widgets, Grommets and Sprockets group as before.

3. Click on the Sprockets tab. The group remains selected and the Sprockets worksheet is now active.

4. Apply the comma style to the range B9:E11. This was covered in: *Lesson 4-3: Format numbers using built-in number formats.*

5. Adjust the widths of all columns so that they fully display their contents. *This was covered in: Lesson 2-9: Re-size rows and columns.*

6. Apply the *Title* style to cell A1, the *Heading 4* style to cells A2, A6 and A9:A11 and the *Heading 3* style to cells B5:E5 and A8:E8. This was covered in: *Lesson 4-9: Use cell styles and change themes.*

7. Adjust the height of rows 2, 3 and 4 to tidy the top part of the price list.

8. Click on each of the other two tabs to ensure that columns are also wide enough for their content. Adjust if needed.

	A	B	C	D	E
1	**Price List**				
2	Prices Effective:		20th March 2008		
3	When calculating prices the following exchange rates will be used				
5		USD	GBP	EUR	JPY
6	USD	1	1.8383	1.4708	0.00911
7					
8	Description	Dollars	Pounds	Euros	Yen
9	Standard widget	3.75	2.04	2.55	411.64
10	Premium widget	5.50	2.99	3.74	603.73
11	De-luxe gold plated widget	7.95	4.32	5.41	872.67

4   With the group still selected, change some exchange rates and the *Prices Effective* date.

I saved the best bit for last. You can now update all three price lists at the same time. This would be needed as exchange rates fluctuate. When a group of worksheets are selected, any change made to one worksheet is also made in all of the others.

5   Save your work as Widget Supplies Price List-1.

Lesson 6-8: Use find and replace

note

Other ways to display the Find and Replace dialog.

Find

Use the <Ctrl>+<F> keyboard shortcut.

Replace

Use the <Ctrl>+<H> keyboard shortcut.

Excel's find and replace tool is amazingly powerful. There are several bells and whistles that can massively shorten many common requirements.

This lesson will explore all of the features and suggest useful ways in which they can be used to solve real-world problems.

1   Open *Sales First Quarter 2008-4* from your sample files folder (if it isn't already open).

2   Use *Find and Replace* to change the text *Davolio* to *O'Reilly* throughout the workbook.

Nancy Davolio has married Sean O'Reilly and she is very proud of her new name. She's made a special request for you to change her name in the workbook too!

1.   Click Home→Editing→Find & Select→Replace. The Find and replace dialog is displayed.

2.   Type **Davolio** in the *Find what:* text box and **O'Reilly** in the *Replace with:* text box.

3.   Click the Options>> button.

We don't want to only look in the current worksheet but in all of the worksheets in this workbook so select the *Within: Workbook* option.

4.   Click the *Find Next* button. The first instance of *Davolio* is found on the worksheet.

5.   Click the Replace button to replace just this one instance. The cursor moves to the next instance found.

note

Searching only part of a workbook.

If you select a single cell, *Find and Replace* will search the entire worksheet.

If you select a range of cells, *Find and Replace* will only search within that range.

6.   Click Replace All to replace all remaining instances of *Davolio* with *O'Reilly*. Excel prompts that it has made 28 replacements.

7.   Check out the worksheets. Notice that Nancy's surname has now changed in every worksheet.

Sales First Quarter 2008-4

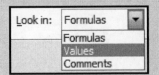
3   Apply the *Good* style to cell G21 on the *January* worksheet.

Click cell G21 to select and then click:

Home→Styles→Cell Styles→Good

The *Good* cell style has a light green background and a dark green foreground.

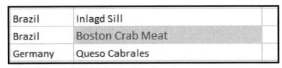

4   Apply the same style to every other mention of *Boston Crab Meat* in the workbook.

1. With cell G21 still visible on the workbook click:

   Home→Editing→Find & Select→Replace

2. Type **Boston Crab Meat** in the *Find what:* text box.

3. Click the Format button alongside *Replace with:* and select *Choose format from cell…* from the drop-down menu.

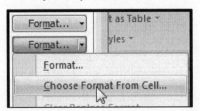

(It is really important that you click the lower of the two Format buttons. If you get it wrong click Format→Clear Find Format to start again).

The cursor shape changes to an eye-dropper. Click on cell G21.

The same format now appears in the *Replace with:* format text box on the Find and Replace dialog

4. Click *Replace All* to re-format all instances of *Boston Crab Meat* to the *Good* cell style. Excel advises that it has changed the format of seven cells.

5. Check out all of the worksheets and notice that every cell containing the text *Boston Crab Meat* has now turned green.

5   Save your work as Sales First Quarter 2008-5.

Session 6: Exercise

1   Close any workbooks that are open.

2   Open *Exercise 6* from your sample files folder.

This spreadsheet shows sales to the USA and UK during the first quarter of 2008.

3   View two copies of the worksheet in the same window and scroll one of the windows so that the first USA sale is visible in the first row.

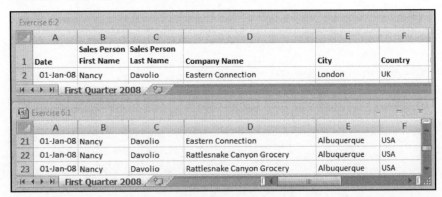

4   Close the *Exercise 6:2* window and maximize the *Exercise 6:1* window.

5   Make two duplicate copies of the First Quarter 2008 worksheet and name them *USA* and *UK*.

6   Delete all of the non USA rows from the USA worksheet and all of the non UK rows from the UK worksheet.

7   Hide the *First Quarter 2008* worksheet tab.

8   Use AutoSum to create a total at the bottom of Columns H and J (Quantity and Total) for both the *USA* and *UK* worksheets.

9   Add a new worksheet and name it *Summary*.

10 Create a summary sheet as illustrated below using cross-worksheet formulas to calculate the totals.

	A	B	C	D	E
1	**USA and UK Sales Summary**				
2					
3	Country	Units	Sales		
4	USA	913	26,572.20		
5	UK	379	7,299.40		
6	Total	1292	33,871.60		

11 Save your work as Exercise 6-End.

Exercise 6

If you need help slide the page to the left

Session 6: Exercise answers

These are the four questions that most students find the most difficult to remember:

Q 9	Q 6	Q 4	Q 3
In the example the following styles were used: A1 Title A3:C3 Heading 2 A4:A5 Heading 4 A6:C6 Total 1. Click cell B4 and type an equals sign into it (=). 2. Click the USA tab. 3. Use the scroll bars to make the total cell (cell H27) visible being careful not to click in the cell area. 4. Click cell H27 and then press the **<Enter>** key. This was covered in: *Lesson 6-6: Create cross worksheet formulas.*	1. Right-click the *First Quarter 2008* worksheet tab. 2. Click *Hide* on the shortcut menu. This was covered in: *Lesson 6-5: Hide and unhide a worksheet.*	1. Click on the *First Quarter 2008* worksheet tab to select it. 2. Hold down the **<Ctrl>** key. 3. Click and drag the *First Quarter 2008* worksheet tab to the right. 4. Double-click the duplicated worksheet's tab and type the tab's new name. This was covered in: *Lesson 6-3: Duplicate worksheets within a workbook.*	1. Click View→Window→ New Window. 2. Click View→Window→ Arrange All. 3. Click the *horizontal* option in the *Arrange Windows* dialog. 4. Click the OK button. 5. Scroll one of the windows to the first USA sale (Row 21). This was covered in: *Lesson 6-1: View the same workbook in different windows.*

If you have difficulty with the other questions, here are the lessons that cover the relevant skills:

1   Refer to: Lesson 1-2: Maximize, minimize, re-size, move and close the Excel window.

2   Refer to: Lesson 1-4: Open and navigate a workbook.

5   Refer to: Lesson 3-1: Insert and delete rows and columns.

7   Refer to: Lesson 2-3: Use AutoSum to quickly calculate totals.

8   Refer to: Lesson 1-7: View, add, rename, delete and navigate worksheet tabs.

10   Refer to: Lesson 1-5: Save a workbook.

Session Seven: Printing Your Work

> The greatest misfortune that ever befell man was the invention of printing.
>
> *Benjamin Disraeli, British Prime Minister and Novelist (1804-1881).*

As we move towards the paperless office printing will become less important.

In the last year or so, screen and rendering technology have improved to the extent that I now prefer to read on-screen rather than from paper.

Perhaps we are not far from the time when all communication will be done electronically, but we're not quite there yet.

Excel has a range of tools that will allow you to present your work as polished and professional printed reports. This session will give you all of the skills you need to control every aspect of printing your work on paper.

Session Objectives

By the end of this session you will be able to:

- Print Preview and change paper orientation
- Use page layout to adjust margins
- Use Page Setup to set margins more precisely and center the worksheet
- Set paper size and scale
- Insert, delete and preview page breaks
- Adjust page breaks using Page Break Preview
- Add auto-headers and auto-footers and set starting page number
- Add custom headers and footers
- Specify different headers and footers for the first, odd and even pages
- Print only part of a worksheet
- Add row and column data labels and grid lines to printed output
- Print several selected worksheets and change the page order
- Suppress error messages in printouts

Lesson 7-1: Print Preview and change paper orientation

1   Open *Sales Report* from your sample files folder.

Make sure that you open the Session 7 Sales Report file a there's also a sample file of the same name in an earlier session.

2   Print Preview the worksheet to see how it will look on paper.

1.   Click Office→Print→Print Preview.

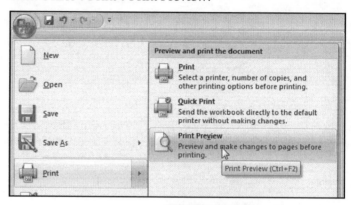

2.   Click the Next page button 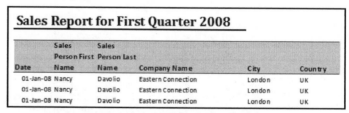 to page through the document.

Notice that the paper isn't wide enough to show all of the columns. Excel tries to help out by printing the columns across two pages.

Sales Report for First Quarter 2008

Date	Sales Person First Name	Sales Person Last Name	Company Name	City	Country
01-Jan-08	Nancy	Davolio	Eastern Connection	London	UK
01-Jan-08	Nancy	Davolio	Eastern Connection	London	UK
01-Jan-08	Nancy	Davolio	Eastern Connection	London	UK

Product Name	Qty	Unit Price	Total
Thüringer Rostbratwurst	21	99.00	2,079.00
Steeleye Stout	35	14.40	504.00
Maxilaku	30	16.00	480.00

You would have to take the two pages, cut them with scissors, and tape them together in order to see all of the rows and columns.

3   Close the Print Preview view.

Click the Close Print Preview button on the toolbar.

Sales Report

4   Change the paper orientation to Landscape in order to print more columns on each sheet of paper.

Click: Page Layout→Page Setup→Orientation→Landscape.

In Landscape orientation the paper is printed as if it had been put into the printer sideways.

5   Print Preview again to see how the report looks in landscape orientation.

The printout is very nearly there now. We still have a problem with the last column which prints out all on its own.

Sales Report for First Quarter 2008

Date	Sales Person First Name	Sales Person Last Name	Company Name	City	Country	Product Name	Qty	Unit Price
01-Jan-08	Nancy	Davolio	Eastern Connection	London	UK	Thüringer Rostbratwurst	21	99.00
01-Jan-08	Nancy	Davolio	Eastern Connection	London	UK	Steeleye Stout	35	14.40
01-Jan-08	Nancy	Davolio	Eastern Connection	London	UK	Maxilaku	30	16.00

Total
2,079.00
504.00
480.00

6   Close Print Preview view.

Notice that after you have executed a Print Preview on a worksheet, the page breaks are indicated by thin dotted lines.

Qty	Unit Price	Total
21	99.00	2,079.00

7   Print a copy of the worksheet with Quick Print.

If you'd like to save the forests (and save the cost of sixteen sheets of paper) you may wish to skip this step.

Click Office→Print→Quick Print.

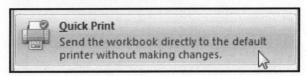

Quick Print
Send the workbook directly to the default printer without making changes.

Even if you didn't actually print the sheet, I'm sure you will believe that the print out would not have been very good. You'd be back to the scissors and tape if you wanted the pages to show that missing last column.

Quick Print will print in Landscape orientation because you've told Excel to do that.

By default, Quick Print will print one copy of the currently selected worksheet in portrait orientation and apply the default margins.

8   Save your work as Sales Report-1.

Lesson 7-2: Use page layout view to adjust margins

Page Layout view is a brand new feature for Excel 2007.

It's a bit like Print Preview as you can see just how your page prints. The big difference is that, unlike Print Preview, you can edit a worksheet in this view. You can also set up many page layout features including margins, headers and footers and page numbering.

We'll be exploring all of this view's features in coming lessons. This lesson will focus upon changing the page margins (the blank areas at the top, bottom, left and right of the printout).

1   Open *Sales Report-1* from your sample files folder (if it isn't already open).

2   Display page layout view.

> The fastest way to do this is to click the *Page Layout* button on the status bar at the bottom right of the screen.

> You can also do this from the Ribbon by clicking:
>
> View→Workbook Views→Page Layout
>
> Page layout shows almost exactly how the worksheet will print.

> The missing Total problem is immediately obvious.

3   Make sure the rulers are on display.

> Unless you've turned them off, you'll see a ruler at the top and left of the page that contains the active cell.
>
> Click cell A1, to make it the active cell, and look for the rulers.

Sales Report-1

note

Changing ruler units to inches, centimeters or millimeters.

1. Click: Office Button→
Excel Options→
Advanced→Display→
Ruler Units.

2. Select *Inches, Centimeters* or *Millimeters* from the *Ruler Units* drop-down list.

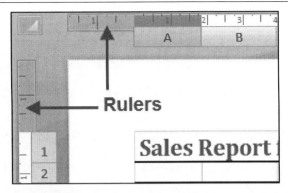

If you don't see the rulers switch them on by clicking:

View→Show/Hide→Ruler.

4   Adjust the left and right margins using the rulers.

1. Hover the mouse cursor over the ruler at the point directly above the left-hand side of the column A header.

   The cursor shape changes to a double headed arrow and the current left-hand margin size is displayed.

2. When you see the double-headed arrow, click and drag to the left to reduce the margin to about one centimeter. You'll probably find it impossible to set exactly 1.0 centimeters with this method and will have to settle for 1.01.

   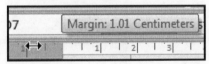

3. Repeat the same operation to adjust the right hand margin to about one centimeter.

   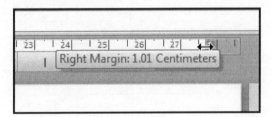

   All of the columns now fit onto one page. Notice that even though the margins are equal, the right hand margin seems too wide. That's because the printout is not (yet) centered on the page.

5   Save your work as Sales Report-2.

note

Can I change the default margin settings?

You can set the default margins, and any other Excel default setting, by changing the default template.

1. Create a template consisting of a blank worksheet with the margins set to the required value.

   Creating templates was covered in: *Lesson 3-14: Create a template.*

2. Save the template to the Excel startup folder with the name Book.xlt.

More information is provided in the sidebar "Can I Change the Default Theme?" in: *Lesson 4-8: Understand themes.*

Lesson 7-3: Use Page Setup to set margins more precisely and center the worksheet

In the last lesson you adjusted the margins using the rulers, and that's often the best way. It is quick and easy and you can immediately see the results of the change on the printed output.

Sometimes you will want the pages in your report to have precise margins. This would be the case when you were going to insert the report into another report (perhaps prepared in Word) and you need the margins to be consistent throughout the publication.

Another common requirement is the need to center the report on the printed page.

1   Open *Sales Report-2* from your sample files folder (if it isn't already open).

2   Display page layout view (if you aren't already in it).

This was covered in: *Lesson 7-2: Use page layout view to adjust margins.*

3   Click Page Layout→Page Setup→Margins.

A rich menu appears showing three standard margin setups along with the last custom margins applied.

Sales Report-2

4 Click the Narrow option to apply left and right margins of 0.64cm.

Notice that all of the margins have now changed to the *Narrow* specification.

5 Set a custom left and right margin of exactly one centimeter.

Let's imagine that this report will be bound within another that uses margins of one centimeter.

Since there's no preset we'll have to apply the margins manually using the *Custom Margins* options.

1. Click:

   Page Layout→Page Setup→Margins→Custom Margins…

   The Page Setup dialog appears with the Margins tab selected.

2. Type directly into the text boxes, or use the spin buttons, to set the left and right margins to exactly one centimeter.

3. Click the OK button.

6 Horizontally center the printout on the page.

The page would look better centered.

1. Bring up the Print Layout dialog again by clicking:

   Page Layout→Page Setup→Margins→Custom Margins…

2. Check the *Center on page Horizontally* check box.

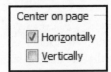

3. Click the OK button.

   The page is now perfectly centered, both on the screen and on any hard copy printed.

7 Save your work as Sales Report-3.

Lesson 7-4: Set paper size and scale

Let's imagine that Landscape mode isn't an option for you.

You need portrait mode and you simply must get all of the columns on each page.

There's only two ways you can achieve this.

1. Buy some bigger paper. As long as your printer can accept it you will have a larger area upon which to print.

2. Print everything in a smaller font.

The second option often works well (as long as you have good eyesight).

You'll be relieved to know that you don't have to manually re-format every font on the page. You can automatically scale the existing fonts to fit.

1   Open *Sales Report-3* from your sample files folder (if it isn't already open).

2   Display page layout view (if you aren't already in it).

This was covered in: *Lesson 7-2: Use page layout view to adjust margins.*

3   Change the paper orientation back to portrait.

This was covered in: *Lesson 7-1: Print Preview and change paper orientation.*

Notice that the columns do not fit upon one sheet of paper.

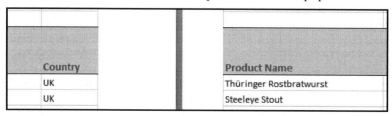

4   Change the paper size to A3.

You will not see an A3 printer option if there are no printer drivers installed on your machine that support A3 (see sidebar).

Click Page Layout→Page Setup→Size→A3.

In the USA and Canada the nearest equivalent of A3 is ANSI B 17X11 (see sidebar on the facing page for more on this). You should still set the size to A3 for the purposes of this lesson.

That works fine. All columns now fit across one sheet of A3 paper.

But what if you don't have an A3 printer, or if the report has to fit on a sheet of A4 (or Letter sized) paper?

5   Change the paper size to A4.

Everywhere in the world except the USA and Canada the normal business letter size is A4.

important

The paper sizes that are available depend upon the printers installed on your machine.

Excel sensibly restricts your choice of page sizes to those that are supported by your printer(s).

If you do not have a printer driver installed that supports A3 paper you will not see this in the list when you click:

Page Layout→Page Setup→ Size

Sales Report-3

trivia

A4 and Letter paper size.

A long time ago everybody used different sizes of paper until the Germans produced a DIN standard (Din 476) in 1922.

So good and great was their DIN standard (that defined the familiar A0, A1, A2, A3, A4 sizes) that it was gradually adopted by every country in the world except the United States and Canada. It is also the official United Nations document format.

As Din 476 was now a world standard, it was ratified in 1975 as ISO 216.

The genius behind the guiding principle of ISO 216 was the German scientist George Lichtenburg (1742-1799). George noticed that if a sheet of paper with an aspect ratio of the square root of two was folded in half, each half would also have the same aspect ratio.

The wonderful thing about this system is that paper merchants only need stock one size of paper (A0) to be able to cut A1, A2, A3, A4...A8 without any waste. It also means that a document designed in any A size will perfectly scale to all other sizes in the series.

A0 has an area of 1 square metre. Fold it in half and you have A1. Fold that in half for A2, then in half again for A3 and so on.

The USA and Canada are the only major countries that use a different system.

In 1995 the American National Standards institute defined a series of paper sizes based upon 8.5"X11" *Letter sized* paper. Unlike the ISO standard, the arbitrary size means that the series has alternating aspect ratios for other derivative sizes.

The ANSI A size (8.5X11) is the nearest to ISO A4 and the ANSI B size (17X11) is nearest to A3.

In America the slightly narrower and longer Letter size (or ANSI A) is the most common.

6 Make the report fit on a sheet of A4 by scaling the print.

Click the Page Layout→Scale to Fit→Scale spin button. Each time you reduce the percentage the worksheet shrinks until it fits the page at about 70%.

Bear in mind that even though it fits the page, it may not be very easy to read at such a small type size.

Another method of achieving the same result would have been to set the Width to one page.

The advantage of this approach is that the content will perfectly fit between the page margins. This will look better and will avoid the need to center the printout on the page.

7 Save your work as Sales Report-4.

Lesson 7-5: Insert, delete and preview page breaks

note

If you don't see the dotted line page breaks, somebody has switched them off.

By default, page breaks are shown as dotted lines in Normal view.

Like so many features in Excel, Microsoft has given users the ability to switch this feature off, though I can't imagine why anybody would want to.

If you don't see the dotted lines then somebody has done just that on your machine.

To bring the dotted lines back click:

Office→Excel Options→ Advanced→ Display Options for This Worksheet→Show Page Breaks

This check box needs to be checked in order to display page breaks in normal view.

After you've either printed a worksheet or executed a Print Preview, you will see thin dotted lines indicating where the page will break.

Sometimes you need to take control of page breaks. This lesson shows you how.

1   Open *Sales Analysis Chart* from your sample file folder.

2   Display normal view (if you aren't already in it).

Click the Normal view button at the bottom right of the screen.

Note that no page breaks are shown. This is because the worksheet has never been printed or previewed.

3   Print Preview the worksheet.

This was covered in: *Lesson 7-1: Print Preview and change paper orientation.*

Print preview reveals that the printout will cut the pie chart in half:

09-Oct-07 Germany	Dairy Products	1,112.00	USA
10-Oct-07 Spain	Condiments	422.40	Venezuela
10-Oct-07 Spain	Grains/Cereals	249.60	Grand Total
10-Oct-07 Spain	Beverages	310.00	
11-Oct-07 Sweden	Beverages	304.00	
11-Oct-07 Sweden	Dairy Products	672.00	
11-Oct-07 Sweden	Seafood	579.60	

We need to solve this problem by inserting a vertical page break.

4   Return to Normal view and note that page breaks are shown as dotted lines.

Click the *Close Print Preview* button and note the vertical dotted lines showing the vertical and horizontal page breaks.

If you don't see any dotted lines somebody may have disabled them. See the sidebar for instructions on how to switch them back on.

▲	A	B	C	D	E	F	G
50	22-Oct-07	Ireland	Dairy Products	200.00			
51	22-Oct-07	Ireland	Dairy Products	122.88			

It is immediately clear where the problem lies. The vertical break needs to occur at the left of column E to solve the problem.

5   Insert a page break to the left of column E.

1. Click cell E1. It is important to choose row 1 otherwise both a horizontal and vertical page break would be inserted.

2. Click Page Layout→Page Setup→Breaks→Insert Page Break

The dotted line moves to the left of the active cell to show the new position of the vertical page break.

Sales Analysis Charts

	D	E	F	G
1				
2	Sales		Sales By Country	
3	154.00		Country	Total Sales
4	86.40		Argentina	762.60

6   Print Preview the worksheet (or view the page in Page Layout view) to confirm that the worksheet will now print correctly.

7   Click the *Close Print Preview* button to return to Normal view.

8   Insert a horizontal page break above row 78.

Row 78 displays the first sale for November 2007.

75	31-Oct-07 Germany	Beverages	216.00
76			37,515.73
77			
78	01-Nov-07 USA	Condiments	616.00

For presentational reasons you want each month to begin on a new page so need to insert a page break above row 78.

1. Click in cell A78. It's important to click in column A otherwise both a horizontal and vertical page break would be inserted to the left of, and above the active cell.

2. Click Page Layout→Page Setup→Breaks→Insert Page Break.

   A dotted line appears above the active cell (row 78) to show the position of the new horizontal page break.

	A	B	C	D
76				37,515.73
77				
78	01-Nov-07 USA		Condiments	616.00

9   Print Preview the worksheet (or view the page in Page Layout view) to confirm that the worksheet will now print correctly.

The page now breaks at row 77 and a new page begins for row 78.

10   Remove the horizontal page break above row 78.

Click anywhere in row 78 except cell E78. If you were to select cell E78 you would remove both the horizontal and vertical page breaks.

Click Page Layout→Page Setup→Breaks→Remove Page Break.

The dotted line disappears indicating that the page will no longer break before row 78.

11   Save your work as Sales Analysis Chart-1.

Lesson 7-6: Adjust page breaks using Page Break Preview

In the last lesson we learned how to adjust page breaks in Normal view. Many users also like to adjust page breaks in Page Layout view.

Microsoft recommends that you don't use either. There's a purpose-built view just to handle page breaks called Page Break Preview view.

I tie my tongue in knots during my classes just trying to say *Page Break Preview view*!

This view allows you to move page breaks (something you can't do with the other views) and to identify which breaks are manually inserted and which are automatic breaks (created by Excel).

1   Open *Sales Analysis Chart-1* from your sample file folder (if it isn't already open).

2   Display Page Break Preview view.

Click the Page Break Preview button at the bottom right of the screen.

You can also select this view from the Ribbon by clicking:

View→Workbook Views→Page Break Preview

If it is the first time you've used this view, a dialog will appear.

Check the box before you click OK and it won't bother you next time.

Page break preview allows you to see which breaks are manual and which are automatic. Breaks shown as solid lines were manually inserted. Breaks shown as dotted lines were automatically inserted by Excel.

Areas that will not print are also easy to see in this view as they are shaded gray.

	A	B	C	D	E
49	22-Oct-07	Ireland	Beverages	85.12	
50	22-Oct-07	Ireland	Dairy Products	200.00	
51	22-Oct-07	Ireland	Dairy Products	122.88	
52	22-Oct-07	Ireland	Produce	1,628.16	

Sales Analysis Charts-1

Notice that your manually inserted vertical break (to the left of column E) is shown as a solid line while Excel's automatic page break (after row 50) is shown as a dotted line.

note

Intelliprint means never having to say you're sorry... for wasting paper.

Intelliprint was introduced in Excel 2003.

Prior to 2003 a worksheet similar to the one used in this lesson would print out several blank sheets of paper (the sheets shaded gray in the Print Preview).

Simply put, Intelliprint means that Excel will never output blank pages at the end of a document.

Prior to the introduction of Intelliprint it was necessary to set a print area to exclude any blank pages. (We'll be covering print areas later in: *Lesson 7-10: Print only part of a worksheet*).

tip

In Page Break Preview you can enter page breaks using a right-click.

It is usually quicker to add page breaks by using the shortcut menu – the menu that appears when you right-click a cell.

1. Right-click the cell that you want the page break to appear above, or to the left of.

2. Click Insert Page Break from the shortcut menu.

3   Move the automatic break from between rows 101 and 102 to between rows 77 and 78.

1. Move the mouse cursor over the dotted blue line between rows 101 and 102 until you see the double-headed arrow cursor shape.

100	13-Nov-07	Austria
101	13-Nov-07	Austria
102	14-Nov-07	Mexico

2. When you see the double-headed arrow, click and drag to move the page break up the page so that the line is between rows 77 and 78.

76		Page
77		
78	01-Nov-07	USA	Cond

Notice that the page break is now shown as a solid blue line.

76			37,515.73
77			
78	01-Nov-07	USA	Condiments	616.00

4   Automatically scale the sheet so that all of November's sales fit on one sheet.

An interesting feature of Page Break Preview is its ability to scale a page to fit the paper. We did this manually in: *Lesson 7-4: Set paper size and scale*. The process is far more intuitive in this view.

1. Scroll to row 128. Notice that there is an automatic page break between rows 128 and 129.

2. Drag this page break to a new position between rows 145 and 146.

   Excel hasn't inserted another automatic break somewhere in Page 3 even though Page 3 is now a lot longer than it was before. The only way Excel can possibly print Page 3 is by automatically scaling it down to fit the page.

3. Print Preview the worksheet and notice that the fonts for the entire report have been reduced. Excel cannot scale a single page in isolation; it scales all pages to keep the font size of all report pages consistent.

4. Close Print Preview.

Excel's automatic scaling system means that it is easy to lose track of what is happening. Sometimes you want to set everything back the way it used to be and start again.

5   Remove all manually applied page breaks.

Click Page Layout→Page Setup→Breaks→Reset All Page Breaks

All solid lines disappear and Excel's automatic page breaks reappear.

6   Save your work as Sales Analysis Chart-2.

Lesson 7-7: Add auto-headers and auto-footers and set the starting page number

Headers and footers are displayed at the top and bottom of each printed page.

If you are printing a long report it is very useful to add page numbers. Other items commonly added to page headers and footers include:

- A title.
- The date and time that the report was printed.
- The report author's name.
- The name of the Excel file that was used to generate the report.
- The full path to the Excel file.
- A company logo.
- Copyright notices.
- A distribution list or the security level of the document (for example you may want to include the word: *Confidential*).

1   Open *Sales Report-4* from your sample files folder.

2   Display page layout view (if you aren't already in it).

   This was covered in: *Lesson 7-2: Use page layout view to adjust margins.*

3   Click in the Page Header area at the top of the screen.

   The page header area contains the text: *Click to add header*.

   > Click to add header

   When you click in this area a new tab appears on the Ribbon.

   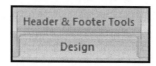

   We will use this tab to access Excel's Auto Header and Footer feature.

4   Add a header that will display page numbers at the top of each page in the format: *Page 1*.

   When you click in the header area you are able to access the *Header & Footer Tools* Design tab.

   1. Click:

      Header & Footer Tools→Design→Header & Footer→Header

   2. Choose the option *Page 1* (see sidebar). Page numbers are now shown at the top of each page.

Sales Report-4

Page 1

5   Add an Auto-footer to show the filename at the bottom of the page.

1. Click in the *Click to add footer* area at the bottom of the page.

Click to add footer

2. Click:

Header & Footer Tools→Design→Header & Footer→Footer

3. Choose the Sales *Report-4* item from the drop down list (see sidebar).

The filename is now shown at the bottom of every page in the report.

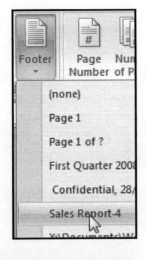

| Montréal | Canada | Steeleye |
| Montréal | Canada | Côte de |

Sales Report-4

6   Change the page numbering so that numbering begins at page ten.

It is very common to print an Excel report and then collate it into another report (perhaps produced using Word). If the pages were to be inserted after page nine we would want Excel to begin numbering at page ten.

1. Click Page Layout→Page Setup→Dialog Launcher.

2. Click the *Page* tab and type the number 10 into the *First page number:* text box.

Paper size:	A4
Print quality:	1200 dpi
First page number:	10

Click the OK button. Page numbering now begins at Page 10.

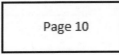

Page 10

7   Save your work as Sales Report-5.

note

You can edit a header and footer on any page.

It doesn't matter which page you add your header and footer to.

You can add or edit header and footer information on any page and it will then automatically apply to every other page.

Later in this session (in: *Lesson 7-9: Specify different headers and footers for the first, odd and even pages*) we'll explore a technique that will allow you to have multiple headers and footers in a single worksheet.

video

You can watch a free video walk-through of this lesson at:

www.LearnMicrosoftExcel.com

note

How to include an ampersand in a header or footer.

In the header and footer area, the ampersand (&) denotes the beginning of a field.

Sometimes you will need to put an ampersand into header text. For example your company might be called:

Marks & Spencer

To do this you need to incorporate a double ampersand into the header to tell Excel to print the ampersand. You would need to type:

Marks && Spencer

note

Headers and footers may have multiple lines.

You can make your header and footer information span as many lines as you need. Press the <Enter> key when you want to move to a new line.

If you use many lines it may be necessary to adjust the top margin as the header can sometimes overlap the worksheet.

Sales Report-5

Lesson 7-8: Add custom headers and footers

Auto-headers and footers provide a quick and convenient method when your needs are simple. Custom headers allow you to combine your own text with report fields (such as page numbers). You are also able to add text to three different sections in the header and footer areas (Left, Right and Center).

1   Open *Sales Report-5* from your sample files folder (if it isn't already open).

2   Display page layout view (if you aren't already in it).

This was covered in: *Lesson 7-2: Use page layout view to adjust margins*.

3   Click on the Page Header area.

Notice that when you click the Page Header area the contents change from *Page 10* to *Page &[Page]*.

Page &[Page]

The Ampersand (&) is called an *Escape Character*. It tells Excel that whatever text follows is a field rather than literal text. The field &[Page] tells Excel to insert the current page number.

4   Change the page header to: *The Gourmet Food Company*.

Click in the center of the header area (where you currently see the page number) and type **The Gourmet Food Company**.

5   Place the date and time on the left-hand part of the page header.

There's no Auto-header for date and time. In this case you'll have to create your own custom header field.

1.   Click in the **left-hand** section of the header area.

2.   Type the text **Printed on:** followed by a space.

3.   Click Header & Footer Tools→Design→ Header & Footer Elements→Current Date.

4.   Type a space followed by **at:** and then another space.

5.   Click Header & Footer Tools→Design→ Header & Footer Elements→Current Time

The left-hand section of the header bar now contains the following text:

Header
Printed on: &[Date] at: &[Time]

When you click away from the Header section the date and time are displayed. The date is displayed in a format dictated by the locale of your operating system. In this example it is the date: 31st Aug 2008 displayed in UK format (day/month/year):

> Printed on: 31/08/2008 at: 14:30

6   Place the page number on the right-hand side of the page header.

This time there is an Auto Header to suit but you can't use it. Auto headers may only be used in the center section of the header. We'll have to make our own using the Header & Footer Elements just as we did for the date and time.

1. Click in the right hand part of the page header and type **Page:** followed by a space (the last space won't appear on screen but don't worry, it is there).

2. Click: Header & Footer Tools→Design→ Header & Footer Elements→Page Number.

3. The right hand section of the header bar now contains the following text:

> Page: &[Page]

When you click away from the Header section, the current page number is displayed:

> Page: 10

Printed on: 31/08/2008 at 14:52   The Gourmet Food Company   Page: 10

---

7   Apply an attractive format to the page header section.

1. Click the left-hand section of the header. The text is automatically selected.

> Header
> Printed on: &[Date] at &[Time]

2. Click Home→Font→Font and set the font face to *Cambria 10 Point Bold*. Note that, following good design practice, this is one of the two theme fonts (see sidebar).

3. Click Home→Font→Font Color and set the color to the *Dark Blue, Text 2* theme color.

4. Apply the same format to the right-hand section of the header.

5. Format the centre section of the header as *Cambria 28 point, Dark Blue, Text 2.*

Printed on: 31/08/2008 at 15:06   **The Gourmet Food Company**   Page: 10

---

8   Save your work as Sales Report-6.

Lesson 7-9: Specify different headers and footers for the first, odd and even pages

If you look at the pages in this book you'll notice that there's a different header and footer for odd and even pages. The first page of each session is also different.

If the sample worksheet needed to be inserted into a publication like this, you'd need to specify three different headers and footers, one for odd pages, one for even pages, and one for the first page.

1   *Open Sales Report-6* from your sample files folder (if it isn't already open.

2   Display normal view (if you aren't already in it).

     Click the normal view button at the bottom right of the screen.

3   Insert five blank rows above row 1.

     This was covered in: *Lesson 3-1: Insert and delete rows and columns.*

4   Insert a manual page break above row 6.

     This was covered in: *Lesson 7-5: Insert, delete and preview page breaks.*

     A dotted line appears above row 6.

     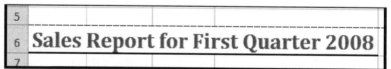

5   Merge and center cells A2:J2 and enter the text: **Sales Report Jan-Mar 2008**.

     This was covered in: *Lesson 4-6: Merge cells, wrap text and expand/collapse the formula bar.*

6   Apply the Title style to the newly added text.

     This was covered in: *Lesson 4-9: Use cell styles and change themes.*

7   Merge and center cells A3:J3 and enter the text *Private & Confidential*.

8   Apply the Heading 4 style to the newly added text.

9   Apply a fill color of *Blue, Accent1, Lighter 80%* to cells A2:A3.

10   Resize Row 1 so that it is three or four centimeters deep.

11   Print Preview the worksheet.

Sales Report-6

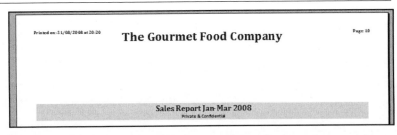

We've created a cover sheet for the report. It doesn't look bad but the header and footer are spoiling things. We need to suppress the header and footer from the cover sheet.

12 **Remove the header and footer from the first (cover) page.**

1. Close Print Preview view.

2. Change to Page Layout view.

3. Click in the Header area of the first page.

4. Click Header & Footer Tools→Design→ Options→Different First Page.

    The header and footer information vanishes from the cover page.

13 **Set a different odd and even page header and footer.**

1. Click in the header area.

2. Click Header & Footer Tools→Design→ Options→Different Odd & Even Pages.

    The header and footer information vanishes from odd pages but remains on even pages.

14 **Remove all header and footer information.**

    We're going to replace the existing page header and footer so delete the contents of all header and footer sections.

15 **Add odd and even page footers so that the page number appears on the right of all odd pages and on the left of all even pages.**

    If you look at the footer of this book, you will see that the page numbers are arranged in this manner.

1. Click in the footer area of one of the pages.

    Notice that when you click in the footer area, Excel indicates which footer you are editing (odd or even).

    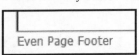

2. Insert a page number into the odd and even page footer area.

    If you're wondering why Excel thinks that even pages are odd, and odd pages are even, see the sidebar for an explanation.

    While the cover page is useful in all reports, the different odd and even page headers will only improve the presentation of reports that will be printed on both sides of the paper and then bound.

16 **Save your work as Sales Report-7.**

Important

Page numbering confusion.

We have set this workbook to begin its page numbering at page 10 (an even page).

As far as Excel is concerned the "real" starting page number is page one (an odd page).

This can cause a little confusion as you will find:

Even Page Header

... at the top of the second page in this report even though it has a page number of eleven and is thus an odd page.

Excel uses the "real" page numbers when it labels the page header and footer areas.

---

note

Print areas do not have to be contiguous.

You may want to print several different sections from your worksheet.

Simply select the non-contiguous (non-adjacent) ranges (covered in: *Lesson 2-7: Select non-contiguous cell ranges and view summary information*) and then use either of the techniques discussed in this lesson to print the selected cells.

trivia

Origins of the term: "One-off".

Many years ago, I studied engineering and spent part of my time discovering the joys of lathes, milling machines, grinders and all of the other paraphernalia found in machine shops.

Sometimes I would wander around the factory where the lathe operators would sit next to their machines – usually reading a book.

They would have a specification drawing next to them with something like "600 Off" written on it. This would mean that they would make 600 parts to the defined specification.

A One-off would be quite unusual as it would be expensive to set-up the lathe to produce just one part.

The term "one-off" is now commonly used in the UK to describe something that happens, or is made, only once.

Lesson 7-10: Print only part of a worksheet

Sometimes you will want to only print a range of cells from a worksheet.

Excel provides two ways to do this. The first method is applicable when the requirement is a one-off. In other words, the change will not persist the next time you print, when the entire worksheet will be printed in the usual way.

The second method involves setting a print area. If you save the worksheet, the defined print area will then persist (until you clear the print area).

In this lesson we'll explore both methods.

1   Open *Sales Report-7* from your sample files folder (if it isn't already open.

2   Display Normal view (if you aren't already in it).

Click the Normal view button at the bottom right of the screen.

We're going to imagine that we need to print a listing of all of January's sales.

3   Select all of the transactions for January 2008 (cells A8:J93).

4   Click Office→Print→Print.

The Print dialog is displayed.

Notice the *Print what* frame. There is an option to print Selection.

5   Click the Print what→Selection option button.

Sales Report-7

6   Click the Preview button at the bottom left of the Print dialog.

Notice that only January transactions (cells A8:J93) will be printed.

7   Close the Print Preview.

8   Click Office→Print→Print Preview to confirm that the entire worksheet would be printed on future occasions.

9   Close the Print Preview.

Now consider the case of a worksheet where you will only ever want to print a selected range. In this case we'd like to set the print area so that it becomes the default for future printouts.

10   Select all of the transactions for January 2008 (cells A8:J93) once again.

11   Set the print area.

Click Page Layout→Page Setup→Print Area→Set Print Area.

When you set the print area it remains active even if you close and re-open a workbook.

12   Click Office→Print→Print Preview to confirm that only the print area will be printed upon future occasions.

13   Close the Print Preview.

This is fine but what about if we want to print the entire worksheet as a one-off? In this case you don't want to clear the print area, but simply to over-ride it for a single printout.

14   Click Office→Print→Print and then check the *Ignore print areas* check box.

15   Click the Preview button at the bottom left of the Print dialog.

Notice that the entire worksheet would now be printed.

16   Close the Print Preview.

17   Click Office→Print→Print Preview to confirm that only the *print area* would be printed on future occasions.

18   Clear the print area.

A print area that was once appropriate may no longer be needed.

To remove the print area click:

Page Layout→Page Setup→Print Area→Clear Print Area

19   Click Office→Print→Print Preview to confirm that the print area no longer exists and that the entire worksheet will be printed on all future occasions.

note

The print area is implemented using a named range.

Excel has a feature called "named ranges". The definition and use of named ranges is an expert-level skill covered in the next book in this series: *Learn Excel 2007 Expert Skills with the Smart Method.*

When you set a print area, Excel simply creates a sheet-level named range called *Print Area* for the currently active worksheet. Each worksheet can have its own print area.

If you do progress to become an Excel Expert, it is possible to define this named range manually and to use it in formulas.

Lesson 7-11: Add row and column data labels and grid lines to printed output

1   Open *Sales Report-7* from your sample files folder (if it isn't already open).

2   Print Preview the worksheet.

There's a slight problem with this worksheet. The first page is easy to understand as it has a column header row to indicate which data is in each column (such as Date, City and Company Name):

Sales Report for First Quarter 2008				
	Sales Person First Name	Sales Person Last Name		
Date	First Name	Last Name	Company Name	City
01-Jan-08	Nancy	Davolio	Eastern Connection	London
01-Jan-08	Nancy	Davolio	Eastern Connection	London

The second page isn't so easy to understand because the column header row is missing:

The Gourmet Food Company			
23-Jan-08	Robert	King	Mère Paillarde
23-Jan-08	Robert	King	Mère Paillarde
24-Jan-08	Michael	Suyama	La maison d'Asie

3   Close Print Preview.

4   Add column headings to each printed page.

1. Click Page Layout→Page Setup→Print Titles.

    The page Setup dialog is displayed with the Sheet tab selected.

2. Click inside the *Rows to repeat at top* text box.

3. Select all of Row 8 by clicking anywhere in row 8.

→8	Date	First Name	Last Name

The row reference appears in the dialog.

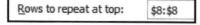

Rows to repeat at top:	$8:$8

Note that you could enter these manually if you wanted to. For example, to print rows 6 to 8 on each page you would enter **6:8** (or **$6:$8**)

4. Click the OK button

Sales Report-7

5   Print Preview the worksheet.

This time the column headings appear for every page in the printout.

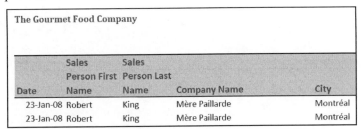

6   Close the Print Preview.

7   Add gridlines to the printout.

Sometimes it is difficult for the eye to track across printed lines. For this type of report it is useful to print gridlines onto the printed page in a similar way to the ones displayed on the worksheet.

Click Page Layout→Sheet Options→Gridlines→Print.

8   Print preview the worksheet.

This time gridlines are displayed upon each printed page:

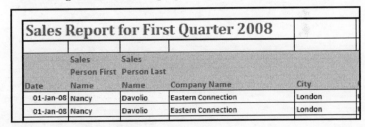

9   Close the Print Preview.

10   Add row and column headings to the printout.

You may want to send a printed worksheet to a colleague and then discuss it on the telephone. It would be useful to be able to ask "what do you think of the value in cell H11?" This isn't possible because row and column headings are not shown on the printed page.

Click Page Layout→Sheet Options→Headings→Print.

11   Print Preview the worksheet.

This time row and column headings are displayed on the printed page:

12   Remove the gridlines and column headings from the printout.

Clear the check boxes that were ticked in the previous steps.

13   Save your work as Sales Report-8.

Lesson 7-12: Print several selected worksheets and change the page order.

1   Open *Palace Hotel Bar Activity* from your sample files folder.

2   Print Preview the worksheet.

Notice that the worksheet prints first downward (listing all activity between 11:00 AM and 4:00 PM for all days.

When it reaches the bottom of the list it moves across to print all activity between 5:00 PM and 10:00 PM and so on.

3   Close *Print Preview*.

4   Change the view to *Page Break Preview*.

Click the Page Break Preview button at the bottom right of the screen.

In this view it is easy to see the page order by looking at the watermarks on each page (the watermark is the transparent large gray text saying Page 1, Page 2 etc).

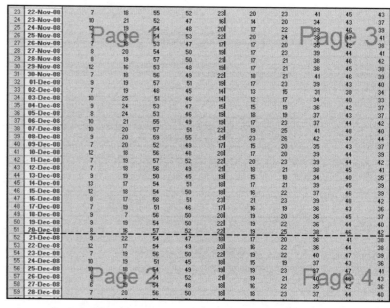

But what if you don't want to print in this order? Perhaps you would like to first print all activity for all times. In other words, you want the above display to make the existing Page 3 into Page 2.

5   Change the print order to *Over, then down*.

1.   Click: Page Layout→Page Setup→Dialog Launcher.

Palace Hotel Bar Activity

2. Click the Sheet tab.

3. Click the Over, then down option button.

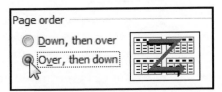

4. Click the OK button.

It can be seen from the page break preview that the order has now changed.

6   Print sales for Jul-Aug and Nov-Dec in one printout.

You can print several worksheets at the same time and they needn't be adjacent.

1. Click the *Jul-Aug* tab.

2. Hold down the **<Ctrl>** key and click the *Nov-Dec* tab.

Both tabs are now colored white

3. Click Office→Print→Print.

The Print dialog is displayed.

4. Note that when more than one sheet is selected the *Print What* frame has the *Active Sheet(s)* option selected.

5. Click the Preview button at the bottom left of the dialog to confirm that the contents of the *Jul-Aug* and *Nov-Dec* worksheets would have been printed.

7   Close the Print Preview.

8   Save your work as Palace Hotel Bar Activity-1.

Lesson 7-13: Suppress error messages in printouts

Excel has several built-in error messages such as the divide by zero error:

#DIV/0!

Sometimes you're quite happy to have these errors appear in a worksheet. For example, divide by zero errors could appear quite normally when there is incomplete data.

Even though the errors are fine in the worksheet, you may not want them to appear in your printed output.

1   Open *Average Revenue per Sale* from your sample files folder.

	First Name	Last Name	Sales	Units	Average Revenue per Sale
	Average Revenue Per Sale				
4	Andrew	Fuller	7,639.30	15	509.29
5	Anne	Dodsworth	-	-	#DIV/0!
6	Janet	Leverling	29,658.60	60	494.31
7	Laura	Callahan	19,271.60	40	481.79
8	Margaret	Peacock	44,795.20	90	497.72
9	Michael	Suyama	4,109.80	8	513.73
10	Nancy	Davolio	-	-	#DIV/0!
11	Robert	King	21,461.60	43	499.11
12	Steven	Buchanan	2,634.40	5	526.88
13			Total: 129,570.50	261.00	

This is an example of a worksheet with errors. In actual fact, you are simply waiting for Anne Dodsworth and Nancy Davolio to send you their sales figures so they aren't really errors.

Divide by zero errors occur because it is impossible to divide any number by zero (that's not quite correct, you can, but the result is infinity).

We'd like to print out this interim report but replace the ugly #DIV/0 errors with a blank space.

2   Replace errors with a blank space in printed output.

1.   Click: Page Layout→Page Setup→Dialog launcher.

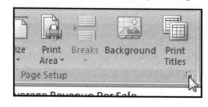

The Page Setup dialog appears.

2. Click the Sheet tab.

3. Click the *Cell errors as* dropdown list and then click <blank>.

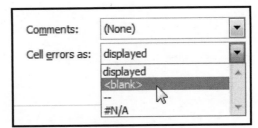

4. Click the OK button.

3   Print Preview the worksheet.

The errors are no longer printed. Blank spaces are substituted.

Average Revenue Per Sale

First Name	Last Name	Sales	Units	Average Revenue per Sale
Andrew	Fuller	7,639.30	15	509.29
Anne	Dodsworth	-	-	
Janet	Leverling	29,658.60	60	494.31
Laura	Callahan	19,271.60	40	481.79
Margaret	Peacock	44,795.20	90	497.72
Michael	Suyama	4,109.80	8	513.73
Nancy	Davolio	-	-	
Robert	King	21,461.60	43	499.11
Steven	Buchanan	2,634.40	5	526.88
	Total:	129,570.50	261.00	

4   Close Print Preview.

5   Save your work as Average Revenue per Sale-1.

Session 7: Exercise

1   Open Exercise 7 from your sample files folder.

2   Change to Page Layout view.

3   Change the left margin to about 1.0 cm using the click and drag method.

4   Click Page Layout→Page Setup→Margins and use the *Custom Margins…* option to set top and bottom margins to 2.0 cm and the right margin to 1.0 cm.

5   Horizontally center the printout on the page.

6   Change the page orientation to landscape.

7   Scale the printout so that all columns fit on one printed page.

8   Change the view to Page Break Preview.

9   Insert a horizontal page break between rows 27 and 28.

10   Move the page break so that it now occurs between row 24 and 25.

11   Change to Page Layout view.

12   Add an auto-header to match the following:

Page 1 of 3

13   Make the data labels in row 1 repeat on every page.

14   Set the print area to A1:J12 and then Print Preview to prove that only these cells would be printed.

15   Clear the print area.

16   Add gridlines to the printout.

					Page 2 of 3	
Date	Sales Person First Name	Sales Person Last Name	Company Name	City	Country	
08-Jan-08	Laura	Callahan	Folies gourmandes	Lille	France	
08-Jan-08	Laura	Callahan	Folies gourmandes	Lille	France	

17   Save your work as Exercise 7-End.

Exercise 7

If you need help slide the page to the left

Session 7: Exercise answers

These are the questions that most students find difficult to remember:

Q 14	Q 13	Q 7	Q 5
1. Select cells A1:J12 2. Click: Page Layout→ Page Setup→ Print Area→ Set Print Area. This was covered in: *Lesson 7-10: Print only part of a worksheet.*	1. Click Page Setup→Print Titles. 3. Click in the *Rows to repeat at top* text box. 4. Either click in row 1 with the mouse or type 1:1 into the box. This was covered in: *Lesson 7-11: Add row and column data labels and grid lines to printed output.*	1. Click Page Layout→ Scale to Fit→ Width drop down. 2. Set the *Width* to *1-page*. This was covered in: *Lesson 7-4: Set paper size and scale.*	1. Click Page Layout→ Page Setup→ Dialog launcher 2. Click the Margins tab. 3. Check the *Center on page horizontally* check box. This was covered in: *Lesson 7-3: Use Page Setup to set margins more precisely and center the worksheet.*

If you have difficulty with the other questions, here are the lessons that cover the relevant skills:

1   Lesson 1-4: Open and navigate a workbook

2,3   Lesson 7-2: Use page layout view to adjust margins

4   Lesson 7-3: Use Page Setup to set margins more precisely and center the worksheet

6   Lesson 7-1: Print Preview and change paper orientation

8,9   Lesson 7-6: Adjust page breaks using Page Break Preview

10   Lesson 7-6: Adjust page breaks using Page Break Preview

11   Lesson 7-2: Use page layout view to adjust margins

12   Lesson 7-7: Add auto-headers and auto-footers and set the starting page number

15   Lesson 7-10: Print only part of a worksheet

16   Lesson 7-11: Add row and column data labels and grid lines to printed output

17   Lesson 1-5: Save a workbook

Index

D

Z

Also Available From The Smart Method

Watch a FREE video walk-through of lessons from this book.

Each and every lesson in this book has been recorded as a video walk-through. See and hear Mike Smart deliver some free sample lessons on-line at:

www.LearnMicrosoftExcel.com

The videos feature a full-size recorded Excel screen with Mike's voice-over as he walks you through each lesson.

If you find that you love the sample videos online why not download or buy the DVD?

You can install the entire video onto your hard drive meaning that every piece of information in this book is always instantly available.

- Over 8 hours run-time.
- Includes PowerPoint slides and Lesson Planner.
- Available for instant download from our website: **www.LearnMicrosoftExcel.com.**
- Also available from **Amazon.com** and **Amazon.co.uk** as a DVD.

Become an Excel Expert with our Excel Expert Skills book.

Also available on video.

- Over 13 hours run-time.
- Available for instant download from our website:
- Also available from **Amazon.com** and **Amazon.co.uk** as a DVD.

The next book in the series builds upon all of the foundation skills you've learned.

There's a whole lot more to Excel, and you'll learn it all with this book. Security, advanced functions and formulas, tables, macros, pivot tables, what-if analysis... and so much more. Search for it at **Amazon.com** or **Amazon.co.uk.**